W9-CBQ-920

THE MESSAGE

Also by Richard Wolffe

Renegade

Revival

THE MESSAGE

THE RESELLING OF
PRESIDENT OBAMA

RICHARD WOLFFE

TWELVE

NEW YORK   BOSTON

Twelve
Hachette Book Group
237 Park Avenue
New York, NY 10017

www.HachetteBookGroup.com

Printed in the United States of America

RRD-C

First Edition: September 2013
10 9 8 7 6 5 4 3 2 1

Twelve is an imprint of Grand Central Publishing.
The Twelve name and logo are trademarks of Hachette Book Group, Inc.

The Hachette Speakers Bureau provides a wide range of authors for speaking events. To find out more, go to www.hachettespeakersbureau.com or call (866) 376-6591.

The publisher is not responsible for websites (or their content) that are not owned by the publisher.

Library of Congress Control Number: 2013943968
ISBN: 978-1-4555-8156-6

To Mum and Dad,
who gave me the book of life;
and to Paula, Ilana, Ben, and Max,
who gave it meaning.

CONTENTS

THE MESSAGE

For I have neither wit, nor words, nor worth,
Action, nor utterance, nor the power of speech,
To stir men's blood; I only speak right on.
I tell you that which you yourselves do know.

—Antony in the Forum, *Julius Caesar*, Act III, Scene ii

ONE

VINDICATION

One Prudential Plaza was more than just the address of the Obama campaign in 2012; it was a state of mind. Tucked in between the bold architecture of Chicago's skyline, the almost sixty-year-old rectangular block was a monolithic relic of a more powerful era. It was the city's tallest building when it opened, in the same year the first Mayor Richard Daley seized power as the city's unrivaled boss. Now its main attractions were its empty space and its expansive views. Looking out the window you could see Grant Park, the site of Barack Obama's victory speech in November 2008. Or you could stare at the screen of a laptop, one of many lined up on beige desks, indistinguishable from the beige walls, which populated the campaign's headquarters on the sixth floor. The deep blue campaign posters stuck to the walls seemed to match the dozens of identical gray-blue chairs where the twentysomething campaign workers toiled away on headsets, fueled by Starbucks. They weren't selling insurance anymore on this floor of the Prudential, but they were still calculating a kind of actuarial risk with every phone call and keystroke.

Two floors above the main operations of the Obama campaign was its election-day boiler room. Unlike its industrial namesake, this boiler room was operating at a higher altitude and intellectual plane: here the brains of the operation were crunching data and junk food in equal measure. Most of the campaign's senior staff arrived just before sunrise. Why they arrived so early, and why they needed to be there, was unclear, aside from their overwhelming sense of anxiety. The actual work was already well under way, organized by state around a series of pod-grouped desks, where staffers focused on real-time challenges. There were lawyers ready to tackle voting irregularities, turnout experts monitoring the voter numbers, and new media staff working on instant communications. It was their job to track the precise targets in each state, district, precinct, and block. They stood out not least because they were sporting deep blue T-shirts, with the words Boiler Room Staff wrapped around the circular sunrise logo of the 2008 campaign.

In contrast, the senior staff had no real job on this day. Their work was mostly fake: an appearance of action, at the climax of a two-year-long presidential campaign. Others were turning out voters; they were listening to the people turning out voters. Sitting around a giant, square-shaped series of tables, in a big back room, they clicked through e-mail and stared at one another. Every hour or so, the data guys would come in with the latest numbers. Their reports were avidly consumed by Jim Messina, the ghostly pale campaign manager; David Plouffe, the wiry former campaign manager; Dan Pfeiffer, the White House messaging chief and Plouffe confidant; David Axelrod, the president's political strategist and keeper of the flame for hope and change; Jen O'Malley Dillon, the grassroots organizer and deputy manager; Brent Colburn, the campaign's communications director; and Stephanie Cutter, the campaign's deputy manager and communications pit bull. Plouffe and Cutter would walk in and out, depending on their schedule of TV interviews at the nearby Fairmont Hotel. But the others were hanging out because they had nowhere else to go on this, the most important day of their careers.

The reports at the start of the day looked promising. Republican turnout was a little higher than the data models had projected. But there was no great cause for concern. The model predicted a win for Obama, and that was all that mattered.

Then, as the morning dragged on, the mood turned anxious. As the data continued to flow in to the boiler room, the turnout flattened. In areas with strong Latino and African-American populations—the very parts of the battleground states where they had devoted so much effort to registering new and infrequent voters—the numbers were trending down. In Cuyahoga County around Cleveland, Ohio, the African-American turnout was down in the part of a state most critical to winning the presidency. The call went out to the ground staff in Cleveland, and the response was clear: turnout was not down at all. In fact, it was so high, and the flow of voters so fast, that it was hard to check them all off the massive voter list that represented the wired intelligence of the Obama campaign. The only thing that was trending down was the campaign's ability to capture data.

"Guys," said Plouffe, for once shedding his normally nervous energy. "It's the only part of the campaign where it's like throwing darts. Even if the turnout is down, we're right where we need to be to win the election."

By early evening, the senior staff was relaxed enough to drop their pretense of cautious optimism; they were delighted at what they saw. When the polls closed in Florida and Ohio, election officials released their tallies of the early votes. In Ohio, early voting had started a full month before election day; in Florida, such voting began little more than a week out. Jeremy Bird, the campaign's tireless national field director, pulled up the county-by-county vote projections for Ohio, where he had led the campaign to a stunning victory four years ago.

The numbers were startling. In every county, the real votes were within one percentage point of the model. It was a little after 6:30 p.m. in Chicago.

"That's when we knew the model was right," said Dan Pfeiffer. "If the model was right, we were definitely winning. We knew where this was going."

For months the Obama campaign had projected deep faith in one thing, and one thing alone. Not the candidate, even though they were still true believers in Obama's abilities and abiding popularity. Not the media and communications team, even though they believed they were the best in the business. But the data and the ground game: the combination of volunteers, organizers, and computer modeling that set them apart from anything else in presidential politics—including themselves in 2008.

For months, as they exuded confidence in their numbers, the media, along with Republicans, had gainsaid and doubted. Such misplaced confidence. So typical of the zealots who were fooled by an untested candidate four years ago.

Now, though, the confidence was rooted in something real.

Two hours after looking at the Ohio numbers, Plouffe was sitting next to O'Malley Dillon when they pulled up the real vote counts from Florida. The tally was 75 percent complete, and it seemed self-evident that they were headed for victory. At the start of the campaign, two years earlier, the conventional wisdom was clear: there was no way Obama could win Florida. Now they were looking at the outstanding votes, which leaned heavily toward

Democratic strongholds like Miami-Dade and Broward Counties. The consensus of the pundits and political insiders could not have been more wrong. For Plouffe, that was almost as important as winning the election itself.

He moved to a side room to call Obama.

"You ought to talk to Jim so he can give you the official news," Plouffe told the president, who was still at his home in Hyde Park. The votes were getting counted far more quickly than four years ago, and the night was moving swiftly to its resolution.

Messina took the phone and Plouffe left the room. The anxious knot of a campaign manager emerged unfrayed a few minutes later.

"That was the coolest thing I have ever done," he announced.

Plouffe returned to the phone.

"Can I tell the First Lady?" Obama asked.

"I wouldn't tell her quite yet," said Plouffe. "I would wait another half an hour."

The only suspense was the precise time of victory and the identity of the state that would breach the 270 mark in the electoral college. Would they carve a trail through Iowa, New Mexico, Colorado, and Nevada? Nevada and Iowa were already in the bag, thanks to huge advantages in early voting. Colorado was less certain, but the boiler room soon heard the *Denver Post* was going to call the state early for Obama. Independent voters were outperforming the campaign's model, even though they were down from 2008. Plouffe had bet the rest of the inner circle that they would end up with 332 votes in the electoral college; with each new state, he was edging closer to nailing the final count. He wasn't shy in pointing out his predictive powers.

The president's senior aides were debating the state of Virginia— where Mitt Romney was faring worse than John McCain had in

2008—when NBC's election desk called Ohio and the entire election for Obama. It was 10:12 p.m. in Chicago, almost an hour earlier than the decisive call in 2008.

The First Family had spent the last several hours at the Fairmont Hotel with friends, watching the TV reports and enjoying a rare moment of privacy after months on the road in full public view. When the senior team arrived from the boiler room, they found three staffers there already: Robert Gibbs, the former White House press secretary; Jay Carney, his successor; and Jon Favreau, Obama's longtime speechwriter. In spite of their confidence in the data and the ground game, they were still deeply superstitious. Gibbs, Axelrod, and Plouffe all wore the same ties they had sported four years earlier, when they briefly and tearfully visited Obama on election night.

This night was far more easygoing. The family, friends, and staff were just waiting for Mitt Romney to place the historic phone call that would end the 2012 election once and for all. Their mood was little short of elated. For the next twenty minutes, they celebrated the election calls made by each of the TV networks.

Obama walked up to his senior aides and hugged them all. "Thank you," he said. "This one actually means more to me than the last one. It feels better."

The call from Romney had not come. As the delay dragged on, some of the president's closest friends grew anxious. "Should we call him?" asked Valerie Jarrett. "What is taking him so long?"

"I don't care if he calls at three a.m.," said Obama. "We just won."

Four years earlier, the new president-elect walked onto an open-air stage in Grant Park to deliver his victory speech behind a thick shield of bulletproof glass. On an unseasonably warm November night, the lights of Chicago's skyline sparkled above a quarter of a million people who surged into the park on the shores of Lake Michigan. Four years later, the Midwestern winter was pressing in as usual, forcing the commander in chief and just ten thousand supporters to take shelter in the sterile convention space of McCormick Place. For the agents managing the president's personal protection, the hall was perfect. For the true believers who had returned him to the bubble of the Secret Service, it was a frustrating place.

There was no bar and they wanted to drink.

Obama stepped on to the stage with his family to the soundtrack of the 2008 campaign: Stevie Wonder's "Signed, Sealed, Delivered I'm Yours." Soon after he kissed his wife and daughters, the newly reelected Obama devoted his longest thanks to his second family. "To the best campaign team and volunteers in the history of politics," Obama said to the hall, heaving with supporters. "The best," he continued, nodding his head. "The best ever.

"Some of you were new this time around, and some of you have been at my side since the very beginning. But all of you are family. No matter what you do or where you go from here, you will carry the memory of the history we made together, and you will have the lifelong appreciation of a grateful president. Thank you for believing all the way, through every hill, through every valley. You lifted me up the whole way, and I will always be grateful for everything that you've done and all the incredible work that you put in."

Then he started telling the stories of some archetypes; some notional characters who might have volunteered for his reelection.

"I know that political campaigns can sometimes seem small, even silly. And that provides plenty of fodder for the cynics who tell us that politics is nothing more than a contest of egos or the domain of special interests. But if you ever get the chance to talk to folks who turned out at our rallies, and crowded along a rope line in a high school gym, or saw folks working late in a campaign office in some tiny county far away from home, you'll discover something else.

"You'll hear the determination in the voice of a young field organizer who's working his way through college and wants to make sure every child has that same opportunity. You'll hear the pride in the voice of a volunteer who's going door to door because her brother was finally hired when the local auto plant added another shift. You'll hear the deep patriotism in the voice of a military spouse who's working the phones late at night to make sure that no one who fights for this country ever has to fight for a job or a roof over their head when they come home.

"That's why we do this. That's what politics can be. That's why elections matter. It's not small. It's big. It's important."

As soon as the president finished, the parties began at the back of the hall. There were formal donor receptions and informal staff celebrations. But Obama's closest aides still could not make their way to a bar for a beer. Jon Favreau, the president's speechwriter, could barely move through the crowd. David Plouffe and David Axelrod were mobbed as celebrities and soaked up everyone's adulation. So the inner circle decided to retire to the Fairmont Hotel for a private party.

By the time they arrived, the hotel bar was long closed, and they gathered in Axelrod's suite. They called down to room service for champagne, but the front desk politely declined their request. Chicago law prohibited drinks at such an hour. At that point, Jen Psaki, the traveling campaign spokesperson, volunteered to walk down to the front desk to negotiate. Did they know that Jim Messina, the campaign manager, was upstairs and thirsty?

"Look, we love you guys," said the woman on the front desk. "We love the president. We are so grateful for the business you've given us and that you're all here tonight and that the president watched it here. But we could lose our liquor license."

"Well, we know the mayor," said Psaki of her old boss, the former White House chief of staff Rahm Emanuel.

"Sorry," said the woman on the other side of the desk. "We can't do it."

The victorious campaign staff devised a new plan.

Each of them returned to their rooms, grabbed a laundry bag or pillowcase, and cleaned out the minibar. They walked back to Axelrod's suite, dumped the laundry bags upside down on the countertop, and turned on MSNBC to find that the election desk had yet to call the result in Florida, where the counting process was as broken as it was twelve years earlier.

It was 3:00 a.m., and they realized they had missed one of the highlights of the night. In all their focus on data and state-by-state results, they had not yet seen Karl Rove's spectacle on Fox News. The architect of Bush's 2004 reelection—the campaign they had set out to emulate in two elections of their own—was dumbfounded by the night's results. He insisted on challenging the decision of Fox's election desk to call Ohio for Obama, and the hubristic clash of Rove's bluster with the voting data was gripping television. They fired up a laptop and watched Rove's meltdown until the dawn. At the height of their powers, some of the greatest political strategists of their generation were cradling airplane bottles of liquor as the cast of MSNBC's *Morning Joe* trickled on set.

They ordered some pizza, which room service promptly delivered and David Axelrod just as promptly dripped all over his shirt. Almost all of them had journeyed together from an unlikely beginning on a frigid day in Springfield, Illinois, almost five years ago. From hope to hell and back again, many times over. Their celebration was pitiful, and they knew it. Such small bottles on such a big night.

After just a couple of hours of sleep, at 9:00 a.m. central time, it was time for a conference call on the fiscal cliff. There was no real chance to rest or celebrate.

Later that day, the newly reelected president of the United States walked into the sixth-floor offices of the Prudential building to talk to his staffers. Jim Messina was so pumped up after introducing Obama that he punched the air as he walked away from the simple microphone stand. There was no bulletproof barrier, no presidential podium, and no teleprompter with prepared remarks. Just Barack Obama, his shirtsleeves rolled up to his elbows, and his silver tie loosened under an unbuttoned collar.

"So, you guys," he began, as his young staffers giggled.

"You know, I try to picture myself when I was your age. And I first moved to Chicago at the age of twenty-five, and I had this vague inkling about making a difference. I didn't really know how to do it. I didn't have a structure, and there wasn't a presidential campaign at the time that I could attach myself to. Ronald Reagan had just been reelected and was incredibly popular. So I came to Chicago knowing that somehow I wanted to make sure my life attached itself to helping kids get a great education, or helping people living in poverty to get decent jobs and be able to work and have dignity. Make sure that people didn't have to go to the emergency room to get health care. And I ended up being a community organizer on the South Side of Chicago where a group of churches were willing to hire me, and I didn't know at all what I was doing. And you know the work that I did in those communities changed me much more than I changed the communities.

Because it taught me the hopes and aspirations, and the grit and resilience of ordinary people. And it taught me the fact that under the surface differences, we all have common hopes and we all have common dreams. And it taught me something about how I handled disappointment, and what it meant to work hard on a common endeavor. And I grew up. I became a man during that process.

"And so when I come here and I look at all of you, what comes to mind is not that you guys actually remind me of myself. It's the fact that you are so much better than I was. In so many ways. You're smarter, and you're better organized, and you're more effective. And so I'm absolutely confident that all of you are going to do just amazing things in your lives. What Bobby Kennedy called the ripples of hope that come out when you throw a stone in a lake, that's going to be you."

He began to wipe a tear from his right eye.

"I'm just looking around the room and I'm thinking, wherever you guys end up, in whatever states, in whatever capacities, whether you're in the private sector, in the not-for-profit, or some of you decide to go into public service, you're just going to do *great things*. And that's why even before last night's results, I felt that the work that I had done, in running for office, had come full circle. Because what you guys have done means that the work I am doing is important. And I'm really proud of that. I'm really *proud* of all of you."

He wiped another tear away. And then another. By the time he wiped away the third, his young staffers were cheering and applauding.

"What you guys have accomplished will go in the annals of history. And people will read about it and they will marvel about it. But the most important thing you need to know is that your journey is just beginning. You're just starting. And whatever good we do over the next four years will pale in comparison to what you guys end up accomplishing for years and years to come."

He exited to the right, wiping his left eye now, as his young staffers cheered wildly. He spent hours shaking hands and talking to every single staffer and volunteer at his own headquarters.

In five years on the national stage, it was Obama's most explicit statement about his own mortality, a sense of his nearing the end of a long journey. But it was also the most meaningful statement about the purpose of his politics. What kind of hope and change did he have in mind through all these campaigns? Why was he so much bolder when campaigning than governing? Obama's campaigns were not just a means to an end, like so many others before. The common endeavor had its own purpose. His time as a community organizer was one long training program—both for him and his community. Now he saw his presidential campaign as one long training program for the next political generation.

A few hours later, his closest aides dragged themselves on board Air Force One for the return to Washington with a president who was in an unusually reflective and talkative mood. Two thousand eight was about an idea, he told them. This time was different. After four hard years, the American people looked at his leadership and his accomplishments and decided to reelect him. It was not a decision based on the hope that he would be able to do the job. They actually *believed* he could do the job.

As they flew back to Washington, the Air Force One pilot, Col. Scott Turner, interrupted the president, alongside some of his crew. They were carrying a giant sheet cake to congratulate their most important passenger. As they posed for photos, the president deadpanned: "There is somebody flying this plane, right?"

* * *

Political campaigns can indeed seem small, even silly. As small and silly as a laundry bag full of minibar bottles, drained to the last drop by a dozen people who had just overcome supersized odds—and similarly large egos—to preserve the vast powers of their historic candidate and president. This is the story of how they did it, in big and small ways. Unlike their first campaign, they could not rely on a high concept like hope; after four years of economic hardship, there weren't enough hopeful voters to assure them of victory. They could not use their candidate's biography to fill out the blank page of a political story; that book was already written. They could not promise sweeping new policies; their ideas for governing were mostly set in stone by four years of policymaking from the Oval Office.

All they could do was craft a narrative that recast their lead character in a different kind of drama. They needed to rewrite the script of so many years of struggle, screwups, and downright failure.

"You want to make it to the big leagues in terms of presidencies," said Dan Pfeiffer, the war-weary White House director of communications. Pfeiffer began the 2008 cycle as a young man but had aged inside the West Wing faster than the president. His personal mission was to stop his boss from turning into, as he put it, a black Jimmy Carter:

"After everything, after the country took such a gamble and so many people invested so much in the president, if it didn't work out, if he was rejected, what would that mean? What would it say to people? What would it say to young people who knocked on doors and got involved in politics for the first time? What would it say to African-Americans and Latinos who waited in line seven hours to vote in 2008 and 2012? On a personal level, this is some-one that has been a gigantic part of our lives. Most of us have spent more time around him and doing things for him than with our own families for the past six years."

Barack Obama was, by now, familiar with hard things. In the rearview mirror, each campaign seemed inevitable and effortless. In actual fact, the path to victory was more than troublesome; it was strewn with failure. In early 2008, few in Washington believed Obama could win in Iowa; few inside the campaign believed he would lose in New Hampshire a few days later. A string of pri-mary victories gave way to primary defeats in Texas, Ohio, and Pennsylvania. A great convention in Denver was swamped by the deluge of intrigue surrounding Sarah Palin's nomination.

The vast crowds at Obama's inauguration were replaced on the National Mall by Tea Party protesters. A year of active and sweeping legislation was followed by the loss of Ted Kennedy's Senate seat in Massachusetts. Health-care reform seemed dead, then was resurrected. The shellacking of the midterm elections in 2010 was swiftly followed by a flurry of victories in a lame-duck Congress, including the repeal of Don't Ask, Don't Tell.

The 2012 campaign began at a point of political despair, in the dark days after the debt ceiling debacle of 2011. That sense of despair never really left the Democratic Party, even as the Chi-cago boiler room team insisted its plan would lead to victory. Negativism and nerves seeped into Obama headquarters in a way that rarely happened in 2008. The building felt like an insurance business because there was so much to lose and the risk of defeat was so real. Victory in 2012 was all the sweeter for that triumph; for defeating not just the other side but the doubters on the inside.

"It was vindication," said Plouffe. "Like Iowa in 2008. Not just vindication of where we saw the race but the kind of campaign we ran. It was vindication of his leadership. It was an up-or-down vote on him. And it was hard. Harder than '08 because of the circumstances. The primary was historic. But this was a two-year battle, and eight months were really intensive, from March through November. This was so different."

Different and difficult: from the biggest policy debate to the smallest personal conflict, the reelection of Barack Obama rested on a team that showed few signs of coming together until it was almost too late. Contrary to the self-conscious mythmaking and the conventional wisdom about the 2008 and 2012 campaigns, the Obama machine was rarely as smooth running as its electoral success suggested. This is the story of the fractious team that boiled down an entire presidency into a simple series of messages. It is not a tick-tock of the 2012 election and all its component parts, but a study of how a small and divided group overcame a monumental challenge: to redefine the reality of a mostly unpopular president at a mostly unhappy time. Their biggest opponent was very rarely Mitt Romney and the Republicans; they were running against the economy and against one another. The fear and loathing of 2012 existed less on the campaign trail than inside the White House and its campaign headquarters.

TWO

THE DEEP END

The 2012 campaign coalesced more than a year before anyone would vote for either Barack Obama or Mitt Romney.

It was not the best place to start: the summer of 2011 was the worst period of Obama's presidency. Worse even than the shellacking of the midterm elections, seven months earlier, when the Republicans won the House. The White House was staring at political polling that plunged new depths of misery, at a time when its principals needed to set an optimistic course toward victory. The task of finding a successful strategy looked almost overwhelming to many loyal Obama aides. At the beginning of a sink-or-swim campaign, they felt like they were drowning in bad news and numbers.

For most of July and August, the president was pissed. He would often suffer cold, dark moods. The Oval Office or the Roosevelt Room would chill with his displeasure, and the subzero feeling might extend a few hours or a few days. But this was different.

In private conversations with friends and staffers, he would lash out at his Republican rivals in regular meetings and at the end of his days, when he would normally wind down. "I have never seen him this mad," said one of his closest friends, shaking his head after what was supposed to be a casual dinner together. Obama cursed the media and what he saw as its gross inadequacies and failings. He hated that people on the right and left said he was weak and feckless, that he caved at every obstacle. He loathed his own predicament and his apparent powerlessness. It tore at every competitive fiber in his skinny frame. He was determined to fight back but knew he was a long way from doing so.

His staff was fried. Even before the polling data came back, they knew the summer of 2011 was little short of a disaster. The only question was whether they had hit rock bottom or not. "There was a concern that the numbers were going to keep going down," said Dan Pfeiffer. "There was a fear that this could be like August of 2005 for Bush, where it just fundamentally changed how people see you. Unlike Bush, there was a lot of reservoir and goodwill about the president personally. It was a foundation we could build upon. And everyone still thought he was trying hard. They thought he was a good person who was telling the truth. But the concern was that people would see he was weak and never be able to see him as strong again."

The source of his apparent weakness was a political freak show with real-world financial impact. From May to early August of 2011, the US Treasury had resorted to what it called "extraordinary measures" to avoid defaulting on its debts in the global financial markets. By shuffling paper assets around, Treasury was buying time for the White House and its sworn enemies among the House Republicans to settle the latest round of a budget fight that was already several months old. Infused by Tea Party supporters and lawmakers from their 2010 midterm victories, the House Republicans were in no mood to settle anything, including a budget deal that would avert default by raising the US government's borrowing limit. Paul Ryan, chairman of the House Budget Committee, told CNBC in early May that a few days of default were worth the disruption to the markets if that led to real budget cuts. "If a bondholder misses a payment for a day or two, or three or four," he said, "what's more important is that you're putting the government in a materially better position to be able to pay their bonds later on."

It was no coincidence that the budget brinksmanship began at the start of the long debate season in the Republican presidential primaries. At just their second debate, in Manchester, New Hampshire, in mid-June, the GOP candidates were openly toying with the idea of default. None of them—including a former business executive like Mitt Romney—could resist competing with the extremist rhetoric of a House Republican like Michele Bachmann on the matter of default.

"I believe we will not raise the debt ceiling unless the president finally, finally is willing to be a leader on issues that the American people care about. And the number one issue that relates to that debt ceiling is whether the government is going to keep on spending money they don't have," Romney told the New Hampshire reporter who was moderating the immoderate debate. When asked if it was okay not to raise the debt ceiling, Romney brushed the notion aside. "What we say to America is: at some point, you hit a wall. At some point, people around the world say, 'I'm not going to keep loaning money to America to pay these massive deficits because America can't pay them back and the dollar is not worth anything anymore.' In that circumstance, we saddled our future, the future of our kids, in a way that is just unacceptable." Romney seemed to be encouraging the bond markets to abandon US debt. In contrast, Bachmann was a voice of reason. She limited her economic policy advice to suggesting that Treasury should avoid default by paying bondholders first before spending any other tax dollars on items like defense or education.

Inside the West Wing there was plenty of dysfunction to match the GOP's. Obama's second chief of staff was supposed to be a management expert, with both private-sector leadership skills and a genial personal style to match. Bill Daley was Bill Clinton's commerce secretary and Al Gore's campaign chairman. He was personally recommended by his Chicago friends David Axelrod and Rahm Emanuel, Obama's first chief of staff.

He was also a walking disaster in Obama's White House. He chafed against Obama's team, preferring to bring in his own staff—a preference that was rejected by the president himself. His working relationship with the rest of the West Wing was little short of dismal. Daley had been running several back channels to the GOP leadership on the debt ceiling and had failed to loop in the White House communications team. So the message team insisted the president was looking for a balanced agreement with some tax revenues as well as spending cuts. At the same time, their chief of staff was negotiating a deal without tax revenues. "Daley's reign was chaotic," said one senior Obama aide. "He had something like three secret processes happening at the same time. The messaging folks were not part of all the processes and so some decisions were made without regard to politics or framed in any way. They were drawing public red lines that we were already crossing in negotiations."

On top of the internal confusion, the White House could not afford to attack the Republicans who were flirting with default. They were too fearful of losing votes for an eventual compromise to avoid the apocalypse in the financial markets. Obama's aides could not negotiate in any meaningful way, and they could not message their position. Their strategy was paralyzed by fear. "We didn't feel like we could call their bluff, because we were dealing with irresponsible and incompetent actors in the House Republicans," said one senior Obama aide. "It was a caucus filled with deeply irresponsible individuals who believed sincerely that it was in the country's best interest to default. The House leadership couldn't count votes to save their lives, and basically you had a Speaker who was very weak with two deputies, in Kevin McCarthy and Eric Cantor, who were actively plotting for his job and were terrible at counting votes. So the whole thing required tremendous interaction from us to get across the finish line." Their greatest concern was that the House Republican leaders were so bad at corralling votes they might cut a deal and lose their own caucus, much like the vote to bail out the financial system in 2008. That House defeat prompted the largest-ever drop in the Dow Jones Industrial Average, at more than seven hundred points. If the West Wing tried to message the debt ceiling deal—either positively or negatively—it might trigger a slide back into recession and jeopardize the world economy. The stark calculation was not that different from the vote on health-care reform a year earlier, when the White House feared defeat so greatly that it surrendered all efforts to craft and execute a message to a broader audience outside the Beltway.

The result was a package of real spending cuts and promises of future cuts, in exchange for a rise in the debt ceiling, in early August. Three days after President Obama signed the deal into law, Standard and Poor's downgraded US debt from its AAA rating for the first time in its history. At least one factor in S&P's decision was that, as its senior director put it, "people in the political arena were even talking about a potential default."

Two weeks later, the Obamas left for their summer vacation on Martha's Vineyard. The stock market had lost between 10 and 15 percent of its value since the start of the debt ceiling crisis in May. The president's aides were so depleted that their daily phone calls were meaningless. "We sat on the beach and vegetated," said one. "People were so tired they couldn't see straight."

This was the point when Obama's reelection team commissioned its benchmark polling for the 2012 campaign. In a sweeping set of data, the team set out to map the nation's mood and the president's prospects of victory, more than a year away from election day. It was not the most optimistic time to be calling registered voters for their opinions about politics and the president. The results would at least be honest, if bluntness and bleakness were guarantors of honesty.

The polling was clear. They were down double digits with three critical groups of voters: white, independent women; lower-income white voters; and younger voters aged between eighteen and thirty-four. Overall, Obama had taken a big hit from the year's struggles over debt and deficits. In early May, when the president revealed to the world that Osama bin Laden was dead, his job approval ratings were in the low fifties: his highest point since late 2009. By the end of August, his *disapproval* numbers were in the low fifties: the worst of his presidency. On the most critical measures of leadership and strength, Obama had suffered his greatest damage— just three months after ordering a stunningly successful and risky operation to kill America's greatest and most elusive enemy.

There was one person inside the West Wing who had seen such desperate lows before, yet who still believed a revival was around the corner. David Plouffe had returned full-time to the president's inner circle in January, after two years of recovery from the grueling 2008 campaign, which he led to such historic success. Both metaphorically and literally, he had taken the place of his old friend and business partner, David Axelrod, who left the White House in January 2011. As chief strategist and keeper of the Obama flame inside the West Wing, Plouffe filled a vital role close to Obama; he even took Axelrod's desk next to the president's private study and the Oval Office.

Plouffe had always believed in a plan. Whatever the plan was, he stuck to it with a cold discipline, caring little for distractions or weakness that might divert attention. Where Axelrod was scattershot or indecisive, Plouffe was focused and driven. Where Axelrod was lyrical and aspirational, Plouffe was blunt and functional. If Axelrod was for Hope, Plouffe was for Change.

And Plouffe wanted above all to change the flawed and floundering message that had fared so poorly in the midterm congressional elections. Plouffe enforced discipline on the message and the general purpose of the White House. He was chief strategist and chief of staff rolled into one. "He was a voice of unquestioned authority," said one senior Obama aide. "Basically what he said went. If there was a policy question, it was Gene Sperling or Tim Geithner or someone on the national security staff. But in questions of strategy and message and posture, his was an unquestioned voice. Every single thing we did for two years, no one did anything without talking to him."

As hypercompetitive as his boss, Plouffe wanted to move the country in the right direction, and lock in the achievements of the last two and a half years. But above all, he wanted to prove that 2008 was no fluke. "First of all, I felt this was a moment in time where the direction of both parties was kind of diametrically opposed. So this wasn't a shades-of-gray election. Second of all, yeah, it was a ratification of what the president had done, his vision. It was a chance to build on the legacy. There was no doubt that if we had been a one-term president, 2008 would have been a nice story. But health care might be rolled back. To be a two-term president gives you a chance to really make a difference and make history."

Even beyond the national focus, Plouffe felt the fight was more personal. This time around, his private fear was of losing the presidency with an electoral defeat in Iowa, where he had invested so much time and emotion in 2007. "You know, I just wanted to see the story through," he said. "My nightmare was always that we would lose with 266 electoral college votes, on a loss in Iowa. We would joke about that a lot: 'The one thing we can't have is to lose because we lost in Iowa. If you were writing a tragic play, that's what would happen to us.'"

Plouffe's challenge was confounding: how could they break out of the game of Washington politics while their candidate was still forced to play the game of Washington politics?

Whether the issue was health-care reform or avoiding default on US debt, the president needed to work with Congress, and that often left him looking weak and unpresidential. His team was forced to accept there was no chance to message themselves out of the mess. "I'll put it this way," said Pfeiffer. "We've always been at our best when we are commander in chief and not legislator in chief. The circumstances of 2011 dictated that we had to spend some significant time as legislator in chief, and we knew that wasn't going to be good. It's never good for us, but it was necessary to avoid a default."

Obama returned from his vacation on Martha's Vineyard in late August sounding like a different man. From the start, he looked more presidential. He came back to the White House a day early to oversee preparations for Hurricane Irene. Natural disasters almost always offered presidents the chance to look as if they were in command, with the singular exception of President Bush's response to Katrina.

He was even more prepared for the natural disaster of dealing with a reckless Republican opposition. Obama had never thought it was a good idea for Republicans to run the country, but he believed in compromise all the same. Now their readiness to walk the minefield of default made him reconsider his approach. "What he saw in the debt ceiling debacle was the danger—in the most vivid way—of handing the country over to the other side, and what it would mean for the country," said Pfeiffer. "He was very focused, very engaged, and very spoiling for the fight. And by 'the fight' I don't necessarily mean the presidential election. I just mean the whole larger debate about the country."

For most of the year Obama had wanted to roll out a jobs plan. He and his messaging team had embraced a forward-sounding slogan about "winning the future." But the notion of investing in the future—in technology and education—was not about the here and now of a sluggish economy. Should they roll out a jobs plan before the debt ceiling or after? Pfeiffer was worried that the debt ceiling crisis would swallow any lasting awareness of the jobs plan. So Obama, in all his frustration, was forced to wait until the summer was over. He was allowed a brief bus tour of states he had previously won in the upper Midwest—a glimpse of the campaign to come. But no more.

Obama wanted to ditch the notion of compromise. The only way out, after a summer of default and discontent, was to confront the Republican Congress: to run as an outsider, rather than as an insider. It was the strategy that defined Obama from the outset in 2008, and that helped him finally win the votes to pass health-care reform in 2010.

He ordered his team to abandon their usual approach of crafting a plan that could pass Congress. He wanted to go bigger. If the GOP wanted to block his jobs plan, then he would tell the country who was to blame. "He wanted to run against Congress," said Pfeiffer. "Primarily the Republicans in Congress." Obama was sensitive to the concerns of Democrats in Congress, especially House minority leader Nancy Pelosi and Senate majority leader Harry Reid. Campaigning against a Do-Nothing Congress was not helpful to them. "That's really unfair to Harry and Nancy, who are actually trying to do the right thing," Obama told his team. "If they had real partners who were serious, then we'd get some things done."

Plouffe set out three tests for success. One: were they able to get any results? Two: did they show the country they had a specific plan to create jobs? Three: did they make it clear who was to blame for why the jobs deal did not move forward? "I was looking for opportunities that would get things done and move the public in our direction," said Plouffe. "We wanted to put the other guys on the wrong side of the door, while the president could look strong. The problem with the debt ceiling was that nobody looked strong. And we couldn't ever have that happen again. It's not that we can't compromise or take criticism. A lot of Democrats think we should get 100 percent of what we want, but we can't. We need to do whatever we do from a position of strength."

In the few days before Congress returned, Obama and his aides blocked out their plans for fall, and the start of the presidential election, from what looked like a position of strength.

He would convene the House and Senate for a speech: his signature move to reset politics in any crisis. He would travel at least a couple of days each week to make his case against Washington's dysfunction. He would talk jobs and then, some weeks later, return to the issue of deficits.

But first, they screwed up.

The White House and House Speaker John Boehner could not agree on the date for the speech. It was a small dispute that was emblematic of much bigger problems: not just the political chasm between the two sides, but the lack of professionalism inside the West Wing. Their first choice of date happened to coincide with another Republican presidential debate. Obama's chief of staff, Bill Daley, believed he had Boehner's agreement to move ahead, but once the date became public, the conservative pressure to pull out was intense. "The Republicans, if they have any hope of winning the 2012 election, have got to put this guy in his place using this as their opportunity to do it," Rush Limbaugh proclaimed. "No doubt about it." Within hours, Boehner had refused the suggested date, citing several votes that evening. In the end, just one vote was held that night. Its subject: "Authorizing the use of the Capitol Grounds for the District of Columbia Special Olympics Law Enforcement Torch Run."

Obama and his inner circle were once again furious. "For a lot of us it was like a huge punch in the stomach," said one of Obama's closest aides. "We had done all of this work to prepare for a new beginning, and we had just fumbled the ball before we started. It was completely self-inflicted." The goal was to project strength, and they just caved again. They switched the date by one day, and they blamed Bill Daley inside the West Wing. Outside the White House, the media blamed the players at both ends of Pennsylvania Avenue. The editorial board of the *New York Times* published an item headlined, "Oh, Grow Up." Republicans lacked a sense of respect for Obama and responsibility for the economy; Obama lacked professionalism and a backbone.

Once again, Obama needed a turnaround speech; one that could revive his political fortunes. He had done the same with his speech on race in the middle of the Reverend Jeremiah Wright fiasco in the Democratic primaries in 2008. He needed to take control of the story line. He needed to look more like a president in command and less like part of the political problem.

When the speech came around, Obama projected the kind of strength his staff had failed to signal in fumbling the date. Congress needed to do the right thing. They needed to pass the jobs bill. His jobs bill. There would be no pretense of equality. He summoned Congress for a presidential address to a joint session of the House and Senate—a mini State of the Union—in early September. In little more than thirty minutes, he used the phrase "pass this bill"—or some variation of it—more than a dozen times. "The people of this country work hard to meet their responsibilities," he told a chamber of happy-clappy Democrats and dour-faced Republicans. "The question tonight is whether we'll meet ours. The question is whether, in the face of an ongoing national crisis, we can stop the political circus and actually do something to help the economy. The question is whether we can restore some of the fairness and security that has defined this nation since our beginning." Within a week of his jobs speech, Obama exhorted Congress to "pass this bill" more than one hundred times in a series of events on the road and inside Washington.

Obama was trying to rewrite the narrative: instead of struggling with an abstract and stubborn economy, he was fighting against concrete and stubborn politicians. The GOP was the embodiment of the broken nature of Washington politics and, by extension, the broken nature of the economy. At the heart of his message strategy was a substitution: if he couldn't tell the story of his own success, he could tell the story of someone else's failure.

Never mind that his jobs bill addressed the economic challenges in relatively small ways. He proposed cutting payroll taxes, as well as increasing spending on schools, roads, and bridges. Everything would be paid for with spending cuts that were yet to be defined by a special congressional committee. The speech was much more of a pivot in politics than policy. "We knew that we were going to claw back a point at a time," said Pfeiffer. "No one's going to see that speech and all of a sudden it was going to be great."

Above all else, Obama needed to neutralize the criticism on his own side. He expected to be hated by the right. He was not expecting to face the same attacks from the left. "It was not a reality-based problem in terms of our real supporters, but we had to get the party back on our side," said Pfeiffer. "In this sort of polarized, Internet, cable-driven media environment, it's impossible to operate if your own side is attacking you. You can't fight a two-front war in politics. I'm talking about folks on the Hill. I'm talking about Paul Krugman, Ed Schultz, Arianna Huffington. The problem was that Republicans were saying something about the president and our Democratic friends were saying the same things and reinforcing that narrative. Basically Fox News and the *New York Times* editorial board for two different reasons were saying the same thing about the president, and that's a huge problem."

So began a behind-the-scenes effort to woo the left while whipping the right at the same time. Soon after the jobs speech, the *New York Times* editorial board published yet another column excoriating the president for his weakness. After each negative editorial, the president would summon his communications team to discuss the critical coverage. It was a deeply unpleasant experience for his staff, who bore the brunt of the presidential outbursts. This time, Obama wanted to do more than vent at his staff. He wanted to talk to Andy Rosenthal, the august editor of the editorial page.

"You know what?" said an exasperated Dan Pfeiffer. "Do it."

Obama walked out of the Oval Office and asked his assistant, Anita Decker, to get Rosenthal on the phone. She didn't have the number. Nor did Pfeiffer. Nor did his assistant.

"Anita, just call the main line," said the president.

"Anita, you can't do that," Pfeiffer interjected. "If you call the main line, they are going to announce on the PA system that the president is on the phone for Andy Rosenthal. We can't do that."

So much for the position of strength. In time, they found the number and the president spoke at length to Rosenthal. He invited him to come to the White House with the entire editorial board, and a couple of weeks later he sat with them for almost two hours, speaking freely, off the record. They wanted to talk about political strategy and the wars, about Iran and housing; he wanted to tell them they were parroting Republican talking points and explain why he had cut the deal with Boehner on the debt ceiling.

Over the next two months, Obama would sit down patiently and solicitously with some of his harshest liberal critics and many other influential progressive pundits. It was the first serious outreach to rebuild his base in his brief political career in Washington. By December Obama was having coffee with MSNBC's Rachel Maddow, Chris Hayes, Ed Schultz, and Joy-Ann Reid; Ezra Klein and Greg Sargent of the *Washington Post*; Arianna Huffington; and Josh Marshall of *Talking Points Memo*. Some came not to listen, but to talk: Paul Krugman, his chief economic critic on the left, dispensed his own advice on what the White House policy should be. Ed Schultz sat listening to others opine before ripping into an impassioned plea for the president to stand up and fight. The forty-fourth president of the United States listened calmly and nodded his head, surprising his aides with a meek appearance that successfully masked how little patience he had for such criticism.

There were few dispensers of advice in New York as prolific and impactful as the one working out of a Harlem office. To Obama's inner circle, William Jefferson Clinton could be the most dangerous adversary or the most potent ally in the Democratic Party. He could undercut a campaign among party donors and elected officials, as he did to his own vice president in 2000. Or he could lift a candidate up in a high-profile display of party unity, which he never quite managed in 2008. While Obama and Hillary Clinton had bonded inside the National Security Council at the White House—under the extraordinary pressures of the Arab Spring and the bin Laden raid—there had been no partnership established between the forty-fourth and the forty-second presidents of the United States.

So on an unusually warm and sunny November morning, a clutch of Obama's closest aides traveled to Harlem to talk—and listen—to one of the party's best political brains. Over the course of two hours, they delivered a special presentation of their benchmark polling data, fielded his questions, and listened to his advice. "He's indisputably brilliant at the strategy piece," said Axelrod. "He looks at polling data like an artist walks through a museum. He sees things other people don't see."

It was an awkward session for most of the Obama aides present. Axelrod was once extensively engaged in Hillary Clinton's

Senate campaign in New York, and Clinton had been instrumental in helping Axelrod and his wife, Susan, set up their foundation to research epilepsy, a condition that had ravaged their daughter. The Axelrods and the Clintons were once personally and professionally intertwined. Then, suddenly, they weren't, as Axelrod became the central political operative behind the presidential rise of one Barack Obama. While Axelrod insisted that he was never anti-Clinton (simply pro-Obama), in the heat of the 2008 primaries it often sounded like a distinction without a difference.

Axelrod was never the most organized or diplomatic person in a room full of strategists: his gentle humor and soft-spoken delivery often masked his competitive need to display his sense of superiority. So he managed to show up late to this most fraught meeting with the former president. Bill Clinton gave the distinct impression that he was not amused by Axelrod's tardiness and was a long way from forgiving his perceived disloyalty.

When they dug into the data, Clinton was fascinated by the polling. The race carried many echoes of his own breakthrough in 1992. The Obama team's basic presentation emphasized themes he had struck twenty years earlier: the viability of the middle class, the fundamental fairness of the economy, the nature of opportunity and responsibility. When he accepted his party's nomination in 1992, Clinton had lamented how "those who play by the rules and keep the faith have gotten the shaft, and those who cut corners and cut deals have been rewarded." Now he seemed pleased to hear his original message echoed back to him by the team that had opposed him so aggressively just four years ago.

Clinton wanted to explore where the race was headed against the likely GOP nominee, and he had his own theories about how Mitt Romney was vulnerable to attack. Given the struggling economy, Clinton believed that Romney was not the best image for the Republican party. He looked and sounded like one of those who cut corners and cut deals. A superwealthy CEO with a lavish lifestyle, he was as out of touch as George Herbert Walker Bush. Clinton believed that line of attack was far more profitable than the notion of Romney as the Republican John Kerry: a serial flip-flopper.

Axelrod disagreed. He believed the two lines of attack were related. Romney was presenting himself as a job creator in a struggling economy. But his time at the private equity firm Bain Capital, as well as his record as Massachusetts governor, suggested that jobs were not his real focus in the private or public sector. To Axelrod, Romney was both out of touch *and* inauthentic. He was taking a beating from his Republican rivals for the presidential nomination, and his personal ratings were turning sharply negative. Only one recent candidate for president had recovered from such negative numbers in a primary season, and he was sitting in front of Axelrod. Whatever Romney's strengths, he would never come close to the political talents of Bill Clinton.

For all their professed devotion to the middle class and the jobless, the greatest brains inside the Democratic Party were not arguing about how to turn around the economy or even how to pass the president's jobs bill. They were debating the best way to turn Mitt Romney into an unpleasant message.

By early 2012, Axelrod had been out of the White House for almost a year, and he spent much of his time wondering how to define the enemy. You didn't need to spend as much money as he did on polling to know that Obama was vulnerable. But their real opponent wasn't Mitt Romney or the Republican Party. "We're not really running against Romney," he said in a Chicago café in the early days of the campaign. "We're running against the economy. And we're running against the outsized expectations that people had of Obama."

As soft as he seemed in personal style, Axelrod had something of a contrarian view of politics. The maximum peril came at times of maximum opportunity; the best glimpse of recovery came at the worst moment of misery. When the economy collapsed with the financial markets late in the 2008 election cycle, Axelrod told Obama he was likely heading for victory as president and defeat in the midterms that followed.

Now he believed that Obama's revival had begun in the crisis that seemed to destroy his standing in the polls. "In a way the message emerged from the wreckage of the debt ceiling," Axelrod said. "Even though we lost the debt ceiling battle, we won the message war. The president said we have got to approach the deficit problem in a balanced way that leaves room for growth; that we need to balance growth with broader prosperity, education, research, and development; and that we have to ask everybody to do their fair share. We can't afford these tax cuts for the wealthy because in order to deal with the deficit, to invest in the kind of things that will make our economy grow, the wealthy have to give up something. That formed the framework for our message going forward. We look like we have a vision for how you grow the economy. The Republicans look like you just cut taxes at the top, cut regulation, and everything will just work out."

Inside Washington, Axelrod had dismissed efforts to focus on the middle class. It sounded like so much Clintonesque pabulum. Its chief advocate was the irritable and irritating Stan Greenberg, Clinton's pollster, who was writing a book with James Carville called, simply, *It's the Middle Class, Stupid!* Greenberg's polling memos were laced with blunt criticisms of Obama's approach to messaging. By early 2010, Greenberg's own message was getting echoed by some of Axelrod's own team of outside consultants. Larry Grisolano had taken over his old firm of political consultants, AKPD, when Axelrod moved into the White House. Even Grisolano was telling Axelrod that he was missing the bigger picture inside the West Wing.

Axelrod held weekly Wednesday night meetings with his consultants in his Washington apartment, but he was increasingly impatient with their dissent as the White House team struggled to find a path through the Tea Party–led resurgence of the Republican Party. "The middle class is being lost here," Grisolano lamented to his old friend.

Axelrod dismissed him out of hand. "You have no idea what we're dealing with here, day to day," he said.

Looking back, Axelrod realized he was wrong. Life in the West Wing amounted to a triage unit, dashing from one life-threatening crisis to another. The middle-class message was indeed lost. Every month inside the White House was an effort to prove the economy was improving. Back in Chicago, talking to people outside the Beltway or listening to endless focus groups, he saw that he had dropped the very thing he was trying to protect. Axelrod had always been a big-picture storyteller. He preferred shaping the grand narrative of a candidate and campaign to the trench warfare of the daily and hourly news cycles. He had styled himself as the protector of the Obama brand but had failed to realize how that brand was undermined daily.

What he heard in the focus groups was a vastly different conversation from the one inside the West Wing. "When you hear people talk, you feel two things," he said at the outset of the campaign. "When you think about the average middle-class

American, what they feel is that above them they see people getting bailouts. Below them they see people getting handouts. And they feel that they are on their own. They feel they are working hard and they're not getting a fair shake, and other people aren't doing their fair share."

The fair shake and the fair share: it was a classic Axelrod turn of phrase. A piece of writing that encapsulated a worldview more than a policy prescription for hard economic times. To the right, it sounded faintly socialist with its insistence on fairness. To the left, it sounded like justice. And to the middle-class voters who would decide the election, it sounded like their plight at a time when wages were getting pushed down and costs were getting pushed up. Economy forces were conspiring to keep them from achieving the American Dream. "We mostly only talk to swing and independent voters who are open to us but not committed to us," said Axelrod. "And overwhelmingly they reject the idea that this is the politics of envy, because they are living in this economy. The point isn't envy; it's one of fairness. They don't want the game to be rigged in their favor. They just don't want the game to be rigged *against* them."

When times were tough inside the White House, Axelrod would hand Obama a copy of a single speech from the distant past. It was the first economic speech of his first presidential campaign, delivered to Wall Street executives at NASDAQ's offices in New York in September 2007. For Axelrod, it was one of the top three speeches his boss had ever delivered—right up there with his convention speech from 2004, when he suggested he could unite red and blue America. Axelrod used the speech as his touchstone: a test of whether Obama was true to his own identity. In fact, his insistence on rereading the NASDAQ speech became something of an eye roller inside the Oval Office.

The speech met with a muted response from the Wall Street crowd. That was the point, after all. Obama started out citing Franklin D. Roosevelt, in the midst of the Great Depression, calling on business executives to undergo a "re-appraisal of values" so that everyone could live in prosperity. It was time, as FDR had said, to "recognize the new terms of the old social contract." Obama had no idea how far the subprime mortgage crisis would plunge the economy into a deep and severe recession a year later. He had no idea how that recession would weaken his presidency and challenge his ability to get anything done in Washington. But he did have an idea of the kind of economic turmoil that had disrupted middle-class Americans for most of the last decade. "I meet these Americans every single day," he explained, "people who believe they have been left on the sidelines by a global economy that has forever changed the rules of the game. They understand that revolutions in technology and communication have torn borders and opened up new markets and new opportunities. They know we can't go back to yesterday or wall off our economy from everyone else. Their problem is not that our world is flat. It's that our playing field isn't level. It's that opportunity is no longer equal. And that's something we cannot accept anymore."

In fact Obama did accept the unfair playing field for most of the first half of his presidency. Wall Street and corporate America looked so weak in his first year that there was no choice but to try to save them. Then the banks and big corporations roared back to health and mounted an aggressive lobbying effort to thwart any attempt at new regulations. In late 2011, the backlash to the backlash had begun. Four years to the day of his NASDAQ speech, protesters set up tents in Zuccotti Park, close to Wall Street. The Occupy Wall Street movement spread to other cities and made the White House hesitant in response.

The plan, in December 2011, was to bookend the jobs speech with another speech recalling that NASDAQ moment. But the Occupy Wall Street protesters made it impossible to deliver such a speech in New York without implicitly endorsing them. Obama's speechwriter came up with a solution. Before FDR, there was Theodore Roosevelt's speech that established his new Progressive Party: that government should regulate business and protect working people from inhuman conditions. This New Nationalism, as TR called it, sounded more than familiar to a president a century later as he argued that government should again be concerned with the public welfare. "I stand for the square deal," said Roosevelt. "But when I say that I am for the square deal, I mean not merely that I stand for fair play under the present rules of the game, but that I stand for having those rules changed so as to work for a more substantial equality of opportunity and of reward for equally good service."

Obama traveled to the same small town—Osawatomie, Kansas—where TR delivered his New Nationalism speech to set the terms of the debate he hoped to have in the next year against his Republican opponent. "I'm here in Kansas to reaffirm my deep conviction that we're greater together than we are on our own," Obama said. "I believe that this country succeeds when everyone gets a fair shot, when everyone does their fair share, when everyone plays by the same rules. These aren't Democratic values or Republican values. These aren't 1 percent values or 99 percent values. They're American values. And we have to reclaim them."

Obama walked off stage to sit down with his go-to interviewer: Steve Kroft at *60 Minutes*. Kroft immediately suggested that many people would think he was a socialist engaging in class warfare. Obama challenged the question. He argued that it was time to be honest about what had happened to the economy. He complained

Republicans had never wanted to work with him. Above all, he tried to shift the discussion away from the unwinnable contest against himself from four years earlier. When Kroft suggested the election would be a judgment on his performance, Obama pushed back hard. "No, no, no," he insisted. "I'm being judged against the ideal. And, you know, Joe Biden has a good expression. He says, 'Don't judge me against the Almighty, judge me against the alternative.'"

His message team was already working on the alternative. After more than a dozen Republican debates, Mitt Romney seemed to be sailing through the wreckage of his rivals' campaigns without facing a serious challenge on camera. Other candidates rose and fell, for sure. In September, Texas governor Rick Perry took a lead in the polls, until he could no longer recall his own policies on stage. In October, the former pizza executive Herman Cain took a brief lead before news broke about multiple allegations of sexual harassment. The former House Speaker Newt Gingrich stole the lead, before Romney's superPAC supporters destroyed Gingrich with millions of dollars' worth of ads. Finally the former senator Rick Santorum sparked into life and then fizzled into obscurity.

At Obama headquarters in Chicago, there were equal measures of disbelief and joy at the GOP contest. They had always banked on Romney winning the nomination, and despite their enjoyment at the freak show of the Republican contests, they were deeply troubled that the former Massachusetts governor was not being challenged by anything like a competent campaign. In 2008, the Obama team had been battle-tested by their ferocious and well-funded opponents on the Clinton campaign. Romney seemed to be emerging without any serious challenge. So Obama's aides decided to intervene themselves.

This was not the first time they had tried to mess with a Republican primary. The figure at the center of the strategy had run the same playbook little more than a year earlier. Jim Margolis was not just an adman. Although he played that role in the Obama campaign, he was also a political strategist in his own right, with a track record that was more successful than most of those around him. In particular, he had scored remarkable victories in the most difficult cycle for Democrats in a decade. Margolis counted two vulnerable Democratic senators in his roster of candidates in 2010: Senate majority leader Harry Reid of Nevada, and Barbara Boxer of California. Both senators struggled to break 50 percent in opinion polls ahead of the midterm elections, and Reid was actually trailing his opponent in the last week of polling.

Margolis was faced with two very different opponents. In Nevada, there was the Tea Party favorite Sharron Angle; in California, there was the former Hewlett-Packard CEO Carly Fiorina. The Reid campaign set about making sure that more electable opponents were too wounded to beat Angle in the primary contest. Among them was a casino owner, Sue Lowden, whom they portrayed as an avaricious, coldhearted, and out-of-touch business executive. The masterpiece was a website and video, produced by national Democrats (rather than the campaign itself), that seized on comments by Lowden about the good old days of health care, when people would sometimes pay doctors with livestock. It was called Chickens for Checkups. Fiorina suffered a similar fate, ending her campaign in defeat as the caricature of an avaricious, coldhearted, and out-of-touch business executive.

Margolis appeared to be, on the face of it, one of the least aggressive of Obama's senior advisers. He kept a lower media profile than his peers, doing no surrogate work on TV shows and rarely getting quoted in print. Yet his ads were not for the faint of heart. Sharron Angle wasn't just a liar, she was "pathological." Margolis clearly understood the president's challenges—his low approval ratings and a poor economy—but he also believed Obama had some key assets: his likability, his accomplishments, and his opponent. "We had the benefit of what Romney did during the primary process," Margolis said. "He consistently looked to the right. He made a judgment that that's what he needed to do to get through the primary. I'm not sure that was good judgment, but it certainly helped us as we moved into the general election. He came out of that process with big issue vulnerabilities and big personal vulnerabilities: choice, immigration, his wealth, Bain, who he looks out for. Fundamentally, we believed this election—despite a lot of the commentary—was about big things. There was going to be a fundamental choice that we needed to lead people to by the end of the election. It wasn't all small ball."

Watching the Republican primary debates, Obama's team grew increasingly frustrated by the lack of blows landed on Mitt Romney. Wasn't it obvious to Romney's opponents how much he flipped and flopped on every substantive issue? Margolis had been part of the ad team behind the Kerry campaign in 2004, when the charges of flip-flopping proved devastating to the Democratic nominee. This time around, Margolis and his team were more than ready to play offense, rather than defense.

So, in late November, they released a four-minute-long web video—more of a TV segment than a TV ad—on a new website called Mitt v. Mitt. The site was helpfully subtitled: The Story of Two Men Trapped in One Body.

"He wants to be president," the video graphics said at the start, "But what does he really believe?" The video helpfully pointed out that Romney opposed the stimulus after he said he was for it. He insisted he would protect a woman's right to choose, before wanting to overturn *Roe v. Wade*. He was determined not to return to the politics of Reagan, before he affirmed his support for the principles of Ronald Reagan. He was happy that Obama was copying his health-care reform before insisting that Obamacare was bad news. In one debate exchange on immigration, the video noted that Romney reversed himself in less than three minutes on the embarrassing question of whether he had ever hired an illegal immigrant. All along, the sound bites of Romney's contradictions were interspersed with journalists—from CNN, Fox News, and MSNBC—wondering out loud how long Romney could survive the flip-flopping charge.

Another few months of this message, and Romney would look and sound like Sue Lowden or Carly Fiorina: a business executive with no heart and no brain.

On the eve of the Republican primaries, in December 2011, the president's message men were happier than they had been for most of the last year. That was, admittedly, a low bar to cross. "Since the debt ceiling debate, which was really the nadir of our whole administration, the dynamic is that the Republicans in some ways defined themselves through that fight," said Axelrod at the time. "Their obstructionism became apparent in ways that began to erode them and gave us something to push off from. They put their entire bet on the notion that the president has failed and the economy stinks and he's the responsible party so he should be fired. And their argument has been eroding as there are signs of progress, and they look more and more negative. They look like they are rooting for failure when there's good news. It seems to me that we're now in the position where we've been able to take a higher hill. It's a combination of realism and hope. We recognize that we have a long way to go, that things are moving in the right direction, but we can't go back to what we were doing before. That's becoming a more and more salient argument."

It might have been salient, but it was also very familiar. Obama had run against Republican opposition before. He had touted signs of progress before. It was only a year since the president himself had traveled the country warning that the GOP had driven the economy into a ditch. Now they were standing by the side of the road, watching him pull the car out, while asking for the keys back. The voters heard that argument repeatedly in the congressional elections of 2010. And they decided to give Republicans the keys to the House of Representatives.

Inside the White House they had seen this same strategy play out too many times before. "We were very worried that we were going to get ahead of where people are," said Pfeiffer. "What's always important to remember is that the key was to stay grounded in people's everyday experience, which is: things are not great right now, but there's a good trajectory. That was sellable. Some things are great: people watch TV, the stock market is up, jobs are being created, they had a job this whole time. But everything costs more, they're making less, and they feel more pressure. So you have to be able to speak to where they are. It's realism in the present, and optimism in the future."

Obama's aides never really talked about what was sellable in 2008. Hope was not such a sellable commodity. You either believed in it or you didn't. Now the election was a choice between realistic optimism and something yet to be defined on the other side. The story they were trying to tell—the message they were trying to sell—was starkly different this time around.

So was the dynamic among the message merchants. They had begun to turn the story around inside the White House:

from the floundering, half-competent reaction to the debt ceiling crisis to the more forceful posture of defining the other side afterward. But that turnaround had only begun thanks to some determined command and control inside Obama's inner circle. They had started their campaign strategy in the depths of default talk, and they were not about to descend into such disarray again. Plouffe was the master of this message, not the pundits, not Bill Clinton, not the Chicago team seven hundred miles away. The sooner they all realized that, the better.

THREE

TEAM OF RIVALS

T he press liked to call their style No Drama Obama.

It was a nice turn of phrase that matched the mood of the candidate in 2008. But it was not completely true. There was plenty of early personal tension, yet it rarely spilled into open conflict. Axelrod and Gibbs tripped over one another as they vied to be the chief message maker, but they eventually figured out a way forward. Valerie Jarrett often annoyed the political operatives as the chief defender of the Obama brand, but that was the role she was given by the Obamas themselves. There was plenty of recrimination as the primaries dragged on. But much of that came from Michelle Obama and was directed at her husband and his supposedly incompetent advisers. If there were resentments at campaign headquarters, they had to remain on a low simmer.

That all changed with the reelection. The personal tensions started earlier and rapidly worsened. They fought in private and in the open. There was plenty of simmering, and often a high boil. The team of rivals rarely achieved a spirit of cooperation and seemed more inclined to bitter, dogged rivalries.

The cast of characters had changed, and so had the plot.

At the heart of the Obama drama was a political operative with the air of a bloodless executioner. Jim Messina originally entered the Obama orbit when the campaign's first manager, David Plouffe, was threatening to quit. The primaries of 2008 were not yet over, but Plouffe was burned out. His wife was pregnant with their second child, and Plouffe was ready to leave as soon as the nomination was settled. Obama convinced Plouffe to stay with the promise that he would find someone to run the day-to-day campaign operation, allowing Plouffe to remain focused on the big-picture strategy.

That someone was Messina: the chief of staff to Senator Max Baucus of Montana, and a street fighter of a campaign manager in a series of Senate races. In Baucus's 2002 race for reelection, Messina was the driving force behind a TV ad that demolished his Republican challenger by suggesting that he was both gay and an embezzler of public funds. (It wasn't clear which of the two charges was considered more damning.) The campaign ad featured the GOP candidate, a state senator called Mike Taylor, in a 1980s commercial for his hair salon. The Republican was shown in disco-era clothes, complete with medallion necklace, massaging a male model's face and then reaching for his lap. Taylor soon dropped out of the race and Baucus sailed to victory. Both Baucus and Messina have publicly and frequently described their relationship as a father-son bond in its closeness and trust.

Obama convinced Messina to leave his political father by calling him the day after Hillary Clinton dropped out of the Democratic primary contest. The sales pitch was neither about hope nor change. "You're really going to get to run a business," Obama told Messina.

Seven days later, Messina was in Chicago with control of the campaign staff and its budget. On his first day at work, Plouffe handed him a list of half a dozen people.

"Fire them," Plouffe said.

So he did. Messina would introduce himself to bemused staffers and ask them to visit his office for a second or two. That was the last conversation they would have with him at campaign headquarters. Other staffers might be unhappy at taking the ax to new coworkers; Messina was not one of them. He was in Chicago to bring some order to an operation that had outlived the structure of the primaries. If that meant he was unpopular, so be it.

Messina had avoided presidential campaigns of cycles past because he preferred the control and camaraderie of Senate elections. He had read all the stories about the Kerry campaign in 2004, and the Gore campaign in 2000, and decided the infighting was unbearable. Chicago in 2008 was totally different. In five months there, he witnessed only one dispute between the two most senior figures: David Plouffe and his former business partner, David Axelrod. "I thought that was the best culture I had ever been a part of," Messina said. Like the two Davids, Messina felt he had finally found a candidate who was worthy of his idealism and his hard work.

He entered the White House as deputy chief of staff and was a central player in the extended, painful saga of health-care reform. Inside the West Wing, he was widely blamed for buying into Baucus's belief that there were Republican senators who would join their effort. As a reward for his efforts, he faced a year-long House GOP investigation into his work on Obamacare, especially the backroom industry deals that greased the way for the legislation.

Just five months after President Obama signed his historic health-care reform into law, he shared his armored limo with Messina in Seattle, where they had traveled for an event to help reelect Senator Patty Murray.

"Everyone says you should run the campaign," Obama told Messina. "How will I replace you?"

Messina asked to defer the conversation until after the midterm elections of 2010. Which was how he ended up in Hawaii at Christmas, wading through the surf with the president of the United States, discussing his next job as manager of the 2012 reelection.

There never was another serious candidate for the position. Plouffe had handed him operational control of the 2008 campaign. And the following year, in the White House, Plouffe had once again told Messina to run Chicago. Implicit in that offer was the notion that the two operatives could maintain their working alliance: Plouffe would set the course and steer the strategy, while Messina would run the machine. Plouffe could stay inside the White House, close to POTUS, while still controlling a headquarters seven hundred miles away.

Messina walked into the empty offices in the Prudential building in March 2011 with a single box of personal items. There was no structure and no staff: not even on paper.

The newly anointed Messina faced his earliest, biggest staff challenges in two of the closest and longest-serving aides to Barack Obama: David Axelrod and Robert Gibbs.

Axelrod had in many ways created Barack Obama as a candidate. He had not just crafted his ads since 2004; he had cowritten his narrative. Obama was just an obscure state senator when

Axelrod, the biggest Democratic consultant in Chicago, gave him the seal of approval to win the Illinois seat in the US Senate. Obama was just a freshman in Washington when Axelrod turned down the Clinton campaign, and everyone else, to steer him to the presidential nomination and the White House. He entered the White House as a friend and keeper of the campaign flame: the high priest of the hope-filled Obama revivalists in a West Wing full of inside-Washington survivalists. As shambling as he was in his outward appearance, Axe—as he liked to be called—was a wily strategist who liked to keep an iron grip on the levers of the message machine. He ran the pollsters and the admen, the speechwriters and strategic communications. Axe was personally and professionally invested in Barack Obama: he represented the lifelong merger of the spirit of Bobby Kennedy's campaign with the racial transcendence promised by Martin Luther King. After Obama delivered a flawless acceptance speech in Denver in 2008, Axe closed his eyes and embraced him with the kind of ear-to-ear smile that suggested he was almost in love with his candidate.

And then he was pushed out.

Not officially, of course. He was just leaving a little earlier than intended. Heading back to Chicago to spend more time with his family and recharge before the campaign. Nothing unusual, really. Just a wrenching expression of disaffection from the president he had fallen for. After two brutal years in the White House, when nobody was happy with the message, he was now on the outside looking in.

Robert Gibbs fancied himself as an Axe-in-waiting. Behind the scenes, he could serve as the strategic storyteller just as smoothly as he could play the role of the spokesman in front of the cameras. He had been Obama's horse whisperer since 2004: his political coach and sidekick on tens of thousands of miles of campaign travel. When the candidate was sullen and grumpy—which was often—he could read his mood and adjust the bubble accordingly. He knew when to punch at their opponents on Obama's behalf and how to crack a stinging joke when his boss couldn't. He entered the White House as a friend and confidant, and he liked to think of himself as an indispensable part of the family. Yes, he was disorganized and rarely returned phone calls from the press. Perhaps that constituted one of the jobs of the White House press secretary. But Gibbs was busy at the side of the president of the United States.

And then he was pushed out.

Not officially, of course. He was just leaving a little earlier than intended. Heading back to Alexandria to spend more time with his family and recharge before the campaign. Nothing unusual, really. Just a wrenching expression of disaffection from the president he had fallen for. After two brutal years in the White House, when nobody was happy with the message, he was now on the outside looking in.

"The president broke Axe's and Robert's hearts," said one member of Obama's inner circle. For those who remained, the departure of Axelrod and Gibbs sent a clear message: they were all dispensable. "He doesn't need anyone," said another member of the inner circle. "Axe and Gibbs were effectively fired. He owes everything to Axe. Everything. He'd never have gotten anywhere without him. I'd like to think he knows that and sees him differently. But I'm not sure." Obama kept a close team of younger male staffers to manage his immediate needs, and that was all he needed. "He needs the guys to play cards and golf, and tell him where he's going next and why," said a former aide. "But beyond that, it's what function you have. And if you can't fulfill that function anymore, or someone can do it better, you're gone. That's hard for those of us who really believe in him. He expects full loyalty. But you need to have your eyes open."

If Barack Obama—or any of his other senior aides—felt a pang about the departure of Axe and Gibbs, they did not show it. David Plouffe took control of the White House message operation, as well as Axe's office close to the Oval, and nobody looked back. Jim Messina took Plouffe's old job in Chicago, and the president tasked him with bringing both Axe and Gibbs back on board in more limited roles. Plouffe and Messina claimed to be just as much of a believer in Obama's brand of hope and change as Axe and Gibbs. But behind their intensely competitive exteriors, they nurtured intensely competitive interiors. Unlike Axe and Gibbs, they were still on the inside ring of Obama's circle of confidants.

Gibbs was in some ways the easier of the two heartbreaks, because he failed to put up a fight. He was making huge amounts of money on the speaking circuit—up to $1 million a year—and toying with job offers in the private sector, including one from Facebook. But that wasn't enough, and the campaign couldn't—or wouldn't—give him what he wanted. He was paid $15,000 a month to jump on some calls, and travel out to Chicago once a week in the early stages. But he made no more than a dozen trips to headquarters in twenty months. He had no appetite to jockey for power with those running the communications team in Chicago. And he was excluded from the senior message meetings in the Roosevelt Room in the White House on Sunday nights. "Robert to this day isn't whole," said one senior Obama aide. "We paid him to do absolutely nothing. What he wanted was to hang out with Barack Obama, and there was no way he was going to be allowed on the plane. The plane was very disciplined and there was no role for him there." Between Plouffe and Jen Psaki, Air Force One had no room for Robert Gibbs. "Typical Obama structure: we knew what we wanted and we weren't going to do something else."

Axe was rather more complicated. The polling and ad operations still lay in his hands. All the president's message men were his friends, former coworkers or contractors, and sometimes all three. He was tasked with crafting Obama's campaign narrative once again. His old agency, AKPD, was still running the TV ad strategy under his friend Larry Grisolano. His old agency partner was none other than Plouffe. But as the campaign began to staff up, and the Republican primaries started to play out, Axe felt doubly excluded. Plouffe and Messina seemed to be joined together in a tight-knit alliance, dictating to everyone—especially Axe—how the strategy would unfold.

In reality, that meant Messina was ordering everyone around. Plouffe wanted to avoid personal conflict at all costs. His intensity masked a certain social nervousness; insecurity, even. The last thing he wanted to do was confront his old, and older, business partner. Besides, he thought Axelrod needed to adjust to a less intense life outside the White House bubble. Once the adjustment was done, he liked to think that everything would be fine. But that would not turn out to be true. "One of Plouffe's great strengths as a manager is that he never says more than he wants to, but when he speaks he's very straightforward," said one senior Obama aide. "That would not be one of Messina's strengths."

The struggle began with Axe's hiring and his contract negotiations. For consultants like Axelrod, election cycles were opportunities to turn candidates into elected officials, and to turn fund-raising dollars into personal wealth. In 2008, none of the consultants knew how big the Obama operation could be. Many of them did not expect Obama to decide to run for president, never mind win the Iowa caucuses and the party's nomination. None of them dreamed Obama could raise the kind of dollars he did in 2008, when he smashed all fund-raising records and opted out of the public finance system for presidential campaigns. So consultants like Axelrod capped their fees, which are normally a tiny percentage of the total spending on their part of the ad budget—whether TV commercials or direct mail.

Four years later, they were not going to make the same mistake. The reelection was forecast to be a billion-dollar campaign, and they wanted their fair share. Axelrod hired a lawyer to negotiate his deal, which was a combination of a monthly fee and what he called "a very, very small percentage" of the overall TV ad budget. For Axelrod, the fees were only part of the story. After almost two years of campaigning solely for Barack Obama, he had spent two years away from his family, working inside the White House. The personal and financial sacrifices were real. Plouffe had made a fortune on the speaking circuit while Axelrod was struggling to find the message during the great recession and the rise of the Tea Party. Everyone else could monetize their 2008 experience except the man most loyal to the president.

Messina took a different view. He did not seem to appreciate Axelrod's decision to hire a lawyer to negotiate a deal. In his mind, nobody was going to get rich from the reelect. Salaries were capped. Donor dollars would not flow like they did in 2008. And while Plouffe officially stayed out of the dispute, he had a reputation as a tight-fisted manager who was loath to waste cash.

As for President Obama, this was just the sort of dispute he hated. In policy debates, he seemed perfectly happy to watch and listen as his closest aides engaged in lengthy argument. His first economic team had been at war with each other on matters big and small from the days of his first transition through the first two years in the White House. But his political team was his blind spot. It seemed unclear—even to his most senior advisers—whether he knew about the simmering disputes inside his political team. Those advisers suspected he knew about the conflicts but pretended they didn't exist because he had no desire to resolve them, and because he hoped they might peter out. Obama wanted consensus on communications and strategy, not personal conflict. And since Axelrod selected and controlled the message teams, consensus was generally what Obama got. "The principal's position is: 'You guys figure it out. Come to me with your recommendation,'" said one communications insider. "Obama generally doesn't like to be in this position when it comes to political stuff. He does not mind disagreement at all on the policy. But he has placed a huge amount of trust in navigating his political career in this team, and in particular David Axelrod, from the beginning, and it's hard to argue with his success. So let's be honest: at the end of the day, Axe controlled who got which contracts. There's not a lot of percentage in disagreeing with him."

Except the contract negotiation was not in Axelrod's control. It was in the hands of Messina and, by extension, Plouffe. Messina told friends that he was acting under the president's direction, which he characterized like this: "I want everybody treated fairly, but I don't want anybody to get rich on this. They're gonna get rich on the books they write afterwards." Many of those who worked with Messina doubted his accounts of conversations with Obama or Plouffe. But he acted as if he was empowered by them, and he was. Messina and Axelrod negotiated hard, as Messina hacked away at Axelrod's demands.

The dispute centered not just on money, or even status. There was a more deep-seated rift beneath the disagreement about terms of employment. For much of his time inside the White House, Axelrod was the keeper of the 2008 flame in the face of intense efforts to extinguish it. His frequent opponents were the Washington insiders represented by his old Chicago friend Rahm Emanuel, then White House chief of staff, and Emanuel's deputy: Jim Messina. As health-care reform staggered through to its signing in 2009, the cozy backroom deals with the industry drove Axelrod crazy: they were anathema to the reformer he had helped elect a year earlier. They would hurt the president politically and undermine health-care reform itself. But Axelrod would lose those arguments to Emanuel and Messina, just as he had lost an earlier debate about getting tough against Wall Street. And the biggest reason he lost those debates was because he often stood to the left of his own boss, Barack Obama.

For the first six months of the campaign's life, the contract talks between Axelrod and Messina led to festering resentment at the heart of the leadership in Chicago. Axelrod made it clear that he felt Messina was not up to the job of campaign manager. He liked to compare the relationship between Plouffe and Messina to the two strongmen running the Kremlin. Plouffe was President Vladimir Putin, the man really in charge, while Messina was his henchman and prime minister, Dmitry Medvedev. Axe respected Plouffe highly, but he did not believe that Messina was an honest broker. He felt that Plouffe had no sense of the day-to-day business in Chicago, while Messina was desperately overcompensating for his insecurity and lack of control.

So Axelrod ran his message team independently of the person supposedly leading the entire operation. Until the fall of 2011, the two most senior figures of the reelection campaign were in open conflict. There would be little trust between them moving forward, and their dispute spilled into other relationships and operations across the Chicago office. Axelrod repeatedly tried to convince other senior aides to bypass Messina, and they believed he was trying to oust Messina altogether. Axelrod had never wanted him to get the job in the first place. Now he was complaining to others inside Obama's inner circle about Messina's shortcomings, but there was no support for a change of campaign manager. Axelrod knew that Plouffe had confidence in Messina, and nobody could come up with a good candidate to replace him. "For a good six months of that campaign, they were trying to wedge him out, which created all of the divisions," said one senior Obama campaign official. "But there was no one else, and Messina had positioned himself with Plouffe. Axe had tried a long time to prevent him from getting that job."

Messina returned fire in much the same way. He could not fire Axelrod—not least because Axelrod had already been pushed out. And he could hardly dismantle Axelrod's team; that team was almost the entirety of the message machine. Instead, they fought by proxy, like cold war superpowers trapped inside the so-called Prudential building.

The plot only thickened with the arrival of a third alpha ego in the highest ranks of Chicago's leadership. Stephanie Cutter was a veteran of the brutal presidential campaigns that Messina says he had read about and wanted to avoid. In the chaotic civil war of the Kerry campaign of 2004, as communications director, she stood out as an aggressive internal warrior with few allies. In the post-election write-ups, notably the *Newsweek* insider account of the election, she was unfairly tarnished as the singular reason for the campaign's multiple failings—as if the candidate and his senior consultants played only minor roles in the message fiasco. Cutter knew how it felt to lose a presidential election against a mighty Republican machine—and what it felt like to lose the internal struggle for power and positive press—and she was determined to avoid either fate again.

In the intervening years she had more than repaired her reputation. She returned to work for her mentor, Senator Edward Kennedy, who had initially placed her inside the Kerry campaign. She helped engineer Kennedy's emotional endorsement of Obama in the early stages of the 2008 primaries, and remained close to the Kennedys through the senator's final struggle with a brain tumor. By the general election phase of 2008, she was drafted into Chicago to repair the battered image of Michelle Obama. The candidate's wife was personally and politically vulnerable as she reeled from the right-wing attack on her as an angry and unpatriotic black woman. And her staff seemed incapable of taking control of Michelle's public profile. From that moment on, Cutter proved herself a trusted and invaluable insider for the Obamas. She helped manage their family transition into Washington, including the selection of schools for their daughters. She gave shape and purpose to the First Lady's anti-obesity campaign, Let's Move, managing its rollout to the perfectionist standards of Michelle Obama herself. It was Cutter who successfully shepherded the first Supreme Court nomination of Obama's presidency, Sonia Sotomayor. Her reward was to enter the White House as a deputy senior adviser, backing up David Axelrod himself.

The only problem was that Axelrod never wrote up a job description for Cutter or gave her any lines of management. Being a senior adviser was fine for Axelrod and his peers, Valerie Jarrett and Pete Rouse. All three were unimpeachable because of their close relationship with the president, and all three ranged freely in their interests and influence. A deputy senior adviser had no such freedom. In an acutely competitive and status-conscious White House, if you weren't on top, you felt like you were on the bottom.

Cutter wanted to run communications inside the White House, but that job was already filled by Dan Pfeiffer, an early staffer on the 2008 campaign who grew personally close to David Plouffe. Pfeiffer and Plouffe shared a peculiar combination of a placid appearance with a deeply driven spirit. They barely seemed to break a sweat while focused on beating the Clintons in 2008, or McCain after that.

Given their similar abilities and ages, Cutter and Pfeiffer clashed from the moment she entered the West Wing. "There was always a direct friction between Cutter and Pfeiffer," said one senior Obama aide. "She would be in meetings and it was obvious that she was the only one who wasn't looped in like the others." Since she wasn't part of the formal structure of the communications team, her rivals found it easy to keep her in the dark.

Cutter joined the new campaign in Chicago carrying the scars of both the 2004 campaign and of working in the Obama White House. She negotiated hard to get the title of deputy campaign manager, and ring-fenced her responsibilities. "She understood the dynamics of the operation," said one of Cutter's trusted friends. "In this kind of operation there are two kinds of people. There are people who make their own rules and suffer no consequences, and then there's everyone else." Cutter set about building a communications team that could do the aggressive work of crushing a Republican challenger even in the midst of a struggling economy that imperiled a sitting president. To ensure its aggression and effectiveness, and to protect her new fiefdom, Cutter controlled everything within her reach. Every piece of the communications team—every press release and statement, every event and response—everything had to go through her. She was unassailable. If she was gone for an hour or a day, nothing could proceed.

Cutter still suffered from her own insecurities, driving away possible friends and giving succor to her likely enemies. Her social manner was abrupt and her resting state seemed irascible. She was the Patton of campaign communications: a brilliant general who crushed her enemies with relish and cared little for the damage she inflicted on herself. She was her own collateral damage. "Stephanie is Stephanie," said one close friend. "She's got her great strengths. Working well within a system isn't one of them, however."

Nobody worked harder than Cutter, and few people wanted to work with her. *Marie Claire* magazine published a profile of Cutter, written by a former White House press staffer, calling her a "human bulldozer." She told the magazine how, growing up in Raynham, Massachusetts, she was treated as an equal to her two brothers. When one brother got a rifle for a birthday, so did she. When one got a hunting knife, so did she. "I know how to throw a punch," she said. And it sounded as if she liked to throw them, too.

Cutter drove herself hard, and she drove her staff even harder. "You can't do everything in that job," said one Obama communications insider. "No question she works her tail off. But no one wants to work with her. Not Messina. Not the young twenty-two-year-olds. She doesn't bring on anyone or give them advice. Even though she's successful and established now. She's just incredibly insecure."

Cutter clashed with her underlings and her superiors. She had little respect for Messina and was not afraid to show it. Her old mentor, Ted Kennedy, had taught her to speak up, no matter what the consequences to her reputation. So she did: she would disagree with Messina on communications strategy loudly and frequently. In her view, Messina lacked backbone, like so many others, and she needed to work around him. In his view, she needed some straight talk about her social manner. "I think it is fair to say we're both the same age," said Messina. "We've known each other for a very long time, and I think we felt an absolute ability to be completely frank with each other in ways that were almost always helpful and sometimes not." To the staffers around them, the battlefield between Messina and Cutter was dangerous territory. "Who wants to get caught in the crossfire between her and Messina?" asked one of Obama's senior aides.

So it was more than a little ironic that Cutter's crossfire hit one of her biggest mentors, and the person who had brought her into the White House and then the campaign.

David Axelrod considered Cutter his closest colleague inside the Prudential. "I begged her to come out to the campaign," he said. "At the end of the campaign I would say she was one of my closest colleagues. So, did we have moments in the course of a long campaign where we had disagreements? Yes. Was she one of my closest colleagues and best friends of the campaign? Yes." Axelrod believed Cutter was an invaluable asset to the campaign, but more of a tactician than a strategist. "Stephanie is a master at the tactics of politics," he said. "She was brilliant on television and she was a great image for us on television because when you think of who our targets were, she was a great image for our campaign. So not only was she effective but she was the right demo for us."

In addition to representing a demographic, Cutter led by sheer force of character. And that was often her problem. "The truth is that everybody's strength is their weakness," said Axelrod. "Stephanie is an incredibly focused and intense person. And sometimes that rubs some people the wrong way. But the upside of her was enormous in terms of driving the strategy of the campaign through our tactics and communications. She's the best, I think."

*   *   *

The staff drama was not confined to Chicago. It leached into and out of the White House, where the message team secretly gathered every weekend in the Roosevelt Room to review the state of the president's reelection campaign. The meetings started out with a wide group: beyond Obama's inner circle, there was the team of campaign consultants and a broad internal communications team.

The Sunday night meetings were highly confidential and sacrosanct: this was the brain trust of the presidential campaign, discussing strategy in total honesty—the equivalent of the Situation Room in the West Wing basement, or the supersecure room inside the Pentagon known as "the tank." The enemy was never supposed to know what happened inside the Roosevelt Room sessions.

They would stay secret for several months, at least as far as the national newspapers were concerned. But first, they would leak to another kind of enemy.

In the late fall of 2011, the president and his team were feeling reenergized by their comeback strategy after the debt ceiling fiasco. So they met to discuss how best to push forward with their new momentum. Obama himself had drawn up a list of his priorities. It was a presidential wish list of the items he felt he wanted to address directly in his second term.

Some he had deferred because of political necessity in his first term; some he had deferred because of circumstances. He wanted to speak out about climate change in a more direct way and tackle a global challenge that he had pushed aside in favor of health-care reform. Between the early days of his first campaign and the start of his time inside the White House, Obama had discarded his rhetoric about slowing the rise of the oceans and dropped all pretense of tackling carbon emissions with a cap-and-trade plan. Now he wanted to return to the issue, to build support for a second-term agenda that would shape his legacy.

The president wanted to talk above all about same-sex marriage. Everyone in his inner circle had known from the outset of the 2008 cycle that he supported same-sex marriage. As early as 1996, when he was running for the Illinois state senate, he told gay supporters that he was in favor of such marriages. But as his career moved to a statewide and then national level, Obama pulled back: he was too cautious, too calculating about political risk, to voice anything but support for what he called "strong" civil unions.

He also wanted to address the Israeli-Palestinian conflict that had made no progress toward peace in his first term. He knew that his initial efforts to push Israel to freeze settlements had won him no friends in Jerusalem and little support in the West Bank. He had withdrawn from his early effort to restart a peace process. Like Presidents Bush and Clinton before him, Obama was looking to a second term to revive his faith in his own peacemaking powers.

The list was a revelation only to newcomers to the inner circle. Within days, one of them leaked the list to some prospective book authors, and Obama was livid. He felt he had already suffered enough from leaks to writers about the dysfunctional nature of his economic team. Now he could barely talk to his own campaign team without one of them singing to an outside journalist.

"I'm disappointed," he steamed, picking up the language his wife used if their children misbehaved. He wanted the meetings to continue because he thought they were important. But they couldn't continue like this. He would tolerate no more leaks, no more Obama books and Washington reads. There would be no discussion of internal strategy. No strategic leaking to make his aides look important. No public settling of scores between competing confidants.

"If you can't keep a secret," he asked, "what are you doing here?"

With that, he stood up and walked out.

Vice President Biden followed up sharply. He, too, was disappointed. The president was angry and they all looked bad. With that, he too stood up and walked out.

Left on their own, the consultants and aides turned on one another. First came the self-righteous protestations of innocence. It had to be the fault of others in the room because they would *never* think of doing such a thing. To several long-standing aides, the loudest outrage sounded the most fake: they protested too much. After several rounds of general blame, Robert Gibbs let loose.

"Somebody has violated the trust of the president, the vice president, and the whole group," he said. "Who the fuck do we think we are? Regrettably somebody in here has decided to make themselves bigger than anybody else in this room. We're all going to succeed or fail as one. Not as a fucking group of individuals."
There had been tensions in 2008 and there had been disputes. But nothing—nothing—had happened like this. Nobody had leaked secret strategy almost instantly. There was no excuse.

The meetings continued with a much smaller group on Sunday nights, every other week. Alongside Obama was the senior staff of his West Wing: the new chief of staff Jack Lew; senior advisers Valerie Jarrett, Pete Rouse, and David Plouffe; deputy chief of staff Alyssa Mastromonaco, the keeper of his schedule; and communications director Dan Pfeiffer. Joining them were the leaders of the Chicago campaign: Messina, Axelrod, Cutter, and media strategist Larry Grisolano.

There would be no more leaks from the weekend strategy meetings. But the leaks continued elsewhere: the atmosphere between the senior staff in the room and those outside was so corrosive that it was impossible to stop them.

On a frigid Chicago night in early January, David Axelrod drove to the United Center to engage in two of his favorite games: watching the Bulls shoot hoops and watching Republicans shoot one another. Instead of staying at home for the first votes in the GOP presidential contest, he chose to tweet about what he called "the whackadoodles" from his plastic seat inside the basketball arena.

It was the four-year anniversary of that extraordinary night in Iowa, when a freshman senator stunned the wise men of Washington politics by winning the caucuses and beginning his long journey to the presidential nomination and the White House. That night Axelrod celebrated with Obama and the Iowa team at a cavernous convention hall, where the candidate hailed it as "the moment when the improbable beat what Washington always said was inevitable." Later, Axelrod's A-team of consultants shared beers in a dark hotel bar at the Holiday Inn in downtown Des Moines. Their moonshot strategy of launching a virtual unknown into a presidential orbit was just beginning.

Four years later, it was the Republicans' turn in the klieg lights of the cameras. Mitt Romney was squeaking out the narrowest of victories in Iowa, by a first count of just eight votes, over a surging challenge by the former Pennsylvania senator Rick Santorum. For now, that sliver of a win was enough to quell the GOP's concerns about Romney. Iowa's social conservatives had half-embraced Romney and his effort to turn his back on his moderate record as a former Massachusetts governor. But the effective tie in Iowa was also encouraging for Obama's campaign headquarters in Chicago: it promised to sustain the Republican contest, including the extreme rhetoric of the TV debates, for weeks and possibly months to come.

Axelrod's plan was to follow the results on his BlackBerry while sitting in his prime midcourt seat. But Cutter was not pleased with his plan: she thought it was inappropriate and undignified for the chief strategist of the Obama campaign to be seen in public on the night of the Iowa caucuses.

Axelrod ignored her opinion and advice. Her controlling desires meant little to him. He had the chance to see the Bulls star Derrick Rose at a sellout game, where he could also stuff his face with a smoked turkey sandwich and sweet potato fries. Rose was a big Obama supporter, and he was torching the Atlanta Hawks that night.

Axelrod could barely contain his enthusiasm at both contests. Turnout seemed low in Iowa, and he wanted to taunt the media—and Republicans—about their predictions of high GOP enthusiasm. He tweeted about the low number of votes, and about Romney losing much of his support from the voters who backed him in 2008. And of course, he tweeted about the Bulls game, and the single-handed turnaround by Rose, who scored 30 points to eke out a 1-point win at the end of the fourth quarter. "One of the closest, most exciting contests I've seen in years," Axelrod tweeted. "Bulls and Hawks tied at 62 with 6 minutes to go. Oh, how are the caucuses?" Unbecoming or not, the chief strategist was competitive with everyone, just like his boss.

But that competitive desire also masked an inner insecurity. Axelrod fretted about his status, not least after getting pushed out of the West Wing, and he loved to be courted by TV producers. The fleeting fame of TV punditry offered some comfort from the harsh critique that came from internal political disputes and external political failures.

Cutter also fretted about her status, not least after failing to get the job and power she wanted in the West Wing. Her comfort lay in maintaining the tightest grip on the campaign's communications, including the kind of TV punditry she also found flattering.

Two months after the Bulls game, Cutter and Axelrod clashed over a single booking on *CBS This Morning* in a dispute that was less about television and more about control of the Obama campaign. They were both insecure about themselves and each other, when the call came for a simple appearance on morning TV. Cutter was frustrated by an unresolved question inside Chicago: was the campaign engaging with the GOP primaries or not? Her job was to provide definition and focus, while Axelrod's task was ill-defined in its strategic vision. Axelrod could dream big, while Cutter needed to execute small. Both were more than ready to argue face-to-face and out in the open, in contrast to Messina, who preferred to wage his disputes in secret.

The campaign researched every piece of the message machine, and the findings on TV appearances by Obama's surrogates were not encouraging for Axelrod. Focus group data suggested that the campaign needed more women on television. Women voters would be a dominant part of any victory in a tough political year for the president. But his surrogates on TV were mainly men like Axelrod. When the request landed from CBS, a young staffer passed on the booking to the highest-profile woman, who just happened to be his boss: Stephanie Cutter. To cover herself, Cutter asked Axelrod if it was okay for her to take the slot, and he agreed.

An hour later, Axelrod discovered a crucial piece of missing information: CBS had first asked for him but were rejected by campaign staff. Axelrod marched into Cutter's office at the Prudential building to demand an explanation. Why did nobody tell him what was happening? Why was he in the position of looking so bad in front of his media friends?

"CBS asked for me, not you," Axelrod thundered.

"I didn't know that," Cutter explained. "I was asked to do it. I didn't know what the request was."

Axelrod was furious. He was convinced that Cutter was trying to steal the limelight. She claimed she wasn't. But she was trying to displace him in the rotation of talking heads that counted as surrogates for the campaign. They were both unsure of their own status and unsure of their own purpose.

The dispute was big enough that word spread through campaign headquarters. Messina scheduled a dinner with Axelrod and Cutter, but Axelrod was unable to attend. When Messina and Cutter sat down, the campaign manager had a direct order that purportedly came straight from the White House.

"Plouffe says we need to get Axe off TV," Messina said.

Cutter was skeptical. She thought Plouffe might have said that Axelrod was doing a lot of TV. But Messina was surely using Plouffe's mild observation to pursue a bigger agenda. She did not trust Messina. Perhaps he was manipulating Plouffe's words, or perhaps he was simply manipulating Plouffe's understanding. Either way, he seemed to be using her dispute with her former mentor as a means to advancing his own agenda against a rival power inside Chicago.

For the team at the Prudential, this was the phony war period of the election. They had no green light to move ahead with the full campaign, at a time when the Republican primaries showed every sign of dragging on for months. The overarching strategy was set but was not yet in motion: they needed to tell not just their own story, but the story of Mitt Romney. They would message him as part of the problem, not the solution, in a miserable economy. It would be a slow, steady grind. "We had our strategy set very early, and we never deviated from it," said one senior campaign staffer. "It wasn't hope and change, obviously. It was more: 'We've got a job to do, let's go do it.' "

The reality was rather different from the way they bragged to themselves. In the early weeks and months of 2012, there were skirmishes that threatened to make them deviate from the campaign plan.

Presidential campaigns like to start their massive ad spending with what they call foundational commercials. The idea is to invest heavily in the core themes of the election debate, as they see it. For a new candidate, as Obama was in 2008, those core themes start with character and biography. The admakers try to tell a story about who the candidate is and how that character will translate into leadership.

They planned to do the same in 2012, albeit with less focus on character. After all, there was nothing they could say about Obama's biography that had not been told already. And there was nothing they could say about his character that would supplant the impression gained by four years of voters watching him on television almost every night. Yet they still had a story to tell that would set the tone for the election cycle, and they had been refining it for months, ready to roll out when the time was right.

But first, the time was wrong. Just two weeks into election year, in mid-January, Axelrod was deeply worried about attack ads funded by the billionaire brothers Charles and David Koch.

Americans for Prosperity spent $6 million in battleground states with a long, sixty-second ad arguing that Obama had given tax dollars to Solyndra, a solar panel manufacturer, in exchange for campaign dollars. The ad featured urgent, conspiratorial music and ended with Obama in sunglasses, throwing his head back in laughter, as he walked alongside none other than Axelrod. "Tell President Obama: American workers aren't pawns in your political games," the narrator urged.

Axelrod was troubled. His research data, including extensive focus group interviews, suggested that other outside groups had damaged the president just a few months earlier. The American Crossroads group, shaped in large part by Karl Rove, had repeatedly accused Obama of lacking leadership and failing to deliver on his promise of national unity. If left unanswered, the ads could inflict real damage on the president.

Now the Koch brothers seemed to be emulating the earlier ads, attacking Obama while the GOP candidates were going after one another during their primary contests. When Axelrod looked at battleground states where the Koch ads were not airing, the president's numbers were markedly higher. "We were nervous about just letting the ads sit out there," he told me over coffee and eggs in a Chicago restaurant soon after the commercials first aired.

Axelrod's response was a strangely contorted thirty seconds that tried to be defensive and offensive at the same time. Spending several hundred thousand dollars in six battleground states, the ad punched back at the Koch brothers before boasting about Obama's ethics and jobs record:

"Secretive oil billionaires attacking President Obama with ads fact-checkers say are not tethered to the facts," the ad began to ominous music in a minor key, against a screen full of white text on a black background.

Then the music switched suddenly to an upbeat major key, over a full-color photo of the president and his aides in the Oval Office. "While independent watchdogs call this president's record on ethics 'unprecedented,'" the narrator said. Seconds later, there was video of workers installing solar panels and wind turbines spinning against a golden sky. "And America's clean-energy industry? Two point seven million jobs and 'expanding rapidly.' For the first time in thirteen years our dependence on foreign oil is below 50 percent," the narrator continued. "President Obama. Kept his promise to toughen ethics rules and strengthen America's energy economy."

The ad managed not just to undermine the credibility of the attacks but to question the patriotism of those who would do so. "We tested the ad and it seemed to be impactful," Axelrod concluded. "So I think we effectively neutralized it. The truth is that our numbers in the states where they ran those ads have improved dramatically. I don't think that's because of the response we ran, but clearly they didn't have a hugely negative impact."

Those kinds of skirmishes were relatively easy to adapt to: there was an attack and a counterattack. But there were other kinds of fights that threatened to overwhelm the message strategy and reshape it fundamentally.

Just two days after the Solyndra response, Obama's health secretary Kathleen Sebelius announced she was moving forward with a requirement for most health-care plans to provide women with free contraceptives. In doing so, the Obama administration was rejecting a blanket exemption requested by the Catholic Church for all affiliated universities, hospitals, and charities.

In the hyperventilated language of the start of an election year, the debate over birth control and health insurance was neither a medical nor a moral issue. It was much simpler than that. Either Obama was declaring a war on religion or conservatives were declaring a war on women.

What followed threw the GOP candidates off their chosen message strategy to focus on the president's economic failings. Mitt Romney condemned the rule as a blow to Catholics, while his main opponents at the time—Newt Gingrich and Rick Santorum—delighted in the chance to talk about the similarities between Romney's health-care reforms and those of Obama. This would be the final phase of the insurgency against Romney, when Gingrich and then Santorum would steal brief poll leads before fading against the onslaught of Romney and the supposed outside groups aligned with his campaign.

For the next three weeks, the White House floundered for a solution. The debate was already several months old inside the West Wing, pitting Obama's female advisers against their male counterparts. On one side were women such as Sebelius, Valerie Jarrett, and deputy chief of staff Nancy-Ann DeParle, who had managed the health-care reforms from start to finish. On the other side were men such as Vice President Joe Biden, the former chief of staff Bill Daley, and the deputy national security adviser Denis McDonough. It was a debate that forced a choice between women's health advocates and the Catholic bishops who could influence battleground voters.

Obama's aides acknowledged their own boss had been part of the problem. In a meeting with Archbishop Timothy Dolan of New York in November, the president had left the impression that he would be more flexible than his stated policy. Obama's closest aides believe he was never fully prepared for a discussion about contraception at the meeting with Dolan. "They didn't say he was going to talk about contraception, but to talk about what we're doing on world hunger and to have dialogue," said one senior Obama official. "Well, they should have known and probably did know that he would raise contraception. We should have had the people involved say, 'If he raises it, what are you going to say and how will you handle it?' But that did not happen. Obviously, it was raised and the president probably got more forward leaning than probably was our position, because that is what politicians do, right?"

For his part, Obama was frustrated at the situation and furious with his staff. This was an unforced error after months of recovery since the debt ceiling fiasco. He had wanted to avoid another salvo in the culture wars, but that was precisely where the policy had ended up. "The president's view was: how the hell could this happen? That was as angry as I have seen him at his staff for a mistake," said another senior aide. "Because he had a view of how it should go, what he wanted, and we did not achieve that for him." Among his political aides, the decision was clear: it made more sense to keep women happy than Catholics. On the other side were people like Biden, whose view of electoral politics was seen as distinctly outdated inside the West Wing. "The people who believed that we should take the more conservative position were looking at our electoral map from 1992," the senior aide said. "It's people who grew up in a different era of politics, where the Catholic, white, Reagan Democrat vote was decisive."

The Catholics they needed were progressives, not conservatives. But the president and his aides were losing Catholic support across the board, even from those who had supported Obamacare.

When Sister Carol Keehan, the CEO of the Catholic Health Association, told the White House she opposed the new contraception rule, the game was over. The only way to dig out of their own hole was to force insurers, not Catholic employers, to pay the cost of the free contraceptives. The bishops were not happy, nor were conservatives.

But the backlash to the compromise reshaped much of the message for the remaining nine months of the election. Sensing Obama's difficulties, Republicans pushed ahead with more extreme positions on contraception. Senator Roy Blunt drew up a "conscience amendment" to the health-care reform law, allowing any employer or insurer to opt out of any provision on the grounds of any moral objection. At the same time, the Virginia state legislature passed a bill forcing women to get an ultrasound—including a probe inserted into the vagina—before having an abortion. The final act started with a decision by House Republicans to refuse to allow a Georgetown law student, Sandra Fluke, to testify on the contraception issue. Instead, the House hearing included only men on the panel of expert witnesses. Fluke testified instead at a special hearing of just House Democrats, prompting conservative bloggers to heap abuse on her for having a sex life. That led to a stunningly sexist tirade by the bigoted radio host Rush Limbaugh, who trashed Fluke as a slut and prostitute, and demanded to watch her sex life on video. Within days, advertisers were dropping Limbaugh's show and Republican leaders were forced to distance themselves from his comments. Romney disagreed with "the language" used by Limbaugh, while Santorum called him "absurd."

The pile-on saved Obama's message team and showed them a path to victory. "We always knew if we didn't win the gender gap, we were not going to win the presidency," said White House communications director Dan Pfeiffer. "That's not just true for us. That's true for every Democrat. After the contraception fight when everyone went to the right and the Republicans backed the Blunt amendment, we saw their numbers fall dramatically among women. We realized what an opportunity it was, in particular after Santorum rose to the top of the Republican primary. We recognized what a turnoff that was to independents and independent women, in particular. We didn't intend to have a fight with the Catholic Church. But it created the environment for Santorum and Romney to race each other to the right on contraception. Our opponents got us out of our mess by overplaying their hand."

In the early days, the Obama messaging strategy was unformed. Their own candidate was a highly public figure, but his campaign positioning had yet to be rolled out. Their opponent remained undecided. There was no positive track to follow about Obama and no negative track to follow about his likely challenger.

So Obama's communications team set about an under-the-radar strategy to prolong the primary contest by pushing out—often through third parties—the kind of research that could hurt Romney. The Chicago team was deeply frustrated by the lack of serious campaigning by Romney's rivals: there seemed to be no opposition research and no effort to expose the record of the GOP front-runner. The solution was to weaken the likely nominee with an extended contest that would push the candidate and his party further to the right.

Sometimes they attacked one of Romney's rivals just to make it look like they were concerned about their candidacy, so as to promote them as a viable alternative to the former governor. For a brief time, Obama's campaign team hoped that Texas governor

Rick Perry might mount a serious and prolonged challenge against Romney. Texas Democrats had warned Chicago not to underestimate Perry, and his political profile seemed to suit a Tea Party–driven GOP more than the formerly moderate Romney. In the early fall of 2011, as Perry continued to lead Romney, Chicago pushed out a carefully written memo that tied Perry and Romney together. On the face of it, the goal was to damage both Republican candidates. But the real intention was to elevate Perry and sustain his candidacy, even as he was losing altitude. Campaign press secretary Ben LaBolt accused both Perry and Romney of embracing policies that would hurt the middle class—especially on Social Security and immigration reform. LaBolt cited Perry's description of Social Security as "a Ponzi scheme" and said that Romney wanted to privatize some parts of Social Security. He also condemned both men for opposing immigration reform and its path to citizenship. Chicago had no idea that Perry would collapse little more than a month later, when his TV debate performance was excruciatingly bad: he could not recall the details of his own spending cuts, especially a pesky list of three federal departments he would shut down.

In 2008, the Obama campaign prided itself on not trying to win the day in the press. That kind of short-term thinking was precisely the opposite of the longer-term strategic play they had in mind for their campaign and their candidate. Four years later, the new Obama team was trying to do both: to play the long game while also trying to win the day.

They set about pushing oppo research on the Republican candidates, but found that the news media was interested in airing their research only if there was a video release from Chicago to accompany it. The campaign released several dozen videos as a way to push forward its message in ways that a simple press release would fail to do. Reporters who deleted or ignored press releases were more likely to treat video with respect.

In one week in April, the campaign sent out two video releases in quick succession. At an Associated Press lunch of influential media leaders, Romney attacked Obama for his critique of the Republican budget plan laid out by the House budget chair Paul Ryan. Rather than rebut Romney line by line, Chicago chose to release a video instead, titled *Mitt Romney versus Reality*, undermining Romney's credibility and some of his favorite attack lines against Obama. In less than ninety seconds, the Obama campaign spliced together Romney's assertions about Obama's record with a clip of Obama stating the precise opposite. So a sound bite of Romney claiming that Obama traveled the world to apologize for America was followed by Obama saying that he would never apologize for America's way of life. Another Romney assertion that Obama had taken military options against Iran off the table was rebutted with a clip of Obama saying he would never do so.

A few days later, Chicago demonstrated a classic example of the impact of video. The press shop e-mailed a *Boston Globe* story about a three-minute campaign video marking the six-year anniversary of Romney signing health-care reform into law in Massachusetts. It could have simply e-mailed reporters the video, but the newspaper story about the video held greater credibility. The video made the argument that Romney's health-care law was the model for Obama's. The story included this line, from Jonathan Gruber of MIT, asserting how the laws were identical: "The core of the Affordable Care Act, or Obamacare, and what we did in Massachusetts are identical. It was to President Obama's credit that he said, 'You know what, the policy might have been introduced on the right, but look, here's something that really worked.'" What really worked was a video press release filtered through a news story and reprocessed as a press release.

That represented one of the simpler ways to manipulate the media with a chosen message. The more complex way was a cloak-and-dagger operation that involved leaking documents to the press through a third party. Subterfuge was especially helpful when dealing with the *New York Times*, which frustrated Chicago by refusing force-fed opposition research. The *Times* maintained that its standards were high, and rightly so.

But there were times when only the *Times* would do. In early May, an explosive package of materials landed at Obama headquarters: a presentation of a proposed Republican strategy for tying President Obama to inflammatory statements by Rev. Jeremiah Wright, his former pastor. The strategy was prepared for Joe Ricketts, the founder of the brokerage TD Ameritrade and the family owner of the Chicago Cubs baseball team. In stark black lettering, the strategy deck was called "The Defeat of Barack Hussein Obama: The Ricketts Plan to End His Spending for Good." It detailed a $10 million plan to stoke racial fears by associating Obama to Wright's "black liberation theology." To preempt charges of race-baiting, the plan included hiring what it called "an extremely literate conservative African-American" to become its spokesperson. The strategy sounded like much of what passed for regular debate on Sean Hannity's prime-time show on Fox News.

Obama's aides knew they needed a swift and high-impact response, and few news outlets could deliver that as well as the *New York Times*. Since the *Times* would not readily accept the documents from the campaign itself, Obama's staff passed the documents to someone gingerly described by the *Times* as "a person not connected to the proposal who was alarmed by its tone." The story noted that the strategy was presented to Ricketts's family members and associates. It also noted that Ricketts's daughter Laura was a top contributor to none other than the Obama campaign. The Ricketts plan—which was only in the early stages of discussion—was strangled before it could breathe.

Mitt Romney was still two weeks away from clinching enough delegates to secure his party's presidential nomination. His campaign—and their well-funded allies—seemed oblivious to the notion that Chicago would try to strangle his message just as they had the Ricketts plan: before anyone could truly hear it.

FOUR

THE AMERICAN DREAM

Campaign consultants tend to hate the slogans that define their efforts. They see the bumper stickers and banners as some kind of gross oversimplification of their more sophisticated strategy of gross oversimplification. For some reason—mostly professional pride—they think the reduction of an entire campaign to a handful of words is unbecoming; whereas they think the reduction of a complex policy debate to a thirty-second attack ad is entirely legitimate.

Obama's team hated the creation of their first slogan in 2008: Change We Can Believe In. It emerged not from a stroke of genius or from group consensus, but rather from the absence of anything better. It was a default option that encapsulated the contrast with the Clintons in the primaries of 2008, both in terms of change and credibility. It carried the lofty rhetoric so admired by David Axelrod, who thought it was the antithesis of the microtargeting strategy of the counterpart he loathed on the Clinton campaign, Mark

Penn. The slogan survived mostly because the Obama campaign was unwilling to spend any more time and money on finding a replacement.

Four years later, the same team chose another lofty slogan, albeit one that was more concise: Forward. Its rollout came with a seven-minute video of the same name, narrating the last three years as a time when Obama "never lost faith" in America and "never stopped believing in us, and fighting for us." Obama's closest aides—especially the message men who controlled his research and ads—found the slogan entirely forgettable.

For one man—the candidate and president—Forward was a vast improvement on its predecessor in 2008. "Unlike four years ago, he liked it right out of the gate," said Plouffe. "He didn't like Change We Can Believe In. Forward made sense. It fit. I have never been a believer that slogans matter very much. But we put it in our ads. It was in the stump speech and Romney ended up being the great alternative to moving forward. Whoever we were going to run against was going to be backwards looking. But Romney was made for this role."

The irony was that another left-of-center leader had used a similar slogan in his recent reelection campaign: British prime minister Tony Blair, as he won a third term in 2005. Blair's slogan—Forward, Not Back—was the work of none other than the much-loathed Mark Penn, who proposed that Democrats use the same slogan in the midterm congressional elections in 2010. Penn argued that incumbents face a referendum, when they needed to frame their reelections as a choice. Blair used the slogan to emphasize the choice facing his voters, even as they were disillusioned with his position on the war in Iraq.

Blair won a historic third term by a narrow margin of less than three percentage points, and he left power just two years later. Forward might squeak out a victory for a wounded leader and party. But it was an empty marketing message, not one that could build or sustain a movement. It was neither promising nor pointed, like the 2008 slogan; it was prudent and functional. In the face of all the disputes between Obama's senior campaign staff, as well as an economy that was still the cause of deep dissatisfaction among voters, Forward just did the job.

Forward was merely the latest example of a long tradition of political and commercial messaging in America. Political advertising feels like it has been with us forever. The ads blanket our elections to such an extent, and with such uniformity, that it's easy to forget how new they are, or where they came from. But their ability to shape our understanding of ourselves, our issues, and our country should not blind us to their origins. Those origins offer clues to the nature of the sheer power of campaign commercials.

There is a paradox about these political ads: even as we distrust politicians and profess to dislike the propaganda of their advertising, we allow them to shape our opinions and our votes. If they didn't work, campaigns would not spend so much time and money to produce them. Politicians and pundits all lament the huge amounts of money consumed by campaigns in today's elections, yet they rarely treat the biggest driver of those costs with the same disdain. That's because the political insiders are as addicted to ads as the voters.

The reason for this paradox lies in the allure of such ads: they promise a candidate the chance to control the message and win power. Voters like to be flattered with the notion that their decisions at the ballot box can reshape history. Donors like to feel their money is buying them access to candidates, which it is. And consultants like to grow wealthier by charging fees scaled to the amount of money spent on their advertising.

How did the madness of the message take hold?

The first admen surfaced in Boston, Chicago, and New York in the 1850s and 1860s, acting as brokers of newspaper space between publishers and traders selling medicine or dry goods. From the earliest days of advertising, it was hard to tell the bad guys from the good. Their business was either one of deception or one of protecting innocent people from hucksters intent on deception. One pioneer, George P. Rowell, was typical. Born in a log cabin in Vermont, he started work selling ad space for the *Boston Post* before moving to New York and founding the trade journal *Printer's Ink* in 1888. In his autobiography, Rowell wrote that advertising was "one of the easiest sorts of business in which a man may cheat and defraud a client without danger of discovery."

By the early twentieth century, advertisers had displaced peddlers and snake oil salesmen as the chief purveyors of physical perfection. Soap, laxative, tobacco: advertisers turned their products into tools for a better life.

If ads could convince people of the power of toilet powder, could they persuade people to change their votes?

Presidential campaigns since the mid-1800s have used symbols, imagery, and songs to tell the stories of their candidate. In the 1840 contest between President Martin Van Buren and his challenger, William Henry Harrison, the image of Harrison's log cabin became paramount. In banners and pins, Harrison's log cabin—rather than his two-thousand-acre estate—was testimony to his decency and common sense. Such symbols became commonplace: Abe Lincoln had his split rail, and Theodore Roosevelt became associated with the teddy bear, bull moose, and big stick.

But advertising did not prove its powers of mass persuasion

until World War I, when admen deployed their skills in support of the military draft. The intensive cheerleading of the time appeared to shape the national spirit—in contrast to German propaganda, or Russian chaos, the American ads seemed to unify a young nation in agreement about its own goodness. Uncle Sam wanted *you* to enlist, so that men could prove their manliness, defend the nation's honor, or travel the world. Advertising helped recruit more than four million men, leading *Printer's Ink* to proclaim after the Armistice, "the war has been won by advertising, as well as by soldiers and munitions."

The advertising that emerged after the war promised not just physical perfection but national improvement. Listerine was a general antiseptic until copywriters in 1920 reinvented it as a whole new product category to deal with a new medical problem. Mouthwash would not just cure you of the sinister-sounding halitosis; it could unlock the secret of success in life, love, and business. Its manufacturer, the Lambert Pharmacal Company, watched its annual profits explode from $100,000 to $4 million in just six years. Advertising's triumph was to sell a way of life: specifically, the American Dream.

This was the newfangled world in which the radio entered the American home. In 1924 there were three million radios in the country; within a decade there would be ten times more. The radio itself was the symbol of personal success: of modernity and class mobility. At first, admen were reluctant to enter the home with radio commercials: the living room was an intimate space, a refuge from commerce and worldly affairs. But the intimacy of the space was too tempting: radio sponsorship, rather than direct advertising, was deemed acceptable.

In politics, the master of the new medium was FDR. His fireside chats transformed the notion of campaigning, political communication, and the powers of the presidency. Roosevelt could reach millions in their homes while his predecessors traveled the country for months on end to reach similar numbers with stump speeches in the public square. Personal campaigning by presidential candidates was largely unacceptable since the earliest days of the Republic: direct communication with voters was the purview of the Congress. FDR's fireside chats reached more than 60 million listeners, or half the population—an astonishing figure by the standards of any era. "In the olden days, campaigns were conducted amid surroundings of brass bands and red lights. Oratory was an appeal primarily to the emotions and sometimes to the passions," FDR said in one radio address in 1932. "Today, common sense plays the greater part and final opinions are arrived at in the quiet of the home." It was no coincidence that in this darkest hour of the Depression, the writer James Truslow Adams coined the phrase "the American dream, that dream of a land in which life should be better and richer and fuller for every man."

FDR delivered the first television address in 1939 at the World's Fair in New York. The following year, TV covered its first political conventions, but it would take another decade before the medium could reach across the country. The first presidential campaign to exploit TV advertising was Eisenhower's in 1952, when little more than a third of homes owned a television. Rosser Reeves, a partner at the ad firm Ted Bates and Company, devised a campaign to counter the Democrats' argument that the economy had recovered from a Republican Depression. In the Democratic narrative, Republicans were against Social Security and full employment, while Democrats were for the working people and prosperity.

Reeves devised an alternative strategy based around targeted advertising, a homespun message, and a trustworthy candidate. Reeves argued that Ike could win by concentrating his advertising on forty-nine counties in twelve key states. His ad format was what we would now call a town hall, a question-and-answer exchange, called Eisenhower Answers America. Ike promised to cut government spending and control inflation and the cost of groceries; he also promised to expand Social Security and military spending at the same time as cutting taxes. Reeves drew on the polling work of George Gallup to identify the issues of most concern to voters, and in so doing created what the Democrats called the "cornflakes campaign."

Just eight years later, the contours of today's political messaging were already clear. John F. Kennedy beat Richard M. Nixon in his first debate, and not just because he looked younger, less sweaty, and more clean-shaven. He won because his ad team cut a four-minute commercial that replayed the debate's best moments, to highlight how Kennedy was in command while Nixon's eyes and complexion looked shifty. Kennedy also sounded like a small government liberal rather than the conservative caricature of a liberal. "I know that there are those who say that we want to turn everything over to the government," said Kennedy. "I don't at all. I want the individuals to meet their responsibilities. And I want the states to meet their responsibilities. But I think there is also a national responsibility."

In the next cycle, Lyndon Johnson skewered Barry Goldwater with ads on Social Security and national security. One ad cited his rival's multiple interviews about transforming Social Security into a privatized, voluntary system. Foreshadowing today's Republicans, Goldwater later insisted that all he wanted to do was ensure that Social Security remained solvent. There was the infamous *Daisy* ad, with a girl plucking flower petals before the mushroom cloud of a nuclear detonation. *Daisy* was pulled after one airing, but its associated controversy showed that ads could reach voters simply by making news. In fact, the message behind *Daisy* was never dropped: there was another, shorter ad that started with a nuclear explosion, with a much more explicit connection to Goldwater: "On October 24, 1963," the narrator intoned, "Barry Goldwater said of the nuclear bomb, 'Merely another weapon.' Merely another weapon? Vote for President Johnson. The stakes are too high for you to stay home."

If those LBJ attacks were harsh, one ad stood out for its subtlety, by simply citing the Republican attacks on Goldwater during their own primaries. A faceless man walks across what is supposed to look like the floor of the GOP convention in San Francisco. He stops to pick up the discarded posters of the defeated candidates who trashed Goldwater as an extremist. One of those posters was of Governor George Romney of Michigan. "In June, he said Goldwater's nomination would lead to the 'suicidal destruction of the Republican Party,'" said the narrator. "So, even if you're a Republican with serious doubts about Barry Goldwater, you're in good company." Goldwater was unrepentant about his positions fifteen years later in his book titled *With No Apologies*. The title was notably similar to Mitt Romney's 2010 polemic, *No Apology*.

LBJ's ads broke with tradition by never mentioning that he was a Democrat. Instead of leveraging the party machine and identity, Johnson was trying to broaden his appeal across the country. Just like Obama in 2008, his campaign featured Republicans who were now backing the Democratic candidate: "Republicans for Johnson."

Meanwhile the Republicans for Goldwater were proving as helpful as the Ricketts plan against Obama. One group called Mothers for a Moral America created a thirty-minute film depicting two Americas. One was Johnson's America: a place where there was sexual immorality, alcohol, and black people rioting.

The other was Goldwater's America: a place where clean young white people cited the Pledge of Allegiance, where the flag flew and the Statue of Liberty stood proud, and black people picked cotton in the fields. Republicans disavowed the movie but Democrats happily used it in fund-raising efforts.

Nixon's return in 1968 was characterized—at least by Nixon himself—as an embodiment of the American dream. In his acceptance speech, later replayed in his campaign ads, Nixon cast the Republicans as the party of individual initiative against the Democrats' faith in government. His campaign was not the first to deploy TV ads, even as his ad team—including a young Roger Ailes, who would later go on to create Fox News Channel—was memorialized in Joe McGinniss's *The Selling of the President*. At the heart of the TV campaign was an updated concept of Eisenhower's question-and-answer sessions, featuring Nixon taking questions from an audience of carefully selected voters. With all the artifice of advertising, even a candidate like Nixon could look authentic, given the right format, staging, lighting, and makeup.

The job of reselling a president follows a simpler but tougher path than introducing a new candidate for president. There are no gauzy bio ads because the candidate is already well-known. On the plus side, there are no hidden surprises in the candidate's bio precisely because the president is so well-known. The ad team has to struggle with a complex and often messy record in office, boiling down four years of governing into thirty seconds of television. But they don't have to prove their candidate's policy credentials with a series of wonkish prescriptions for the country and the world. As the first TV campaigns quickly discovered, the arena of political advertising does not lend itself to either an earnest debate or a nuanced message.

A generation before Obama sought reelection, Ronald Reagan set the contemporary standard for a president seeking a second term. The ad dynamic of the 1984 contest is still in many ways the model for reelection contests today. Reagan's campaign followed a similar path to Nixon in 1972, assembling an all-star Madison Avenue team including Hal Riney of Ogilvy and Mather and Philip Dusenberry of BBDO. Roger Ailes, a TV producer turned Nixon adviser, acted as a consultant to the team.

The Reagan team wanted to avoid the hard-edged tone of the 1980 contest, preferring to focus on picturesque, glowingly lit clichés of American suburban life. The masterpiece was called *Prouder, Stronger, Better,* and it was narrated by Hal Riney himself, in golden-syrup tones that could reassure small children. The one-minute ad started with, among other images, a farmer on a trac-tor, a boy on his newspaper rounds, and a suburban businessman climbing into his station wagon. A just-married couple ran out of church, and the bride was hugged by her grandmother. Children looked in awe at the Stars and Stripes as it was hoisted above them, while a firefighter and senior did the same on their own.

"It's morning again in America," said Riney. "Today, more men and women will go to work than ever before in our country's history. With interest rates at about half the record highs of 1980, nearly two thousand families today will buy new homes, more than at any time in the past four years. This afternoon, sixty-five hundred young men and women will be married. And with infla-tion at less than half of what it was just four years ago, they can look forward with confidence to the future. It's morning again in America. And, under the leadership of President Reagan, our country is prouder and stronger and better. Why would we ever want to return to where we were less than four short years ago?"

Riney narrated the second groundbreaking ad of the reelection cycle. It was an exercise so laden with imagery, and so free of the language of policy and politics, that focus groups could not figure out whether the ad was about the environment or gun control. *Bear* was actually about the Soviet Union, and its release was timed with the second presidential debate, on national security. A huge grizzly bear lumbered over some rocks, through some trees, across a river, until it reached a man with a gun slung over his shoulder. "There is a bear in the woods," said Riney. "For some people, the bear is easy to see. Others don't see it at all. Some people say the bear is tame. Others say it's vicious and dangerous. Since no one can really be sure who's right, isn't it smart to be as strong as the bear? If there *is* a bear?"

The Mondale campaign's ad response sounded even more familiar to those following the political debate in the Obama years. *Loopholes* was typical of Walter Mondale's argument on the stump and on TV. It started with a black-tie dinner party complete with silver candlesticks and platters of food. "Over the last three years, those making $200,000 a year got a $60,000 tax break. Thousands of profitable corporations pay no taxes," the narrator said over sinister music, before Mondale appeared at a campaign event. "I refuse to make your family pay more so that millionaires can pay less," the candidate said to a cheering crowd. Then, in language that the Obama campaign would echo, the narrator returned. "This is the debate: fairness. Will we all pay our fair share? Mondale will close tax loopholes and simplify the tax code. Mondale/Ferraro. Fighting for our future."

If ads determined the outcome of elections, the threat of millionaire dinner parties was far weaker than the allure of happy suburbia. Reagan swept every electoral college vote, except for Mondale's home state of Minnesota and the District of Columbia.

The George H. W. Bush campaign of 1988 copied much of the ad language of the last Reagan cycle. There were soft visuals of American family life, and there was the ominous confrontation with the bearish Soviet leader Mikhail Gorbachev: "Somebody is going to have to find out if Gorbachev is for real."

However, the standout moments were two ads about crime. The first was a low-quality spot by an outside group, called the National Security Political Action Committee, about William Horton, an African-American murderer who had raped a woman and stabbed her fiancé while on furlough in Massachusetts, the home state of Bush's challenger, Michael Dukakis. A month later, the Bush team—controlled now by Roger Ailes—aired its own ad, with higher-quality visuals, referring to the furlough program without mentioning Horton or showing his photo. Both ads triggered widespread coverage in the media, amplifying their message through free coverage across news outlets. The coverage helped define Dukakis as a weak executive, incapable of leading the country, and his support among white voters never recovered. The combined message by a shadowy outside committee and an official campaign foreshadowed the world after the Supreme Court's 2009 ruling on a case involving Citizens United: a world where there was no real distinction between campaigns and their allied outside groups, which were funded by unlimited and anonymous donations.

The success of the Horton ads served to constrain the Bush team four years later. Each attack on the Clinton campaign evoked the dark arts of the 1988 ads.

Clinton, on the other hand, could indulge in the one-minute bio ad of *Journey*, which framed his personal story—the boy from

Hope, Arkansas, who just wanted to help other people—as the embodiment of the American dream at a time of economic hardship. "I was born in a little town called Hope, Arkansas, three months after my father died," Clinton said, speaking to the camera, between several Ken Burns–style shots of old family photos. "I remember that old two-story house where I lived with my grandparents. They had very limited incomes. It was in 1963 that I went to Washington and met President Kennedy at the Boy's Nation program. And I remember just thinking what an incredible country this was, that somebody like me, you know, who had no money or anything, would be given the opportunity to meet the president. That's when I decided I could really do public service because I cared so much about people. I worked my way through law school with part-time jobs, anything I could find. After I graduated I really didn't care about making a lot of money. I just wanted to go home and see if I could make a difference. We've worked hard in education and health care to create jobs and we've made real progress. Now it's exhilarating to me to think that as president I could help to change all our people's lives for the better and bring hope back to the American dream." Clinton's emotional ads stood out all the more against Ross Perot's rambling thirty-minute economic lectures, complete with cardboard graphics.

The next two presidential cycles, at a time of peace and prosperity, produced ads that were by now clichés. There were "Morning in America" scenes of suburban families and sun-bathed shots of candidates and presidents touting their records in office, with uplifting, faintly patriotic music and flags unfurling in the wind. Those positive ads were alternated with darker, text-heavy attacks, intoned over sinister music. The exchanges amounted either to name-calling or traditional lines of attack. Bob Dole was "desperate," while Bill Clinton was an "unusually good liar." Al

Gore wanted to expand government, and George W. Bush wanted to wreck Social Security.

It took the carnage of 9/11 and Iraq to return presidential ads to their roots and to map the future for the Obama team in 2012. President George W. Bush did not start with the high approval numbers of President Obama, but after the terrorist strikes of 9/11, his personal ratings reached stratospheric levels of 90 percent. Three years later, at the start of his reelection effort, the numbers told a very different story for both men. By late April of their reelect years, Bush and Obama were struggling at just under 50 percent approval. The two presidents—whose characters and challenges contrasted so sharply—would fight for another term in similar circumstances, perilously close to the waterline of negative job ratings. As each man approached the day of his reelection, he faced voters who thought the country was on the wrong track by more than a ten-point margin.

The Bush-Cheney team in 2004 faced a rapidly deteriorating situation. There were no weapons of mass destruction in Iraq, and the country was spiraling quickly into a brutal civil war. They started their ad campaign with a foundational spot that reminded voters of the start of the Bush years: a recession, the bursting of the dot-com bubble, and the 9/11 attacks themselves. The situation was hardly "Morning in America," but it was at least getting better: "Today, America is turning the corner," the text said on screen. "Rising to the challenge."

But the real standouts of the 2004 campaign went far beyond the retelling of the Bush record. One opinion poll, taken after the election in six battleground states, identified three ads that influenced voters the most. Just one was produced by the Bush campaign itself: *Wolves* was a conscious echo of Reagan's *Bear* ad, using the metaphor of a pack of wolves prowling in a forest to evoke the threat of terrorists. Unlike the Reagan team, Bush's admen were more explicit in explaining the threat, from both the terrorists and their opponent, John Kerry. "In an increasingly dangerous world, even after the first terrorist attack on America, John Kerry and the liberals in Congress voted to slash America's intelligence operations by $6 billion," a female narrator said over a suspenseful rather than threatening soundtrack. "Cuts so deep they would have weakened America's defenses. And weakness attracts those who are waiting to do America harm."

The other two came from outside groups. One was a sixty-second positive story that was drawn from a local newspaper story of the president's visit to the town of Lebanon, Ohio. While working the rope line, he met a young woman whose mother died in the 9/11 attacks. The photo of him hugging and comforting Ashley ran not just in the newspaper but on the highly trafficked *Drudge Report*. "He's the most powerful man in the world and all he wants to do is make sure I'm safe, that I'm okay," said Ashley Faulkner in the ad. When the Republican group Progress for America aired the ad for its donors, half of them ended up crying.

The second ad generated far more media commentary and sent the Kerry campaign into a tailspin. Swift Boat Veterans for Truth organized themselves after one of its leaders, a retired admiral, read the Kerry book *Tour of Duty* by historian Doug Brinkley. The admiral was so angry at the book that he set about reviving the decades-long arguments about Kerry's Vietnam record and his later opposition to the war. The Swift Boat ads were an exercise in character assassination. "I know John Kerry is lying about his first Purple Heart because I treated him for that injury," said one veteran in the ad *Any Questions?* "John Kerry lied to get his Bronze Star. I know, I was there, I saw what happened," said a second. "He betrayed all his shipmates. He lied before the Senate," said a third.

Kerry himself was confused and frustrated by the attacks, even though he had heard the same in every race he had run for public office. His political strategy was to stay positive for fear of alienating independent and swing voters. But his lack of response seemed to confirm the substance of the attacks and the suggestion that he was a weak leader. The disputes between the candidate and his senior campaign aides were deep, and his vacillation under fire made the antagonism far worse.

So the candidate, on a brief vacation in Nantucket, decided to buy some new sports equipment and do what he liked to do to unwind: he went windsurfing. Neither the press nor his campaign aides knew what the candidate was planning to do, but a local TV crew chanced upon the presidential candidate at sea. The resulting video was a godsend to the Bush campaign, which turned the windsurfing pictures into a metaphor for Kerry's policy reversals, or flip-flopping. "In which direction would John Kerry lead," asked the male narrator over the strains of the Blue Danube waltz. "Kerry voted for the Iraq war, opposed it, supported it, and now opposes it again. He bragged about voting for the $87 billion to support our troops before he voted against it....John Kerry: whichever way the wind blows."

Against a weak opponent and a disorganized campaign, the Bush team eked out a narrow victory of just 2.4 percent, helped by a series of ads that defined the other candidate as much as their own. Their allies had successfully turned their rival's biographical strength into an electoral weakness; a strategy that was not forgotten by the Obama team eight years later.

On a dreary February morning in downtown Chicago, David Axelrod peered over his coffee and newspaper to survey the state of political ads in this reelection year. The Republican primary ads had turned harshly negative as the PACs supporting Mitt Romney tried to eradicate the threats from successive rivals: first Gingrich, then Santorum. Axelrod noted drily how the Romney superPAC Restore Our Future was airing attacks created by Larry McCarthy, the same adman who created the most notorious ad of any presidential campaign in recent years. "It's telling that the Willie Horton admakers are now heading up the superPAC," he said. "The reason George H. W. Bush went negative is because he had to back in '88. He was seventeen points behind and he had nothing to lose. He was either going to take Dukakis out or he was going to lose. And he had to be willing to take the disapprobation that came with that. That was, I think, the philosophy the Romney people took in Florida with Gingrich. But I think he's paid the price for that with independent voters. I also think his craven pursuit of the right-wing vote and his severe conservative rhetoric just made him look like a garden-variety politician, and the last thing independent voters want is a guy who is going to pander to the most dogmatic ideological interests in his party, and so he's paid a price among independents for that as well."

In this cycle, it would be tempting for Obama to deploy the same harsh ads, but there was a cost to doing so: the Obama brand was supposed to be about common ground and optimism, about unconventional politics, and not be predictably careerist.

Four years earlier, that meant holding back from personal attacks on Hillary Clinton, even though they dominated the private conversations between Obama, his friends, and his aides. "When you think about our primary campaign against Hillary, we mentioned her by name in two radio or TV ads in the whole primary," said Axelrod. "Yes, in the general we took McCain on. But I think tone is important just because of who Barack Obama is. We are not going to run ads, at least the ones we have control of—and I trust that the other guys on the outside will be thoughtful about what they do—we're not going to run ads that are inconsistent with who Barack Obama is. Will we run ads that are tough? Yes. Will we run ads that draw a contrast? Yes. Will they be gratuitous and over the line? No. I don't think that helps us. And we don't need to gild the lily. There's plenty there."

Looking back, Axelrod loved the kind of ads that attacked by proxy. There was a JFK ad against Nixon in 1960 that simply re-aired a line from Eisenhower at a press conference, when the president trashed the notion that his vice president had taken any big decisions. ("If you give me a week I might think of one," Ike chuckled to a reporter. "I don't remember.") He loved the LBJ ad four years later that eviscerated Goldwater with quotes from his primary rivals across the fake convention floor. "It didn't feel hard-edged," he noted. "It used their words. And basically it gave a permission structure to moderate Republicans to walk away from Goldwater." Other LBJ ads skewered Goldwater with his own quotes about cutting off the eastern seaboard or his apparently flippant remarks about nuclear weapons.

He admired, from a distance, the way Roger Ailes had destroyed Dukakis in 1988 ("brutally effective") and the way the Bush team hammered Kerry in 2004 ("a very good job"). Some of those same Bush people—Stuart Stevens and Russ Schriefer— were now running the strategy and ads of the likely GOP nominee. Axelrod seemed nonplussed. He and his business partner, David Plouffe, had studied the lessons of 2004. They invested heavily in door-to-door outreach in 2008, and it had worked. Now they were ready to deploy the Bush approach to reelecting a beleaguered president. Stevens and Schriefer were no longer the heirs to the Bush campaign legacy, in Axelrod's mind. "Unfortunately they're running Romney's campaign," Axelrod deadpanned. "But we're running their argument."

In his first presidential campaign, Obama liked to hold up the example of Reagan as a model of how a single leader could transform the political landscape for a generation. He aspired to do the same for progressive politics, so it was only natural to consider how Reagan had messaged his way to such a resounding victory in his reelection. Axelrod loved, above all, "Morning in America": "The brilliant thing about that ad is that it was a celebration of America in which Reagan was associated with American verities and virtues," he gushed. "In addition to signaling progress, it was steeped in Americana and it never really mentioned his name, I don't think." In other words, Axelrod loved the fact that Reagan was selling the American Dream: the chance that a simple vote could open up a world of economic and social progress.

His boss, on the other hand, preferred the darker, more menacing version of the Reagan campaign. "I'm not a believer in the *Bear*. I think it was one of those ads that professionals love. For a lot of people it was a little too abstract," said Axelrod. "But you know, the president loves that ad."

How do the best campaign ads stack up against the work of their commercial counterparts? To the Mad Men of Madison Avenue, the work of the political admakers was never going to rise to their standard. "I don't even call it political advertising. It's really video news releases," says Donny Deutsch, chairman of the Deutsch Inc. ad agency, who worked on the Clinton campaign ads in 1992. "On Madison Avenue, what makes a great ad is the nuance, the creativity, the heartstrings, what makes you laugh and cry. In politics, it's communications warfare. It's not as much about the creativity as the speed of reaction and singularity of the message. It's the decision making behind the message."

FIVE

DEFINITIONS

The numbers did not look good. It was the official kickoff of President Obama's reelection in May 2012, more than a year after the campaign had really started. The event was an indoor rally in what should have been an energized corner of a battleground state: a high-profile start to a period of intensive campaigning. Four years earlier, the roaring rallies were the hallmark of the insurgent Obama campaign, as the upstart senator filled arena after arena with fans from floor seats to the nosebleed galleries.

Now, on the friendly territory of the Ohio State campus in Columbus, the president was staring at empty space. In an arena that could seat more than eighteen thousand people, one-fourth of the rows were vacant. Two years earlier, on the same campus, Obama had staged an event with Governor Ted Strickland that drew two and a half times more people than he could see today. The empty seats were a symbol of a bigger hole: unemployment had just ticked down from 8.2 to 8.1 percent, basically unchanged from where it was at the time of his inauguration.

Obama's aides were unusually anxious to please reporters: they visited the confined press seats on Air Force One and checked in on their filing room at the rally. They pointed out that the audience numbers were at least beating Romney's turnout, and that unemployment in Ohio was at least better than the national statistics.

That was pretty much the case the president himself was making on stage: as bad as it's been, I'm still better than the other guy because there was a time, not so long ago, when we all believed in something better.

"If there is one thing that we learned in 2008," he told the Columbus crowd, "it's that nothing is more powerful than millions of voices calling for change. When enough of you knock on doors, when you pick up phones, when you talk to your friends, when you decide that it's time for change to happen, guess what? Change happens. Change comes to America. And that's the spirit we need again. If people ask you what this campaign is about, you tell them it's still about hope. You tell them it's still about change. You tell them it's still about ordinary people who believe that in the face of great odds, we can make a difference in the life of this country. Because I still believe, Ohio. I still believe that we are not as divided as our politics suggest. I still believe that we have more in common than the pundits tell us; that we're not Democrats or Republicans, but Americans first and foremost. I still believe in you, and I'm asking you to keep believing in me. I told you in 2008 that I wasn't a perfect man, and I would never be a perfect president. But I promised that I would always tell you what I thought. I would always tell you where I stood. And I would wake up every single day fighting for you as hard as I know how. And I have kept that promise. I have kept that promise, Ohio."

There were many Obama supporters who had simply stopped believing. Still About Hope was not the kind of slogan to fire up the numbers he would need to hold on to the White House.

To stir the crowds, Obama needed first to remind them what had happened over the last four years. His campaign's focus groups revealed the perils and the opportunities he faced. At the very beginning of the campaign in 2011, the groups suggested strongly that Obama was very vulnerable to defeat. Had more Republican contenders seen that research, the GOP field would surely have been stronger. "The focus groups were very dark from the very beginning," said one senior Obama campaign aide. "There was really palpable economic anxiety. There were rays of light that they didn't directly blame the president for it all. But nobody, no persuadable voter, felt comfortable with where their finances were. They were very concerned, and that was a red flag at the beginning that this thing was going to be really tight and way tighter than the conventional wisdom."

Obama was still personally popular with voters—especially independent and swing voters—who believed that he cared about them and understood their problems. Only the most partisan of Republicans hated him. But voters also expected their problems to have eased by now, so many years after the financial crisis. Digging deeper into the mind-set of the focus groups, Obama's message team noticed a contradiction that was their best hope: voters knew that Obama had been dealt a bad hand, but they had forgotten just how bad it was. When reminded of the depth of the crisis, they agreed that they had pushed it out of their minds, along with the president's accomplishments: like the recovery of the auto industry, or the killing of Osama bin Laden, or the return of troops from Iraq. "All of the accomplishments, once communicated, helped remind people of what the president had done and the progress that had been made," said Jim Margolis, Obama's leading admaker. "Otherwise, voters tended to forget and would say to themselves, 'Gee, I expected more. I had hoped for more. We should be further along.' So recounting the accomplishments was an important part of the story that needed to be told."

The result was sixty seconds of TV commercial called, simply, *Go*. As the first significant buy of the election, it set the tone for the positive track of the ad campaign. The ad was a highly public effort to nudge the narrative of the focus groups and the last four years into a story line that could unfold in later ads.

"Two thousand eight: an economic meltdown," the male narrator began over pictures of what looked like job seekers, and the kind of foreboding, piano-laden soundtrack normally associated with attack ads. "Four point four million jobs lost. America's economy spiraling down. All before this president took the oath." It was fully fifteen seconds—half the length of a normal campaign ad—before Obama was pictured at his first inauguration. "Some said our best days were behind us," the narrator continued, over pictures of a Tea Party protest. "But not him. He *believed* in us, *fought* for us. And today, our auto industry is back, firing on all cylinders. Our greatest enemy brought to justice by our greatest heroes. Our troops are home from Iraq." The music grew steadily more positive and upbeat, as the narrator explained how many jobs had been created.

Then came the final twist, in the last fifteen seconds: the most hotly debated fifteen seconds of ad script inside Obama's team: "We're not there yet," the narrator concluded. "It's still too hard for too many. But we're coming back. Because America's greatness comes from a strong middle class. Because you don't quit. And neither does he."

Obama's message and media team agreed on the argument for context. Voters needed to be reminded and reeducated about the last few years. That was the easy part. The harder question was: how could you rewrite this story to their candidate's benefit, without making at least two risky claims? It would be all too easy to cut an ad suggesting the economy was better than voters believed it to be, and that Obama was taking all the credit for the hard-earned recovery.

Behind the scenes, the one-hundred-word script was rewritten and reworked dozens of times to refine the perspective. Starting with the campaign research data, Obama's senior media and polling aides would agree on a macro-level mission for an ad like *Go*. One of the ad teams would write a script, which would then be tweaked by the polling and research advisers, before heading into more focus group sessions run by Obama's longtime research adviser, David Binder. The whole effort was coordinated and controlled by Larry Grisolano. The final scripts would be subjected to a group grilling by conference call, involving all the ad and message teams working on the campaign: Axelrod himself, Grisolano's AKPD, Margolis's GMMB, Dixon/Davis Media Group (which cut the first response ad on energy policy, three months earlier), Mark Putnam (who created a thirty-minute TV special near the end of the 2008 campaign), and Mike Donilon, an adviser to Joe Biden who was one of the best admakers in Democratic politics. The group would agree on a cut just before sending the ad back into focus group sessions again.

What emerged from the message machine was very finely calibrated. President Obama had long been frustrated in private by the lack of credit he was given—either in the polls or by pundits—for the rescue of Detroit. He had tried and failed repeatedly to make the case that the auto industry was in far better condition because of his policies. Now, at the start of the intensive phase of his reelection effort, the political landscape looked quite different. The auto bailout was deeply unpopular with voters when it was first proposed in late 2009, but the numbers had turned around three years later: from 54 percent negative views about the auto rescue to 56 percent positive views.

"I think a lot of us believed that there was a character dimension to staying with the automobile industry," said Margolis. "He stood up when most people told him to sit down. And he said, 'We're going to do it regardless of the political risk.' That tells you something about the man." Binder's focus group research showed this was a powerful underlying argument for talking about the auto bailout in 2012: voters had changed their minds because the president's policies had worked. "Tonally, we spent a lot of time working this through," said Margolis. "The president didn't beat his chest saying, 'Look at what a hero I am. Aren't you lucky I saved auto manufacturing?' Rather, we made it a story about the perseverance of the American worker. The president believed in you, and you turned around the automobile industry. This was a core insight. As we looked at the data, we had a lot more room to talk about our progress when it was done in the context of what Americans had accomplished, rather than what the president had accomplished. In short, Barack Obama gave you the keys, but you did the driving."

Sitting inside the West Wing, close to the Oval Office, Plouffe loved *Go*. It was assertive, without being arrogant or out of touch, and it spoke to his competitive nature. "It set that tone," he said. "There was a grittiness to it. It was less about the president than about the American people. He's by their side fighting through this. And there was a guarded optimism to it, which I think really hit home for people because that's what they were feeling. Out of despair, still uncertain, cautiously confident. And they're proud of their role in fighting through all this."

Each major ad spawned several spinoffs that used the same research and tone to deliver more specific messages to battleground states. *Go* gave birth to *Brian from Ohio*, in which Brian Slagle, identified as an Ohio autoworker, told the story of the industry's collapse and his fears for his young family. As he drives to work in the predawn darkness, we see him at the wheel saying, "Obama stuck his neck out for us, the auto industry. He wasn't going to let it just die. And I'm driving in this morning because of that. Because of him." The thirty-second ad ends with him walking through the gates of his factory to start work. The power came not just from the industry's survival but from the fact that one of its rescued workers was giving full and personal credit to Obama. "We were always pretty careful about how far we went," said Margolis. "We would let other people talk about the president and what he had done. That's an entirely different thing from us praising ourselves."

This positive phase lasted through the month of May and reversed the air wars that had been waged, at low levels, for the last several weeks and months. Romney and his Republican outside groups were outspending Obama and his allies by more than two-to-one. In the first week of May, the GOP forces spent almost $4 million compared to $1.7 million by Obama. That flipped over in the second week, as *Go* and its offspring were released. In the second week of May, Obama spent $6.6 million while the Republican numbers stayed almost flat. For the next two weeks, to the end of the month when Romney officially secured his party's nomination, the two sides almost matched each other dollar for dollar.

Costing more than $25 million, the month-long positive ad run did not, on the face of it, change very much. The Obama campaign focused its polling efforts on a group of battleground states, tracking every last piece of data it could scrape from the only states that mattered. As in 2008, the national polls so beloved by the media were all but ignored by Chicago headquarters. At the start of May, the battleground polls conducted by Obama's leading pollster, Joel Benenson, showed the president leading Romney by three points: 49 to 46. After a month of intensive ads, Obama was ahead of Romney by four points: 49 to 45. The president's polling numbers had gone nowhere. Political advertising is something of a black box. If you don't spend enough money on it, your possible defeat will be blamed on the lack of ads. If you do spend enough money on it, you may see no change whatsoever in your polls.

The internal debate inside Obama's media team looped back time and again around a core question of leadership. Not the president's leadership, but their own. How far could they go in leading voters on the critical challenge of the economy? Should they mirror public opinion to demonstrate how attuned they were, or try to push the voters toward a new understanding? Could advertising in fact move the needle at all, as they promised each candidate at the start of every costly fund-raising cycle?

On one side of the debate about economic messaging was the outside advice from the longtime Clinton pollster and strategist Stan Greenberg. In a memo early in 2012, Greenberg wrote (alongside James Carville, Clinton's first campaign manager) that he had tested four messages. The first described the election as a make-or-break moment for the middle class and called for investment in education and training. The second argued for the fair shot and fair shake that Obama had been outlining for the last several months. The third told the story of the deep crisis when the president took office and explained the progress since then. The fourth leaned forcefully into the notion that "America is back," as the president had done in his State of the Union Address at the start of the year. Greenberg argued that the first two messages worked best with the independent and swing voters who would decide the election. The second message on the economic turnaround underperformed the first two by ten points, while the final message—America is back—was "weaker than even the weakest Republican message."

Obama's aides had always found Greenberg's advice and presence to be personally aggravating, and this was no exception. "We had to be careful about the oversell," said Plouffe. "But this Stan Greenberg theory that says, we should basically have just said, 'Nothing's good.' It was a ridiculous argument to suggest that somehow we couldn't suggest that what we did made a difference. We're an incumbent running for reelection. That was divorced from reality."

They wanted to say it was Morning in America, but it barely felt like the predawn. If they couldn't say America is back, could they at least say America is *coming* back? For six months—from the fall of 2011 through the spring of 2012—the message team had been engaged in an unresolved debate about where to draw the line on the biggest issue facing voters. The point of contention was about what they called "accomplishments": the case that Obama had made things better. Axelrod was concerned that too much emphasis on the accomplishments would lead to blowback: it wasn't what the voters felt or experienced. Margolis believed that if you didn't tout the accomplishments, the voters would never feel good about how far they had traveled. Empathizing with voters about the lousy economy would never change the narrative. The debate often played out as the team watched the early cuts of their campaign ads. In the middle of *Go*, the narrator explains there have been more than 4 million jobs created since the recovery began. That indisputable statistic was itself the topic of heated debate. "Do you think people are going to buy it?" asked one media team member. "Does it just feel like we're pumping it up too much? If you're talking about the number of jobs, do people really feel like we're creating jobs out there?"

The answers were not clear from the much-vaunted focus groups. Voters would admit they had forgotten the context, and agreed that the newly elected President Obama faced a dire situation. Then they would pivot quickly to a position that seemed to blame him, too. "When the stock market was crashing, he really did have a shit sandwich handed to him," said one senior Obama aide, recounting the typical focus group response. "But you know, I really thought things would be better by now."

Obama himself leaned far more toward a sense of accomplishment than many of the aides shaping his message. For the first two years of his presidency, Obama wanted desperately to convince voters that no matter how bad things seemed, he was getting stuff done to make the economy better. After his admitted shellacking in the midterm congressional elections, Obama learned that his record of legislative accomplishment was not enough. He couldn't tell them to wait a little longer for the final payoff. He just had to wait a little longer himself, before voters would give him the final payoff of his own reelection.

"You gotta meet people where they live," said Plouffe, who took each ad to Obama personally—every video that required the candidate to say he approved this message—which meant that he also heard every presidential reaction to the media team's output.

"I think he was very proud of what we had done to help stabilize the economy," Plouffe explained. "So he was always eager to make the positive case about different industries or different improvements. But he had a pretty good sense of where people were. He would ask from time to time: 'Are we communicating enough about recovery?' He was always making sure there was a balance out there; it just can't be against Romney. He always brought that perspective to things."

If Obama's perspective had improved, his message team could easily lose their own sense of perspective. For a team that handled something called media, they were acutely uncomfortable with media coverage—if that coverage focused on someone else inside the campaign. Those tensions were only heightened by the close interest paid to such coverage by none other than the president of the United States. Obama had learned to loathe the kind of process stories featured prominently by political reporters. To him, they indulged far too much in score settling and loose talk about secret strategy. Whether the stories appeared in magazines or in books, the candidate felt they never looked good.

So at the start of the rollout in early May, the senior campaign team jumped on a *New York Times* profile of Jim Margolis. This was supposed to be the start of the positive ad track, notably *Go* itself. Instead, the *Times* portrayed the campaign as ready to spend "a considerable chunk of their advertising budget" on aggressively negative ads. "Forget hope and change," the story began.

The tone and the leaking continued through May, ending with a classic of the genre in *New York* magazine, called "Hope: The Sequel." The subtitle was not much better for the enforcers of discipline inside the White House: "For Obama & Co., this time around it's all about fear." Quoting liberally from anonymous aides and former aides, the story set up the campaign strategy against Romney as follows: "'He's the fifties, he is retro, he is backward, and we are forward—that's the basic construct,' says a top Obama strategist. 'If you're a woman, you're Hispanic, you're young, or you've gotten left out, you look at Romney and say, "This fucking guy is gonna take us back to the way it always was, and guess what? I've never been part of that."'" The story quoted another anonymous aide enjoying the prospect of the Ricketts plan to revive the Reverend Wright issue, for the simple reason that the plan would energize the Democratic base. "Nothing could more garishly illustrate a bedrock truth about the campaign that lies before us," the magazine quipped. "It will bear about as much resemblance to 2008 as Romney does to Nicki Minaj."

Such displays of machismo prompted dismay among the campaign's leading figures: from Obama himself to the two Davids, Axelrod and Plouffe. Since the 2008 campaign, Axelrod had warned against process stories. They looked and sounded like traditional political hacks if they talked about the process, rather than the unconventional candidate called Barack Hussein Obama. The *New York* magazine story underscored just how damaging such a focus on process could be. Yes, the campaign to date had been frustratingly slow for the operatives in Chicago and the consultants on the sidelines. But now that it was ready to move into high gear, there was no excuse for leaking strategy. "That *New York* magazine article angered a lot of people because it was a giant vomit of undisciplined quotes," said one senior White House staffer. "We never saw anything like that in all of 2008, and it's the kind of thing that made Axelrod and Plouffe's head explode: people talking about our tactics, talking about our strategy, saying things about Romney that reflected badly upon us, the hubris. The whole thing was sort of asking for trouble." Back in Washington, Obama's closest aides blamed the leaking on the clash of egos that dominated the disputes in Chicago. "That is a product of the friction in the campaign, because in 2008 no one ever felt compelled to talk to a reporter because they thought someone else was going to take credit for what they did or say something bad about them," the senior staffer said. "You get into trouble whenever people feel like they have to talk to protect themselves."

Perhaps Obama's aides were excited about the strategy because they had just made what would be the boldest decision of the campaign. The president and his inner circle prided themselves on making a few big bets. Those gambles were the hallmark of their unconventional nature: their readiness to overturn political convention and build a broader appeal than their rivals. Four years earlier, Obama had gambled by running for president against the Clintons; by investing so heavily in Iowa; by taking his campaign overseas; by going live on TV with a thirty-minute broadcast late in the election; by rejecting public funding for his general election. This time around, as a sitting president in a struggling economy, there were far fewer options for risk taking and there was far less appetite for risk.

The one variable he could control centered on money. Obama and his senior team knew they were going to be outspent. The only question was when that would happen. They could wait to watch the tidal wave of ads from the Romney campaign and its allies. Or they could try to change the dynamic before Romney and his backers could get their act together. The success of *Go*—at least the internal satisfaction with the ad and its rollout—suggested strongly that they should go early themselves. Besides, going early was the strategy deployed successfully by the last two reelected presidents. Both Clinton and Bush spent heavily defining their opponents negatively before they could respond after their own primaries.

The difference this time around was that Obama himself had destroyed the zero-sum game that was the public financing of general elections. In the old days, before 2008, a sitting president would spend only as much as his challenger because he was bound by the limits of taxpayer money. Now that decision threatened to undermine his own reelection strategy for one simple reason: he had no idea if he could raise enough money on his own in the fall.

Obama met with his senior campaign team in the wide and windowless Roosevelt Room in late May. His advisers placed a big bet in front of him: accelerate their fall advertising dollars into the summer. Spend more than $100 million destroying Romney's reputation in battleground states, and cross their fingers that they can raise more cash later in the year. "It was as difficult a decision as you can imagine," recalled Plouffe. "We agonized over it. But the prospect of being outgunned in the fall if the money fell off was frightening. We had to stop Romney from getting people to take a positive view of him in a difficult economy."

Four years ago, Obama had surged late in fund-raising thanks to an unprecedented flow of dollars from grassroots supporters online. Now, with middling approval numbers and a struggling economy, Obama could not be sure the same would happen again. In fact the early signs were not reassuring. Even if the online dollars flowed again, they were unlikely to reach the levels seen in 2008.

"What's the worst situation we think we could be in if we do this?" Obama asked.

They could simply run out of money, replied Plouffe.

Obama questioned their bet, but nobody spoke up against it. As anxious as they felt about the situation, there were no real alternatives. They were already bumping up against the 50 percent mark in several battleground states, and there seemed little room for them to grow. Romney, on the other hand, had plenty of upside ahead of him.

"The early spend was meant to prevent the other side from moving," said Plouffe. "We had to preempt Romney's ability to pull voters away from the president. If he converted all of the undecideds from the president, it would not be close. If Romney was more of an acceptable alternative, the polls would change."

As clear as they were about their anti-Romney reasoning, they remained unsure about the viability of their strategy. They could score early victory in the polls by damaging their opponent, but still watch him bounce back late in the campaign by outspending them by huge margins.

"The problem with planning these campaigns is you make certain suppositions about fund-raising," said Axelrod as he wrestled with the strategy at the time. "You may be right and you may be wrong. But what you don't want to do is get caught short at the end. So that's the hardest part of this: to calculate all of this so you don't run out of money. You want to make sure you have the resources when they are needed. You don't want to go on the air and then go off the air."

The bold decision about early spending might just have encouraged them to take on other risks. A few days after deciding to move their money forward, Obama's senior team was looking for a media event to start the rollout of the next phase of the message: defining Mitt Romney before he could define himself. It was their first serious pivot from positive to negative campaigning, and they needed a big kickoff. They concocted a stunt on the steps of the

Massachusetts statehouse in Boston as a place where a campaign surrogate could tell the real story of Romney's record as governor. The only question was who would stand on the steps, in front of several state legislators, to recite the talking points. They needed a big name from the campaign, so Stephanie Cutter suggested her one-time mentor, David Axelrod.

"What do you guys think?" she asked the senior campaign team. "We need an anchor." They all agreed: Axelrod would be the anchor.

The Massachusetts story was one of the biggest missing pieces of the GOP primaries. Romney himself would rarely discuss his single term as the state's governor, not least because his biggest achievement there was the health-care law that served as the model for President Obama's national reforms. Beyond his record as a moderate, Romney's time in the commonwealth represented a rich vein for his opponents, which they failed to mine. Above all, Romney's much-repeated claim to be a fiscally responsible job creator was undercut by his record as governor. Any half-competent campaign research operation could surely figure that out, or so Chicago thought. When Romney emerged from the primaries largely unscathed by his record in Massachusetts, the Obama team happily stepped in.

The foundational period of the campaign strategy involved recasting Romney's story. Romney was marketing himself as the turnaround artist: if he could fix the Salt Lake City Olympics, he could do the same for the national economy. This was a potent argument inside the focus groups, where Obama's aides were alarmed by the voters' readiness to seek some new solution for their economic frustrations. Digging back into Romney's campaign for governor in Massachusetts, as well as his time in office, they noticed a strong echo. He made the same arguments for his own hiring in 2002 and his job performance for the next four years. The frame they used was "you've heard it all before," even though the vast majority of national voters had never followed Romney's claims or boasts in Massachusetts. The imperative was to reposition their new opponent as a fake Mr. Fixit—an archetypal fraud. "The premise was: if you let him be the economic Mr. Fixit, this would be a huge problem for us," said Margolis. "We've got to really raise significant questions about the ability of Mitt Romney to come in and perform economic miracles." Inside the focus groups, undecided voters seemed far more ready to shift their feelings about Romney after they heard about the broken promises of Massachusetts. The notion that Romney was a disappointment resonated much more than traditional attacks on his personal fortune from the ill-gotten gains of private equity.

Chicago was more than prepared to go negative: they embraced it with gusto. After so many months of phony war and internal strife, they could finally do something real. Mid-ranking staff boasted they would continue the Romney attacks for the remaining five months of the campaign. This was not a team that believed in uniting red and blue America anytime soon. They fanned out on TV and in print, reciting the same talking points: Romney had promised to lift job creation, but his state was forty-seventh out of fifty states in job creation during his time as governor. Manufacturing jobs declined, while government jobs increased. State spending and debt went up, not down. The discipline in the message repetition was impressive.

What was far less impressive was their battlefield awareness. The first engagement with the enemy made a mockery of their planning and strategy. The event leaked on Twitter the night before Axelrod traveled to Boston, where Cutter had already begun work on the day ahead. She met with legislators who would be the backdrop to the press event, but she was concerned enough about the leak to send advance staff to the statehouse in case there was trouble.

It was only when Cutter and Axelrod neared the statehouse that they could see for themselves just how much trouble lay ahead. "You know, there are a few protesters there," one of the advance team told Axelrod in the car, before they turned the corner to witness the scene. The statehouse was just a few blocks from Romney's headquarters and there was nothing to stop the GOP candidate's staff from showing up to make their feelings known. "There was, as we used to say in my newspaper days, a band of marauding youth standing behind the press," said Axelrod. "The podium was probably not more than ten feet from this mob. So I had supporters behind me. These guys in front of me. And I felt like I was in the Roman Colosseum basically."

It was too late to walk away. Axelrod tried to enjoy the surreal scene, the absurdity of the disaster, and the challenge of the protesters. But his halting, intellectual style was no match for the marauding youth. They held signs telling him to go back to Chicago, that he was a broken record, that they wanted Mitt. They even brought along a dog wearing a Romney T-shirt. "Axel-fraud," they chanted, refusing to silence for a second as the TV cameras and microphones struggled to track the scripted comments about Romney's record as governor. Axelrod tried to be witty, recalling a recent gaffe by Romney's political consultant Eric Fehrnstrom, that his candidate could treat the end of the primaries like an Etch A Sketch, erasing his positions ahead of the general election. "You can shout down speakers, my friends," Axelrod retorted, "but it's hard to Etch A Sketch away the truth." A supporter lifted up his microphone because it was hard to hear him shout above the din.

Back at the White House, the reaction was less than amused.

Plouffe was angry at the lack of discipline and felt that Axelrod was placed in an impossible position. The president thought the event was amateurish, and he called Axelrod to tell him it was not exactly helpful. "I see you had an interesting day," he said drily. Axelrod could only agree.

Cutter brushed off the White House concern, as she brushed off most other criticism. She had survived worse in 2004 and was determined to survive anything else this election could throw at her. But she underestimated just how deep the concerns were about the Chicago communications and events team. Obama and Plouffe believed the campaign was not performing well and needed greater adult supervision. Jim Messina in Chicago agreed, seizing on the event that came to be known in the West Wing as Axelfraud. He could rein in Cutter and Axelrod in one swift move because of the televised embarrassment on the steps of the statehouse.

In fact Messina, too, was a source of deep concern. "The president felt like things needed to be tighter," said one senior Obama aide. Obama was particularly concerned that the campaign was telegraphing all its moves. "Stop doing that," he told his message team at the White House. "We don't have to tell everyone what we're doing." There was a widespread feeling around the president that the team in Chicago did not share the spirit of 2008, an understanding of the Obama brand, or the kind of cohesion and competence that allowed a freshman senator to win the White House in the first place.

Obama's team might not be able to beat the economy, but they sure as hell could beat Mitt Romney and the Republicans. Their challenge was to change the subject at the forefront of voters' minds; or at least to nudge that subject into a better light. David Axelrod believed the race was just like 2004, when Bush faced a crisis on Iraq, just as Obama faced a crisis on the economy. To underscore his point, he liked to tell the joke of two guys who chance upon a bear in the woods. "One guy freezes and the other guy bends over and goes into his bag and takes out his gym shoes and starts lacing them up," says Axelrod. "And the first guy says, 'What are you doing? Are you crazy? You can't outrun that bear.' And the second guy says, 'I don't have to outrun the bear. I just have to outrun you.' So the electorate was a bear, but all we had to do was outrun Romney. And the same was true for Bush: he had to outrun Kerry. Beyond that, I understood why Bush won that election because, at the end of the day, he was authentic, people related to him. They thought Kerry was inauthentic. They couldn't relate to him. They didn't quite know who he was. It seemed pretty apparent that Romney could run into those same difficulties because he had contorted himself to retrofit himself for the new conservative Republican Party."

Axelrod was not the only member of Obama's senior team to learn survival lessons from the president they had comprehensively trashed both on the campaign trail in 2008 and inside the White House. Plouffe had modeled the 2008 ground game on the Bush campaign's voter outreach in 2004. Cutter had learned about message discipline from being on the losing side of that cycle with the inauthentic Kerry himself. The Obama team felt no qualms in copying the methods and strategy of politicians and operatives they professed to loathe.

The hope-and-change candidate spent close to $50 million in negative ads through June, starting with a long sixty-second ad introducing the new Republican nominee. Axelrod had heard Romney's claims that he knew how to create jobs and he had a hunch this was nothing new. He asked the campaign's research team to look back at what Romney had claimed when he ran for Massachusetts governor six years earlier. "It was uncanny what they came up with," Axelrod said, "because you could have run the same tape. I also knew from the research that had already been done that his economic record was pretty middling. And there was this one number that really stood out and we polled it. It was a killer that he was forty-seventh in the nation in job creation. Because his whole campaign was pegged to: 'I know how to create jobs.' So I had this idea that we should—the best way to hang him was with his own words. That was to me an effective spot in terms of going at his core." Just like the Goldwater ads he loved so much from 1964, the Romney ads relied on quotes from the Republican candidate as much as facts from a narrator.

The ad *We've Heard It All Before* began with a younger Romney in a C-SPAN video of a governor's debate in 2002: "I speak the language of business. I know how jobs are created." Then the narrator recited a litany of dismal economic facts and statistics about the state under Romney's governorship: losing forty thousand manufacturing jobs, outsourcing state jobs to call centers in India, cutting taxes for the superwealthy ("millionaires like himself") while raising taxes and fees on the middle class. The ad then cut to a CNN interview with Romney from the current race, saying, "I know what it takes to create jobs." The narrator delivered a long punch line: "So now, when Mitt Romney talks about what he'd do as president . . . remember: we've heard it all before. . . . Romney economics: it didn't work then and it won't work now."

In battleground states, voters watched a series of shorter ads demolishing Romney's Massachusetts record. There was one on the one thousand fees he introduced for services like school buses and driver's licenses. The tagline was the same on each of the shorter ads. "Romney economics: didn't work then and won't work now."

For Margolis, who cut many of these ads, the goal was to go beyond the traditional message of presidents seeking voter reaffirmation: stay the course, or don't change horses midstream. "I never liked the horses analogy because I think there had to be a greater risk, there had to be a greater threat," he explained. "And this was not like: 'Here are two guys. Which one do you think has the faster horse to get us across the river?' This was: 'That guy wants to turn the horse around and go back.' Quite simply, Mitt Romney's proposals are the same ones that caused our economy to crash. And the last thing that you want to do is embrace that set of priorities, that prescription for this country. You're never getting across the river with that guy."

What surprised Obama's team was that Romney had no response to what was an entirely predictable move by the president's men. Bob Dole and John Kerry were both defined by their presidential opponents before they could make a move. So they were perplexed that Romney did not release an ad campaign to tell his own story. Obama's aides believed this was one of their biggest advantages of the election: Romney refused to introduce himself and his life story to the voters. Inside Chicago, they speculated that Romney's Mormon religion was so widely unknown across America—and even distrusted by the evangelical base of the Republican Party—that much of their opponent's life was off-limits. In fact, the Romney campaign tested various messages with focus groups and discovered that voters said they were less interested in Romney's personal story and more interested in hearing about what he would do in office as president.

"My view is you build on biography. Biography authenticates

your message," said Axelrod. "In this case, so much of his biography was walled off. He couldn't talk about his faith, which was hugely important to him. He couldn't talk about his business, because his business was controversial. So all they could do was speak at twenty thousand feet about him being a successful businessman, or at least so they felt. And he didn't want to talk about Massachusetts, because his principal achievement was health reform. So that didn't leave a lot for them."

For several weeks in June, Obama was outspending Romney and his allies by more than $3 million a week. The result in the campaign's internal polls of battleground state showed that Obama had moved down one point from 50 to 49 points, while Romney had also moved down one point from 48 to 47 points. After all those millions of dollars and all the man-hours expended on the message, it was still just a two-point race.

The first month of attacks on Mitt Romney represented just a softening up of the other side. The follow-up was intended to deliver the knockout blow on Romney's time at Bain Capital. The private equity firm grew out of Bain and Company, a hard-driving company of management consultants. Romney established the firm in 1984 to put into practice the kind of ideas about efficiencies and new markets that the consultants were selling to other businesses. If their advice was so good, they should be able to make money for themselves and their investors. That strategy turned out to be true: Romney made his considerable personal fortune as the executive who controlled the firm, which reported an incredible 173 percent annual return until Romney left full-time management in 1999.

Yet his time at Bain had also dogged Romney in his previous efforts to win elected office. Bain had helped create successful businesses like Staples, the office supplies retailer. And it had helped close down successful businesses, often taking substantial returns on investments whether the company was profitable or on the verge of collapse. In 1994, when Romney challenged Ted Kennedy for the US Senate seat in Massachusetts, Bain Capital was the basis for a series of devastating ads that all but decimated the Republican campaign. They were simple ads of regular working folks from Marion, Indiana, who used to be employed at SCM Office Supplies. That was, until 1994 when Bain arrived in the shape of American Pad and Paper, which first cut their wages and benefits before closing the plant a year later at the loss of two hundred jobs.

Bain invested $5 million in American Pad and Paper but recouped its investment early through so-called management fees that amounted to $2 million a year. The business strategy for the rest of the 1990s was to borrow large amounts of cash to buy other companies, inflating sales numbers ahead of a stock market listing that added more than $45 million to Bain's returns. American Pad and Paper went into bankruptcy in 2000, six years after Bain bought SCM and just four years after its stock market listing.

The closure of SCM was just a bump in the road on the way to giant returns and the ultimate collapse of the company. But its political value survived, sitting in a virtual vault of attack ads for successive campaigns to open whenever Romney ran for office.

"I would like to say to Mitt Romney," said one former SCM employee over melancholic music in a Kennedy ad, "if you think you'd make such a good senator, come out here to Marion, Indiana, and see what your company has done to these people." The ad showed several workers describing how they lost their benefits, wages, and insurance. "Basically cut our throats," said one woman. Another ad allowed SCM workers to destroy Romney's claim at the time that he had created ten thousand jobs. The ads were relentless and effective. Romney was tied with Kennedy in early September; after the ads ran for several weeks, he was 5 points down in October, and he lost the election the following month by 17 points.

The Obama campaign's TV team had barely begun airing its positive ads, led by *Go*, when the digital team started laying the foundation for the future Bain attacks. This would be a campaign that merged positive and negative tracks, using paid-for advertising and free media coverage together. And they knew the Bain attacks would trigger huge interest from the news media. The echo chamber would cost them almost nothing.

The digital media team cut a full six-minute online video telling the story of another company cut down by Bain: GST Steel in Kansas City, Missouri. The video began with Joe Soptic, a steelworker for thirty years, who described the plant as "a city inside of a city." Soptic continued to tell how they had a reputation for quality and American manufacturing. "We weren't rich," he said, "but I was able to put my daughter through college. That stopped with the sale of the plant to Bain Capital." Jobs were cut, along with quality. The company racked up debt while Bain drew down cash for its own returns. Bain invested $8 million and took a $36 million dividend a year later, funded by $125 million of debt. It bought another steel company and doubled its debt again. Eight years after Bain arrived, GST went into bankruptcy, and the owners cut pensions along with health-care benefits for pensioners. "It was like a vampire," said Jack Cobb, another former GST worker. "They came in and sucked the life out of us." In style and substance, the ad was much like Kennedy's ad from eighteen years earlier. But it was longer, with documentary pictures of the shuttered plant and old video footage of the working steel mill. Since it was online, its production and streaming costs were negligible compared to the heavy team effort of the TV ads and the dollars required to buy airtime. The next week, the Obama team followed up with an ad about SCM Office Supplies in Indiana, just like the Kennedy ad.

The reaction was precisely what they intended, triggering what Obama's team viewed as a feeding frenzy in the media. Conservatives claimed the ad was an attack on capitalism, proving Obama's socialist credentials and their own candidate's business acumen. Progressives believed the ad proved that Romney was part of what Texas governor Rick Perry had called "vulture capitalism": a job destroyer, not a job creator. The media judged the ad to be harsh, but loved the spectacle of a presidential fistfight that was only just beginning. This was what reporters had yearned for since the winding down of the GOP primaries.

The response from Democrats—even political allies of the president—was caustic. Cory Booker, the Newark mayor and rising Democratic star, appeared on NBC's *Meet the Press* to defend Bain Capital for having done "a lot to support businesses, to grow businesses." He said the Bain ads, like the Ricketts plan, were "nauseating." He called on Obama's team to "stop attacking private equity," finishing with a flourish: "It's a distraction from the real issues. It's either going to be a small campaign about this crap or it's going to be a big campaign, in my opinion, about the issues that the American public cares about."

Inside the White House, Obama's aides were furious. Booker was supposed to be one of their surrogates; a young African-American reformer in the mold of Obama himself. Valerie Jarrett, one of the president's closest advisers and a friend to the Obama family, phoned Booker in what she called "a moment of pique" to let him know her displeasure. Obama's aides were already upset that Chicago was telling the press that they were going to go negative on Romney in ways that Obama would dislike. Now those negative tactics had backfired badly, and they blamed Stephanie Cutter. "This is probably mostly Cutter," said one senior Obama adviser. "The campaign had a tendency to say, 'Hey, everyone, big negative Bain push coming.' No one can control Cory Booker going out and crapping on us. That was not anyone's mistake on the campaign. It just made it worse. There was a general sense that we were constantly saying, 'We are about to do something very negative and un-Obama-like. Please watch us and cover it that way.'"

Negative ads still made Obama himself uncomfortable. They just didn't match his self-image, even if he was ultracompetitive to the point of accepting the need for negativity. He was not happy with the heavy focus on attack ads and videos, even though he accepted them as part of the mix.

Within hours Booker had cut and posted an online video "explaining" his *Meet the Press* comments by mostly recanting them. It made for uncomfortable viewing on its own. Booker ended up justifying the Obama campaign's attacks because Romney was using his jobs record as his main reason to be elected president: a complete reversal from his position that morning on TV.

The next day, President Obama was hosting the NATO summit in Chicago, when the first question of his press conference focused not on national security, but Bain and GST. Instead of backing off the nauseating attacks, Obama rejected Booker's notion that the debate over Bain was part of a small campaign about crap. "I think it's important to recognize that this issue is not a 'distraction,'" he said.

"This is part of the debate that we're going to be having in this election campaign about how do we create an economy where everybody from top to bottom, folks on Wall Street and folks on Main Street, have a shot at success and if they're working hard and they're acting responsibly, that they're able to live out the American Dream.... And the reason this is relevant to the campaign is because my opponent, Governor Romney, his main calling card for why he thinks he should be president is his business expertise. He is not going out there touting his experience in Massachusetts. He is saying, 'I'm a business guy and I know how to fix it,' and this is his business. And when you're president, as opposed to the head of a private equity firm, then your job is not simply to maximize profits. Your job is to figure out how everybody in the country has a fair shot. Your job is to think about those workers who got laid off and how are we paying for their retraining. Your job is to think about how those communities can start creating new clusters so that they can attract new businesses. Your job as president is to think about how do we set up an equitable tax system so that everybody is paying their fair share that allows us then to invest in science and technology and infrastructure, all of which are going to help us grow."

Obama continued to lose surrogate support. Deval Patrick, Romney's successor as Massachusetts governor and another Democratic star, kept close to his Boston supporters by saying he had friends at Bain. He told MSNBC's *Morning Joe* that Bain's record had been distorted, although he conceded there were legitimate questions about Romney's accomplishments. President Bill Clinton appeared on CNN to say that Romney was "a man who's been governor and had a sterling business career" who "crosses the qualification threshold" to be president.

Still, the anti-Bain message stuck. In Chicago, the campaign team could rationalize the exchanges in two ways. The messy rollout was obviously unhelpful because it smacked of indiscipline. Second-guessing a presidential campaign was never a good thing, as Al Gore had found when Clinton was publicly criticizing his strategy late in the 2000 election.

On the other hand, the controversy sustained the story and helped it reach voters who might never have paid attention. "Cory Booker kind of helped," said Ben LaBolt, the campaign's national press secretary. "He penetrated it into regional markets in a way that it wouldn't have otherwise. It didn't lead to the cleanest roll-out of the campaign, but it laid out a predicate for the length and intensity of the stories that helped us introduce arguments about Romney, Bain, and outsourcing."

Obama's allies happily picked up the story and turned it into something that Cory Booker might find several notches worse than nauseating. Priorities USA Action was a much smaller super-PAC than those allied to Romney and conservative donors. Run by two former White House officials—Bill Burton and Sean Sweeney—it found itself woefully outraised by its GOP counterparts. In January at the start of the election year, it raised just $59,000 as Democratic donors shunned the kind of outside group that Obama himself had previously disdained. The following month, Obama signaled that he was ready to support the group, because they were so heavily outgunned by their Republican rivals. By June it was raising $6 million a month: a far better performance but still a long way behind the groups aided by Karl Rove and the billionaire Koch brothers.

Despite the fund-raising gap, Priorities USA punched above its weight with the kind of ads the Obama campaign shied away from. *Stage* took the concept of former Bain Capital employees a step further. In place of several ex-workers, the ad used just one: Mike Earnest, who had been employed at the paper plant at Marion, Indiana. Earnest told the story of how, out of the blue, he was ordered to build a thirty-foot stage one day. A few days later, some men stood on the new stage to address all three shifts working at the profitable company. Their jobs were gone; the plant was now closed. "We all just lost our jobs," he said. "We don't have an income. Mitt Romney made over $100 million by shutting down our plant and devastated our lives. Turns out that when we built that stage, it was like building my own coffin. And it just made me sick."

The ad's simplicity held much of its power to shock. The Obama campaign tested the ad—even though it had no role in its production—by taking it to focus groups. "The most effective ad we tested was the Priorities USA *Stage* ad," said Jim Messina, the campaign manager. "They didn't raise enough money to run it the way they should have. But it was an amazingly effective ad." Back at campaign headquarters in Chicago, the senior team loved the way the sixty-second ad captured the message they were trying to push forward. "It enveloped so much of what we were trying to say about Romney," said one senior campaign official. "He wasn't looking out for you; he only cared about his profits, and he would do whatever it took to score one for himself—even if it's at the expense of you. With these middle-class faces, everyone saw themselves in it, particularly coming out of a pretty deep recession. A lot of people knew what it was like to be laid off. Romney wasn't providing any type of reassurance to people."

It took another month before the Romney team cut an online video to respond to the steel plant video, but it was unconvincing and just fueled the story. It featured a former GST vice president called B. C. Huselton saying, "Did it all work out? No. Did we make a difference? I think we made a big difference." The campaign posted the video, then pulled it down without explanation. It finally reposted the video in September, just two months before the general election. The message battle was lost; the damage was done.

Behind the scenes, the Obama ad team was a sprawling mess. Controlling its output across all outlets and all markets turned into a giant undertaking. The division of labor was not always clear, and the various teams were not always aligned. Sometimes an ad that should never have aired would slip through the net.

In Chicago, Obama's political and media strategists knew they had to overperform among African-American voters. If they could turn out a few extra points in the African-American community—a few points above the census model, and several points above black turnout in the midterm elections two years earlier—they stood a chance of pulling off a remarkable victory. So they set to work on a radio ad that would target African-American voters in particular. Shaped by the work of their sole African-American pollster, Cornell Belcher, the campaign commissioned an ad from Fuse Advertising, a black agency in St. Louis, Missouri. The ad—which aired on some of the biggest shows on black radio, including the *Steve Harvey Show* and the *Tom Joyner Morning Show*—tried to convince infrequent or discouraged black voters to stand up for the first black president.

"Four years ago, we made history," the narrator said to a funk-heavy soundtrack spliced together with audience cheers. "Now it's time to move forward and finish what we started together. We have to show the president, we have his back." Then the harmonized singers kicked in: *"We've got yo' back!"* The ad cut back and forth between sound bites from the president's speeches and *"We've got yo' back!"* "Have the president's back and register to vote," the narrator continued. "Go to gottavote.org to register now. That's gottavote.org."

Inside the campaign to reelect the country's first black president, there was an embarrassingly low number of African-Americans in the senior ranks. Prominent and wealthy black donors told Obama's aides, as well as his operatives in Chicago, that they would not take part unless and until there was African-American representation in headquarters. Jim Messina embarked on an intensive search to fill the hole, asking Valerie Jarrett for her advice on the role she herself played in 2008. There were few candidates who were prepared to give up a year's worth of salary, and unwind their outside work, to commit to the campaign full-time. It took several months before Messina could recruit just one figure to the innermost circle of leadership: Broderick Johnson, a former lobbyist and personal friend of the president, who visited Chicago weekly.

With no senior African-Americans in the campaign's chain of command, there could be no real supervision of ads targeting African-American voters. The first black radio ad was nothing Obama himself would ever approve. "It was like something out of *Soul Train* from the 1970s," said one senior Obama aide. "It was so bad. The worst was that it started out with the president saying, "I'm Barack Obama and I approve this message." The jingle wasn't even *your back* but *yo' back*." To cap it all, the ad never spelled out the website address. *Gottavote* was supposed to have two Ts. As conservative pundits and websites trashed the ad as supposedly racist or simply pandering to black voters, the Romney campaign bought out the web address gotavote.org with just one *T*. If you mistyped the name, you ended up at a site asking you to donate cash to the Romney campaign. Obama's aides promptly killed the ad.

For the much-vaunted, much-improved Obama campaign, there was no clean shot at crafting the message. Whether they were staging events in Boston, rolling out attacks on Bain, or targeting black voters, they stumbled early and often in ways that did not bode well for success. It was one thing to fail as the start-up campaign that surprised a party and a nation through the primaries of 2008. But the Obama campaign was supposed to have learned its lessons and built a far bigger and far better machine in 2012. Instead the machine could be surprisingly tone-deaf and technologically inept as it engaged for the first time with the enemy.

SIX

THE DIGITAL DIVIDE

"Half the money I spend on advertising is wasted," said John Wanamaker, a Philadelphia retailer in the late 1800s who was a pioneer in newspaper advertising. "The trouble is, I don't know which half." The line rings so true, and remains so popular, it has variously been attributed to Henry Ford and Lord William Lever, the soap baron who cofounded what is now Unilever.

More than a century later, the Obama campaign could not afford to waste half its money. The president's aides knew they were going to be outspent by a combination of Mitt Romney and Republican outside groups. (They would end up spending more than $500 million on ads, some $150 million less than Romney and his allies.) Their only strategy lay in trying to stretch out their dollars: to figure out which half of their advertising budget was wasted, and narrow down the missed targets to a minimum.

Sitting in a dark Chicago restaurant close to the Prudential building on a frigid February afternoon, the man tasked with minimizing the waste was feeling excited. Larry Grisolano was a bear of a man, with an imposing physique eased by his gentle manner and wry smile. He was tired of the old-style Senate campaigns where you would cut an ad, wait for a response, then go back and forth for a couple of months until election day. This campaign would be different. By merging the media strategy with voter and digital data, Grisolano and the team could reengineer the construction of the entire message machine. Like the general manager of the Oakland A's, Grisolano could be the Billy Beane of political ads, overcoming a huge money disadvantage with the help of a new and rigorous approach to statistical analysis.

"This is Moneyball," Grisolano said. "Now we can take an ad buy for twenty thousand swing voters in Northern Virginia and know their mathematical likelihood of seeing the ad. Nielsen just gives age and gender, which is very basic. But the data team has mathematical probabilities of the perfect ad mix on various shows to hit those swing voters. And if the ads don't reach them, we can use digital to target them."

Back in the digital dark ages of 2008, the campaign's data was stovepiped. The volunteers knocking on doors were largely on their own in terms of messaging and reporting back what they found. This time, the volunteers spoke the same language as the ads on TV and the videos online. And the information they gathered on the doorstep was critical information in shaping the statistical analysis and voter modeling back at headquarters.

"TV is a very blunt instrument. It consumes a lot of money," said Grisolano. "But what really interests and excites me is that we now know what the response is. We can measure everything."

Grisolano was himself one of those young volunteers who knocked on doors. Growing up in Burlington, Iowa, he got involved in politics because there were so many presidential candidates who came to visit. His parents weren't particularly political, but something about the 1980 campaign hooked him as a sophomore in high school, and continued to pull him in as a college student. Three years later, he quit college to work on Tom Harkin's Senate campaign, which still ranked—thirty-five years later—as one of the greatest races he ever worked on. He took so much time out of college for campaigns that it took him seven years to graduate. "At that time there was barely a campaign industry," he recalled. "I didn't know campaign consultants. The guy who did ads for Harkin, for instance, never became a long-term presence in the ad business. So over the course of time that I was kind of getting involved in working in races, this whole industry was building up around me."

He met David Axelrod in 1988, working on Senator Paul Simon's presidential campaign. Axelrod had quit his job as a reporter for the *Chicago Tribune* to work on Simon's first Senate campaign in 1984. But this freshman senator—unlike Grisolano's client a generation later—failed to win the presidential nomination: he finished second in Iowa to Dick Gephardt, came in third in New Hampshire, and lost the nomination to Michael Dukakis. Axelrod later hired Grisolano, and they worked together at his consulting firm for a couple of years before Grisolano moved to California. There he specialized in the state's ballot propositions— the so-called initiatives, where there are no candidates except the issues at hand. Research is paramount in these narrowly focused campaigns, and each ad is exhaustively focus-grouped. Axelrod cut ads for Grisolano's initiatives, and at the end of 2006, he called Grisolano to tell him he might need to return the favor. "I think my guy is gonna run for president, and I want to have our research and media be as tight and methodical as we were in these initiative campaigns," Axelrod said. "I'd like you to come out to Chicago and kind of honcho that process."

Grisolano had read *The Audacity of Hope*, Obama's second book, and felt the candidate captured the mood of the country. The Clintons seemed like more of the same partisanship as the Bushes, while Obama represented a chance to do things differently. Grisolano was an early Obama fan. In the late 1990s his wife at the time was studying law in Chicago, when he was looking for a new book to read in their bedroom. She recommended something obscure written by her law professor: *Dreams from My Father*. "I read this thing and was just blown away," said Grisolano. "It was a really moving book. So I kind of followed Obama after that."

One of the myths of 2008 was the technological prowess of the Obama team. There was little doubt that Chicago was far better organized and technologically proficient than the McCain team. But that wasn't saying much. The experience of 2008 was not especially helpful in crafting the strategy in 2012. Facebook in 2008 was a fifth of the size and efficacy it would have four years later. Back in 2008, Twitter had barely begun to gain traction: the campaign posted a handful of tweets through the twenty-one-month election. Obama's team had modeled its main URL—my .barackobama.com—on MySpace: a white elephant in the world of social networks. The most viral online video of the 2008 cycle was produced by recording artist will.i.am independently of the Obama team. The primaries were so improvised and extended that there was little chance to build any coherent database nationwide. By the time the funds and national organization kicked in for the general election, there were only three months left to build an integrated technology. So it never really happened. Besides, Obama's digital team felt entirely underwhelmed by the voter files handed over by the Democratic National Committee when their candidate finally secured the nomination.

With two years to build world-class technology, the 2012 Obama campaign had a singular goal in mind: to build a gigantic file about every voter in every battleground state. They started with a basic voter file showing name, address, age, party affiliation (in many but not all states), and voter participation in previous elections. That information was layered with census data showing ethnicity, income, and education. Then the campaign bought commercial data on top of that with two thousand characteristics, including magazine subscriptions. Finally, and most important, they added in six years of data from the Obama campaign: whether you contributed, displayed a lawn sign, and how you responded to every phone call and door knock.

Each voter was assigned a probability score of their likelihood to be an Obama supporter. A zero score meant that you were going to vote for Romney. A 100 score meant you were for Obama. If they didn't have a good enough handle on you, they could make thousands of phone calls or knock on hundreds of doors to refine the modeling. The more data they collected, the more they refined the model, confirming predictions or updating analyses as they went along.

Their targets were the ones squarely in the middle: the mathematically defined swing voters. Most of Chicago's essential efforts were designed with them in mind: understanding who they were and trying to persuade them to move closer to the 100 score. Volunteers knocking on doors in Cleveland were trying to find people in the range of 45 to 55 scores. Direct mail went to the addresses of 45-to-55s in Virginia and Ohio. And the TV ads so carefully crafted and focus group tested needed to reach those same targets. If Chicago couldn't reach them on TV, they tried to find them online. Advertising was moving from what they called dumb TV (broadcast to millions of undifferentiated viewers) to a combination of smart TV and digital (targeted to specific voter types). If it succeeded, political advertising would never be the same again.

Voter scores existed in 2008, to be sure. But the scores were directional rather than precise. People with a score under 50 were generally not voting for Obama. But it proved very hard to tell a 45 apart from a 65. And that was precisely where the election was going to be contested in 2012. This time around, the modeling needed to be laser targeted.

Grisolano realized the power of this data and the salvation it offered. "When you are this deadly accurate, it's like you're a mattress salesman and everybody walking by on the sidewalk has a percentage on their forehead which is the likelihood that they're gonna buy a mattress today, right? That's how valuable this is," he said. "So I knew we had this asset. I knew we had this resource. Our preoccupation in this campaign was that we were going to get outspent by the other side. This was the first time this was going to play out against us. We were preoccupied with how were we going to deal with that problem. Nobody wants to be outspent, but if I have to live with it, I can tolerate being outspent among people who are 65, 70, 75 percent likely to vote for us. I can tolerate being outspent among those who are 35, 20, 15 percent likely to vote for us. But I don't want to be outspent by those 45-to-55s or those 40-to-60s. So I've got to figure out a method to make sure that I'm concentrating the resources on that group and allowing the disparities to occur with the other groups."

How could you concentrate on that target group in the soft middle? More data was the answer: nobody knew more about TV viewers than the cable companies. Grisolano knew about the data stored in set-top cable boxes, but he was no technical expert. When he sat down with the campaign's tech team to explain the challenge, he had no idea how complicated the task would be. It took several months to match the set-top data with the campaign's massive voter file, not least because of privacy restrictions. The set-top data did not give out simple names and addresses, but it did allow the campaign to match thirty variables to each customer. It would take several more months to map those profiles to the TV shows and to figure out the cost of advertising to reach a narrow subsection of all the data.

What emerged was utterly new. No ad team in American politics had ever seen a list of TV shows, by geographical market, with a ratio listing how many target voters would be watching, divided by the cost of reaching them. The message men were handed a cost-per-target ratio that allowed them to hunt for bargains. Grisolano passed the data on to the ad buy team run by Jim Margolis, and what they discovered were shows and media markets that had never been the focus of presidential advertising before.

In previous cycles, the campaign pollster would identify the undecided voters, or what the Obama team called the up-for-grabs voters. In a typical 800-person poll, that would normally be 20 percent of the sample, or 160 people. The only useful information for the ad buyer would be a demographic slice: say 40 percent of the targets were women under forty, so the ad team needed to find a show in the right market that oversampled women under forty. But that meant advertising to a lot of women under forty who were already committed to one candidate or another, and that meant wasted money. "The ratings themselves aren't granular enough to find our targets. The research that is traditionally employed is not granular enough to find our targets," said Grisolano. "So we ended up knowing exactly who our targets are and being able to go into the set-top box, which is far more granular, to find exactly what they were watching. When you do this, you are out of the business of saying, 'Lean a little bit toward women.' Because what you're saying is, 'I care about the women on the list, and I don't care about the women who are off the list.' This is a complete shift in the advertising paradigm. Traditional advertising is media-centric: here's the program, who is watching? This is voter-centric, or consumer-centric. I'm saying this is the entire list of people I care about, what are they watching?"

This kind of data crunching was simply not possible in 2008. The data was not available, and even the computing power required was hard to find outside of astrophysics labs on university campuses. Much of the set-top-box data came from Rentrak, a media measurement and research company, which gained critical mass among local stations across the country only in late 2011.

The value lay not in the data itself but in how actionable it was. Among news channels, Chicago identified a clear hierarchy. MSNBC represented the worst value for Obama, because its viewers were close to 100 scores. Fox News—at certain times on certain shows—represented some undecided in the middle-scoring range. CNN beat both rivals in reaching the soft underbelly of swing voters. However, news in general was a bad place to buy advertising. Regular news viewers were informed people, and the kinds of voters they were searching for were less so. "This was one of the biggest differences between our buys and Romney's buys," Grisolano explained. "If you were watching the evening news in Columbus, you might see five or six Romney ads to every one of ours. If you could hold on until prime time through all of that, it was a lot closer and we were about even. But if you moved over to the cable dial, it would be more like the five or six of ours to every one of theirs. This is a manifestation of us trying to find those inefficiencies."

Where were the uninformed, undecided voters watching television? Sports were big, because they reached large numbers of people who avoided news. In other cases, the audience organized itself by politics, even though the shows featured no politics. There were few evangelicals who were likely to watch *Family Guy*, for instance. Other shows defied reasoning. Reruns of black-and-white shows and sitcoms on TV Land showed up again and again as overindexing undecided voters. Obama's team bought ads to reach two thousand people on the Syfy network at 3:00 a.m. because they represented great value for low-information, undecided voters. In normal advertising, the overall audience set the price of the ads; for the Obama campaign, the value lay in the number of undecideds they could reach. Like stock market traders looking for a steal, the Obama team hunted down this kind of market inefficiencies to save millions of dollars.

They also identified the cheaper corners of more expensive channels. Most advertising on cable is sold by the national network, but some is sold locally. In certain local spot markets inside the biggest battlegrounds—like Columbus, Ohio—the rates spiked through the spring and summer. So the Obama team responded by doing something counterintuitive for a campaign that liked to target so intensively: they bought the national networks instead of the local spot markets. Their analysis showed that the sum of the local markets was around the same as the national buy. Overall, the Obama team outspent and outsmarted the Romney team, in terms of national dollars and the number of networks they tapped for their local spot markets.

The newfangled ad-buying strategy needed vastly more spending to support it. Where the Romney campaign had two or three buyers, the Obama team had a team of thirty buyers. As a presidential campaign, they had the legal right to buy at the lowest unit rate for TV ads, unlike the outside groups. And they had the desire and expertise to buy at lower rates than Romney's campaign itself. Even before they went head-to-head with the content of the ads or the kind of targeting they employed, the Obama team was stretching its dollars further than their rivals. That would even be true on the same shows on the same night. If the lowest rate was not available on *60 Minutes*, for instance, the Obama team would not simply jump to the stated rate. They would go back and forth three or four times to get the best price possible. "You will find in exactly the same show, they're spending three times as much money as we are for the exact same spot," said admaker Jim Margolis. "We were almost always spending less." On the Sunday before the election, Romney's team spent $1,100 for an ad during *Face the Nation* on CBS in a single station in Raleigh, North Carolina; Obama's team spent just $200 for the same ad space on the same show at the same time.

That search for more efficient media outlets translated into fewer traditional news interviews for the candidate, too. Obama's communications team preferred local and regional media to national media, because it was far more efficient in reaching undecided voters in battleground states. They also preferred interviews with entertainment shows for their reach among infrequent and uninformed voters.

The consensus among reporters covering the campaign and the White House was that the Obama team simply preferred to dodge difficult questions by picking late-night and daytime chat shows. But that was not the experience of Obama's aides, who felt that the predictable news interview questions about the state of the race were easier to handle than the offbeat questions posed by talk show hosts. That proved especially true as the campaign drew to a close in October 2012. "The truth is that we were struck by the fact that he did interviews with the three network anchors in a three- or four-week period," said Dan Pfeiffer. "He did interviews with [Scott] Pelley, [Diane] Sawyer, [Brian] Williams, [Jay] Leno, and [Jon] Stewart. And Leno and Stewart were by far the most substantive interviews the president did."

Obama felt dismayed that the news anchors had blown their chance to go big. This was a big election about big issues, at a time of war and recovery from a deep financial crisis. But all the anchors wanted to talk about was the horse race, the polls, and the gaffes. Brian Williams started his interview by citing a story from the inside-the-Beltway newspaper *Politico*. "In the Stewart interview they talked about all kinds of tough topics, from housing, to climate change, to gay marriage, to drones," said Pfeiffer. "There is all this talk about how the president never answered questions about drones. The only media figure who asked the president about drones, in all the interviews he did, was Jon Stewart. Prior to that it had been a random person in a Google hangout after the State of the Union, and no one else had. The Leno interview is actually worth watching for how substantive it is. I mean, he did housing, Wall Street reform, Afghanistan, Syria. It was really an amazing piece, and it was all entertaining as it happened."

For all their technological prowess and vision, the teams involved in the giant digital project that was the Obama campaign were often doubtful and distrustful of one another, and frequently descended into downright hostility. They were forced by circumstance, and a shared belief in the candidate, to work together as part of a monumental start-up business that needed to scale rapidly into one of the biggest digital enterprises in the nation. Beyond that, they could barely stand one another.

While they set out to solve the problems of the 2008 technology, they invariably created new, very different problems in 2012. "There were a lot of mistakes in '08. But we definitely figured out how to make different ones this time," said Joe Rospars, the campaign's chief digital strategist. "There weren't many that were the same, actually. Some of them were made in pursuit of solutions, perhaps a misfired solution at challenges from '08. It was very different this time. But it was in many ways only marginally better from the field-organizer experience or the end-user experience as a volunteer. A lot of things were awesome. But a lot of things were a year late and barely scratched the surface of what we should have done."

Their technological challenges were compounded by their ego clashes. If the Obama campaign was truly the disciplined operation its staffers imagined it to be, the new media world of Rospars and the old media world of Grisolano would have been closely coordinated. Instead, they were separate and distinct, and intentionally so. Grisolano, coordinating all research and advertising, wanted to bring the massive output of online videos into his world, even farming out web video to the TV consultants. He wanted there to be message discipline and development, and that meant control under his direction. "Larry really talked himself red about that," said one senior Obama campaign staffer. "He didn't want any internal video team. Anything."

That conversation was shut down by Messina, who handed oversight of the new media team to Cutter. "There was a huge fight about that," said Messina. "In many ways, they never really resolved the fight between the new media team and our TV con-sultants. That was something I had to personally enforce. But we had to allow them to go innovate and not be controlled by the old media deal. Stephanie played a huge role because she ended up becoming the editor and she would approve their stuff. So it was very edgy, but it had to be done." Grisolano managed to carve out digital advertising as part of his turf, and that budget doubled from 5 to 10 percent of the overall ad spending between 2008 and 2012. His focus was especially on people who weren't watching television but were still undecided voters in the middle range of the voter scoring.

But the best online ads were the digital videos themselves—and they were managed separately under Rospars. To the dis-may of the old media team, the online videos seemed to speak mostly to the base—firing up core supporters with sharp-toned speeches by people like Cutter herself—rather than the swing vot-ers the campaign needed to attract. But Messina was insistent that the two media teams should stay separate. "In the end, there is a transition going on," he said. "The new media has taken over, and that leads to hard feelings. And in the end, everyone wants to control it."

However, the digital disputes were not confined to the media teams. Rospars and his team also clashed with the developers who formed a supposedly all-star tech team inside the Pruden-tial building. Much of that dispute hinged on the vastly different worldview held by the people Messina had hired. Rospars and his team had grown up on the Howard Dean campaign in 2004: a group of politically edgy operatives who pioneered online fund-raising to lift an obscure and volatile Vermont governor to the cusp of winning the Democratic nomination. Jeremy Bird, the national field director, was another highly driven, highly effective organizer of the thousands of foot soldiers who would be knocking on doors and turning out voters. Rospars and Bird had played the same roles in 2008 and understood how to reach their enormously ambitious goals.

But the tech team of developers consisted explicitly, purposefully, of political novices. They were supporting some of the most experienced people in contemporary campaigns: digital media under Rospars, the field operations under Bird, and the analytics operation under Dan Wagner. But the campaign's goal was to build a tech team that had nothing to do with their experience or worldview. Messina found a mentor in Eric Schmidt, the executive chairman of Google, who volunteered extensively, and largely out of public view, as the de facto technology leader of the Obama campaign. A former software engineer with a personal fortune of more than $8 billion, Schmidt's advice was to seek new talent. "We knew we had to blow it up, especially on the tech side, because so much had changed," said Messina. "Eric Schmidt said to me: 'You don't want to hire anyone for the senior tech team who has ever worked in politics before.' We had eight people on our analytics team in '08. We had fifty-something in 2012. So we just needed to completely explode that. Part of what I was worried about the entire time was we would be too wed to our own history. This is true in any organization, especially when '08 was so special and it was the greatest campaign of all time. We would have lost if we hadn't reinvented the wheel."

Messina set about hiring his new tech team with an emotional pitch about Obama's last campaign. "His life is already going to be the subject of a Hollywood movie," Messina would say. "You get to decide how the movie ends." He prided himself on the fact that nobody—including the most highly desired developers in Silicon Valley—turned him down. His chief technology officer,

Harper Reed, was a political novice from Chicago: his most recent job was the same position for the crowd-sourced online T-shirt retailer Threadless.

No matter the talent involved, the two sides of the online team—the tech developers and the politically minded campaign team—were so culturally divided that the arguments were deep and they dragged on for months on end. "The conflict was basically a cultural clash between people who were there from the private sector versus the politics," said Reed. "We were brought in from a different culture and were celebrated as being from a different culture. There was never an opportunity for us to fit in. We were outsiders until the very, very end."

Reed was grilled early on about how many other campaigns he had worked on. The answer was, of course, none. "I honestly don't give a fuck about campaigns," Reed said later. "I really like Barack Obama and I really liked the team. But it's so full of drama. I don't know if it was because it was a reelection campaign, but it was kind of silly. We were there for the exact same thing. You don't have a lot of type-B people in a campaign. It's like going to those bars in New York with all those traders together with the white collars. If you take out the douchebaggery, they are still hyperaggressive. Those are campaign people."

Schmidt told Messina that the disputes seemed normal: the developers acted as service providers and everyone else as the customers, and the customers were always going to be disappointed with this kind of start-up work. And he advised Reed to be less optimistic about delivering tech projects on time: a more pessimistic attitude would be more realistic for his customers inside the campaign. Still, the disputes looked like the result of a digital enterprise that was spinning out of control for as long as a year. Either the campaign's digital projects were too complicated and unrealistic, or their tech projects were poorly executed and misdirected.

A classic example was fund-raising. In the spring of 2011, at the very start of the campaign in Chicago, the digital team under Rospars requested a new system for donating money quickly. They all knew that fund-raising would be a huge challenge in this cycle and feared they would be heavily outspent by the GOP and its allies. Their solution would be to use cell phones to pay by text message or SMS, and to create one-click donation by e-mail and web by saving payment information, just like Amazon. Easier payment tools would directly lead to more cash, as long as the developers built what the Red Cross and other nonprofits had already achieved. Donating money by cell phone would be a first for a political campaign, but in terms of the technology it was not groundbreaking.

As the fund-raising quarters passed by, the digital team grew increasingly angry. No new donor tools were emerging, several months into the campaign, despite the high-profile challenge for the entire fund-raising team. Instead of developing simple one-click payment tools, the tech team engaged in what looked like vanity projects. One example was a debate game that emerged in October 2011. Instead of just watching the GOP debates, you could give your credit card details and pay a set amount each time one of the candidates mentioned a buzzword like *Romneycare* or *social-ism*. The debate game—a webpage called gopdebatewatch.com—earned more words on blog posts than dollars for the campaign. Quick Donate did not emerge until March of the election year itself.

The challenge for the grassroots team was even more acute. The goal was to deliver a digital dashboard for the field operation in the fall of 2011, a full year before the election. Their original version in 2008, called Houdini, had failed spectacularly on the morning of election day. This time around, the tech team was going to build a stable system, using a large in-house team of developers. The results, in the early fall of 2011, were ugly and unusable, and they seemed to miss the point of what the field operation needed to do. By the early spring of 2012, the dashboard project was so late and so unworkable that there were open calls for the tech team's management to be fired and replaced with outside vendors. What became known as Narwhal—a unified, real-time data-gathering operation—ended up as separate tech projects that included the field team's dashboard and the phone banks' call tool. They would all pull data from Narwhal and feed it back into the system.

"By the end, what was built and what stood up at the end worked, and was pretty okay by the very, very end," said one senior Obama staffer. "The problem is that rather than becoming legit in September of 2012, it was supposed to become legit in September of 2011. And then we were supposed to spend another year doing awesome stuff. If Narwhal was failing on election day, that would have been a really big fucking problem. But it didn't. The ambition was bigger than the capabilities of the team."

Reed concedes that the experience was unpleasant but insists that the only test was that the technology worked. "Was it frustrating at times? Incredibly," he said. "Were there times when it almost didn't work? Yes. If we could do it again, we would do it swifter but that's hindsight and it's 20/20." From the beginning, his team believed their primary goal was to avoid the fate of Houdini: a complete outage on election day. "We couldn't have anything go down," he said.

If the Romney campaign—or the GOP through the Republican National Committee—had been competent or planned ahead, they might easily have caught up with one of the Obama campaign's biggest advantages. Instead, they built an app designed to help the grassroots team identify who had voted on election day from their own database of targets. The app was called Orca, the only known predator of Narwhal, and it was no equivalent of the Obama team's architecture: it represented merely one campaign tool, where Narwhal constituted an entire system that could lead to the creation of a dozen tools. It also failed dismally on election day, as the Obama tool had done four years earlier.

In reality, the cool tools were nowhere near as effective as the factory of electronic content produced by the Obama digital team. While the communications team fretted over a handful of press releases each week, the digital team blasted dozens of versions of similar e-mails to test which ones were the most effective. While the old media team focus-grouped each ad, the digital team produced scores of online videos each week, adapting them to the data gleaned from supporters' behavior. Direct mail was nothing new in election politics: in fact, it was how Karl Rove built his reputation and fortune on the Republican side. But the cascade of consumer-tested e-mails, social media posts, and videos managed by Joe Rospars and his partner, Teddy Goff, was one of the biggest advantages of the entire Obama operation. The team helped lift the donor base from 4 to 4.5 million between 2008 and 2012, at a time when Democrats were supposed to be depressed and many donors had dropped out completely after supporting Obama the first time around. Between mass e-mail and ads on Facebook and Google, the digital team recruited potential new donors and then converted them into giving money by persistent e-mail.

Eric Schmidt liked to joke that the campaign was successful because of spam. But the e-mail campaign was a highly structured story moving from a welcome phase to urgent calls, as well as more personal messages from Michelle and Barack Obama. Messina gave the digital team ninety days to return any investment they made in acquiring new donors, leaving little time for Rospars and Goff to recoup the cash and go beyond the ad spend. At times of big campaign news, especially good news, the donor numbers would rise in line with the cycle. In times of crisis, the video team was a rapid response unit of its own. The rest of the time, the digital team constituted its own news operation: telling the stories of an election that Obama's supporters would read about only through campaign e-mail and watch only through campaign video. "We're telling a different story of fund-raising than what Nick Confessore is writing in the *New York Times*," said Rospars. "We're talking about the role of money in politics. We're talking about the role of you the individual donor in this campaign."

With almost two hundred people, including thirty working on video alone at headquarters, the digital team was the size of a major media organization in its own right. In 2008, there were just fifteen people working on digital video by the end of the general election. Four years later, the team—which drew on talent from scripted TV, reality TV, ad agencies, and the news media— would cut a dozen versions of each video before settling on a final edit. Then they would slice a one-minute video down to a fifteen-second version for a preroll ad to run in front of other web videos.

The numbers tell a story that will reshape the message of future presidential campaigns for years to come. The two most popular videos on Obama's YouTube channel were seen more than 3.5 million times each. There were dozens of videos that reached between 500,000 and 2 million people each: the kind of numbers that a prime-time cable TV show would be proud of. There was no such thing as too much video or e-mail. In fact, the data suggested that people did not mind a torrent of e-mail and gave no less money if there were more e-mails clogging their inboxes.

The most successful e-mail from the Obama campaign raised $2.6 million on its own and went through eighteen drafts. Its subject line was perhaps the single most successful message of the 2012 campaign. It had nothing to do with Obama's record as president and its focus group testing was a matter of watching its performance against seventeen other versions of the same e-mail. That message sounded like a cross between a challenge and plain old scaremongering, and it captured the essential dynamic of Obama's reelection. The stakes were high, the threat of defeat was real, so the need for action and participation was now: "I will be outspent."

SEVEN

SUMMER HAZE

A s his campaign was spending heavily to destroy Mitt Romney's jobs record in mid-June, President Obama traveled to the Franklin Institute in Philadelphia with two purposes in mind: one high and admirable, the other less so.

The president first walked into a small auditorium to address some 130 graduating students from the Science Leadership Academy, a partnership between the institute and the city's school district. The students cheered as he walked in, and he congratulated them on their graduation. His words were a mixture of inspirational encouragement and older-generation befuddlement.

"As I look around this auditorium, we are tapping into the talents of everybody—women as well as men; folks from every ethnic group, every background—that's also this incredible strength for the United States, because innovation, brainpower does not discriminate by gender or race or faith or background. Everybody has got the capacity to create and improve our lives in so many ways. So you guys are representative of the future. This is a great postcard for what America is all about," he said. "The pace of change these days is so rapid. I'm reminded when I talk to Malia and Sasha that when Sasha was born, most people weren't on the Internet and now she knows more about it than I do. And so, in many ways, your youth and the fact that you've come of age in this new information age gives you an enormous advantage over old fogies like us."

Before he headlined two fund-raisers at the institute, the old fogey spent some time looking at one of its exhibits on the Dead Sea Scrolls. Then, two hours after embracing the future of science and innovation, he entered the Planetarium to speak to a small group of high-paying donors about his view of the presidential contest. Obama started by pointing out that this cycle was even more polarized than the heated exchanges of the 2008 election. Then, he could agree with John McCain on immigration reform, climate change, or campaign finance reform. (The irony seemed to be lost on Obama that he was saying this at his second fund-raiser of the evening.) But with Mitt Romney, there could be no common ground: he was aligned with the radical House Republicans. Government could not solve every problem, but it still needed to invest in the future and the middle class. "The good news is I think the American people agree with us," he said. "They're not following...the ups and downs, the ins and outs of this campaign. But they do have a sense of what's true, and they have pretty good instincts about what works. And they're not persuaded that an economy built on the notion that everybody here is on their own is somehow going to result in a stronger, more prosperous America. So our job is just to make sure that we get that message out, that the facts are presented fairly, that we push back against misinformation. But if we can just have a straight, honest, clear debate about the choices presented, then not only are we going to win this election, but, more importantly, we're going to keep this country moving forward."

His job, and the job of his sprawling campaign machine, was indeed to get the message out: to clarify the choice in the election, to push back against attacks. Inside the White House, for the last three and a half years, he and his inner circle had singularly failed to do just that. They had failed to communicate clearly about the economic stimulus and health-care reform, allowing the biggest legislative achievements to be skewed into caricatures of wasteful government spending and pseudosocialism. Obama himself, as well as his wife, had grown personally, deeply frustrated with the failures of his communications team for the two years leading to the shellacking of the midterm elections, when the House Republicans surged into power.

Now the presidential campaign—the one monumental exercise in messaging that he and his team could control and command better than any other group in politics—would set the record straight and reshape the trajectory of his presidency and the country. His own job now relied on his ability to get the message out.

To propagate the message and clarify the choices before the voter, it was time to move into the second phase of destroying Mitt Romney's credibility. Phase One was to undermine Romney's record on jobs in Massachusetts. Phase Two was to undermine his record on jobs at Bain. Phase Three was to drive home the Bain story by tying it to policies of outsourcing and tax avoidance.

The plan centered on using the work of the research team, led by Liz Jarvis-Shean, as the trigger for several investigative newspaper stories, which would in turn clear the way for TV and digital ads to move public opinion. Ben LaBolt, the campaign's national press secretary, worked for months to convince high-profile news media to run with stories that examined Romney's time at Bain.

In Chicago, they viewed the news media through the lens of how receptive or hostile they were to their spoon-feeding. The *New York Times* was generally hostile but would follow the lead of others. "They would follow up on the follow-up, when it came from a candidate's mouth," said LaBolt. But the *Times* was not nearly as central to their strategy in 2012 as it had been in 2008. "Four years ago we thought that if you got a story on the front page of the *Times*, that was enough to make the evening news," said LaBolt. "That wasn't true this time around. It was much harder for correspondents to get political news at all on TV."

Of all the TV broadcast news divisions, CBS was considered the most hostile and conservative. Chicago distrusted the new CBS morning show, anchored by Charlie Rose, and they believed the network's correspondent Jan Crawford, covering Romney, leaned against them. They complained to David Rhodes, the president of CBS News, to no avail. It was no small irony that Rhodes's brother Ben was a long-serving, die-hard Obama aide who led the communications effort on national security inside the West Wing.

Four years earlier, Obama's senior aides loathed the emergence of *Politico*, treating it as a necessary evil in their lives. They saw it as an overhyped, small-bore operation that would skew the coverage of other media. Its outsized influence among other journalists forced them to engage with journalists and stories they would otherwise disdain. In 2012, *Politico* was displaced by what Chicago saw as an even more overhyped and small-bore online news outlet: *BuzzFeed*. "It annoyed the shit out of us when they wrote about us," said one senior Obama aide. Still, *BuzzFeed*'s large-scale traffic—thanks to its concentration on celebrity news and viral photos—made it a useful channel for reaching a nonpolitical audience about Romney's excesses. As much as they loathed *BuzzFeed*, Obama's message team was delighted that the site featured multiple stories about Romney's $50,000 car elevator.

However, the best example of Chicago's press message work—and the best-timed example, too—was one that landed on the front page of the *Washington Post* just two weeks after Obama visited Philadelphia. Its headline read: "Romney's Bain Capital Invested in Companies That Moved Jobs Overseas." The story was based on what it called "a *Washington Post* examination of securities filings" to tell the story of Bain's track record of relocating American jobs to low-wage countries like China and India. The *Post* tersely pointed out that Romney had recently pledged to protect American jobs by getting tough on China.

The Obama campaign rejoiced; all the more so because the Romney team reacted furiously to its publication. "The outsourcing story in the *Post* was something we had been working for months and months and months to get placed," said LaBolt. "The timing of when it ran was actually really convenient for us, but it was a long ramp-up to get that in the paper." The *Post* had been working on its own leads for several weeks and took the time to complete its own research to confirm what the campaign had unearthed. The week after publication, President Obama repeatedly referred to the story, as well as the explanation first offered up by Romney's aides. After several weeks of not responding to the assault on their candidate's Massachusetts record, the Boston team immediately set about challenging the outsourcing story. Romney's spokeswoman Andrea Saul argued that the *Post*'s account was "fundamentally flawed" because it "does not differentiate between domestic outsourcing versus offshoring, nor versus work done overseas to support US exports."

The response in Chicago was one of disbelief. "Are you fucking kidding me?" said one senior Obama campaign official. "It was so unbelievably irresponsible to think that he was running for president, after having already run for president and having been beaten in the Senate campaign on Bain, and they weren't prepared for this."

The Obama team continued to drive the message across as many news outlets as they could find. On the day the *Post* story was published, President Obama traveled to Florida, where he cited the article at a campaign rally. "Let me tell you, Tampa, we do not need an outsourcing pioneer in the Oval Office," he said. "We need a president who will fight for American jobs and fight for American manufacturing. That's what my plan will do." Obama's aides rolled out past comments and articles by economic advisers to Romney—Greg Mankiw and Glenn Hubbard—who both praised outsourcing as good for the American economy. Stephanie Cutter fronted a new online video from campaign headquarters, highlighting the *Post* story and explaining how Romney's policies would encourage outsourcing. Meanwhile, David Axelrod called Romney "the outsourcer in chief" and the *Huffington Post* obligingly wrote up his comments, recycling the line. The campaign then blasted an e-mail to reporters quoting Axelrod in the *Huffington Post* speaking about a story the same campaign had placed in the *Washington Post*.

Obama's aides like to complain about the introverted and insular nature of the news media in Washington, but it was happy to circumscribe that news media with its own talking points. Outsourcing certainly represented one of the painful long-term trends against American workers, especially in the manufacturing sector. But it was not the root cause of an unemployment rate that remained stubbornly fixed at 8.2 percent at this point, almost unchanged from the first full month of Obama's presidency. It was far easier to discuss the broad sweep of Republican economic policies than to dissect the enduring results of a deep recession caused by a financial collapse.

The Romney camp's legalistic quibbling over outsourcing and offshoring only seemed to energize the president and the vice president on the campaign trail. Four days after the *Post* story appeared, both Obama and Biden continued to attack the nuanced Romney response to the story. At a lunchtime event at the Westin Peachtree Plaza Hotel in Atlanta, Obama seemed like he was enjoying himself with the story his campaign aides had worked so hard to place, as well as its aftermath. "There was an article the other day in the *Washington Post* about how Mr. Romney's former firm—this is what gave him all this amazing success—was a 'pioneer' in offshoring jobs to China and India," he began. "And when they were asked about it, some of his advisers explained, no, there's a difference between offshoring and outsourcing." At this point, the audience began to laugh. "I'm not kidding," he continued. "That's what they said. Those workers who lost their jobs, they didn't understand the difference."

Speaking in a much more important battleground—in Waterloo, Iowa—Biden added some punch to the offensive. "You've got to give Mitt Romney credit: he's a job creator," Biden said, before pausing to deliver his punch line. "In Singapore. And China. And India."

The following day, the Romney team demanded a retraction from the *Post*. Clutching a ten-slide PowerPoint, Romney's aides—including his communications director Gail Gitcho—met with eight editors, including the story's reporter, Tom Hamburger. They argued that the story was inaccurate because the six companies it featured did not send jobs overseas during

Romney's time at the helm of Bain Capital; indeed, they argued that the companies created jobs in the United States during that time. The *Post* refused to retract the story. In Chicago, they could barely believe their good fortune. After watching Boston ignore months of attempts to draw them into a debate, the outsourcing story had finally triumphed. The flap at the *Post* was a clear sign, they believed, that the Romney team could see the damage they were inflicting on the GOP candidate's standing.

Still, Chicago felt perplexed. Why wasn't the Romney campaign mounting a more full-throated defense of the Bain record? Was there some secret plan that Boston was holding close to its chest, ready to deploy at a moment's notice? It was incredibly hard to game out where the Romney campaign would go next, when their responses seemed so inadequate. Surely there was some other strategy at work? "When you are on a campaign, you don't put out your play unless you are trying to predict what their play is going to be after yours," said one senior Obama campaign aide. "So you know where you're going to go next. So you're not making your plays for the short term. You're making them for the long term. If you move here, I'm going to move here. And then I know you're going to move here, so I'm going to come around here. On the Bain stuff, every time we did something, we thought we could predict what they were going to do. But they never played it. Andrea Saul would put out the same statement every single day, thinking they could just make it go away, and we just kept going. They never answered us on Bain."

Republicans struggled to agree on their presidential nominee, trying almost every other candidate before settling on Mitt Romney. They struggled to agree on the nature of the new tax structure they wanted, embracing ideas from sweeping tax cuts to a radically flat tax for all incomes. But on one thing they all agreed: Obama's health-care reform law was not just wrong, it was plainly unconstitutional. They felt confident that the conservative-leaning Supreme Court would surely concur. But just a week after the outsourcing story, the Court ruled the other way. Obamacare was not just constitutional, it now had the one thing that Republicans denied it through its painful passage through Congress: a conservative stamp of approval from the Bush-appointed chief justice John Roberts.

The next two weeks, in late June and early July, represented the last clean shot from the Obama campaign at a slow and underperforming Romney operation—at least in terms of advertising dollars. Chicago would outspend Boston by $25 million to $20 million, as Obama's message team began a full assault on Romney as the archetypal international multimillionaire. One story in *Vanity Fair* connected Romney's personal wealth to the outsourcing-offshoring story, and—even more potently—to the limited release of his tax returns through the primaries. The story detailed mysterious Bermuda corporations, Swiss bank accounts, and continued payments from Bain well after Romney left the company in 1999 to work on the Salt Lake City Olympics. The same day the *Vanity Fair* story surfaced, Chicago released a new ad called *Believes*, which began by citing the *Washington Post* story about Romney's pioneering work as an outsourcer. In contrast, the ad noted, Obama worked as a creator of American jobs, who just happened to save the US auto industry.

There are many differences between a president running for reelection and a challenger hoping to unseat him. Apart from flying in Air Force One and having a deep reservoir of political fund-raisers, presidents can actually *do* things while challengers can only talk about doing things. While Romney talked about getting tough on China, Obama's officials actually filed an unfair trade case against China at the World Trade Organization. The cause: new Chinese duties against American-made cars, including the Jeep Wrangler made in the battleground state of Ohio. The torrent of bad news for Romney managed to overwhelm a June jobs report of weak growth—just eighty thousand jobs added—and an unemployment rate painfully stuck at 8.2 percent.

The Republican response underscored how damaging the attacks had grown. The Republican National Committee launched a website and campaign suggesting the outsourcing argument was all wrong. Romney was nothing like the outsourcer that Obama was. The site's verbose name said it all: obamanomicsoutsourced.com. It suggested that billions in economic stimulus had gone overseas. The campaign was, like its website address, unwieldy and unconvincing—not least because it implicitly recognized how damaging the outsourcing accusation was.

By the week's end, Romney was forced to drop his avoidance of TV interviews to agree to no less than five on-camera interrogations to explain his connection to Bain after he was supposed to have left in 1999. The explanations only seemed to make matters worse. Romney sat down with Jan Crawford of CBS to try to square his public comments about leaving Bain in 1999 with official paperwork that described him as the sole owner of a Bain company three years later. "I was the owner of a, of the general partnership, but there were investors which included pension funds and various entities of all kinds that owned the, if you will, the investments of the firm," Romney began. "But I was the owner of an entity which was a management entity. That entity was one which I had ownership of until the time of the retirement program was put in place. But I had no responsibility whatsoever after February of '99 for the management or ownership—management, rather, of Bain Capital."

His supposed supporters were even less convincing or, for that matter, supportive. Conservatives urged him to release more tax returns to clear up the debate. Bill Kristol, editor of the *Weekly Standard*, told Fox News that it was "crazy" for Romney not to release multiple years of tax returns, rather than just the one he had already released for 2010. Ed Gillespie, a senior Romney strategist, made a complicated situation even more unfathomable by suggesting that the candidate had "retired retroactively to 1999" from Bain, but remained engaged with the company for another two or three years. Whatever Romney's message was about his connection to Bain and outsourcing, it was lost in the noise of conflicting explanations from his own team and concerted attacks from the other side.

After six weeks of sustained assault on Romney's record as a governor and a businessman, the battleground polls were almost unchanged. The four-point advantage Obama held during the positive period of advertising was now a one- or two-point advantage. But that was beginning to change. The continued focus on Romney's credibility about outsourcing and his tenure at Bain was starting to break through. All the Obama team needed were the ads to bring it all together.

The Romney campaign had started its ad run with a series of spots that tried to reassure skeptical voters about the challenger. The traditional path would have started with bio ads, reintroducing this presidential hopeful to the American people after the chaotic contests of the Republican primaries. Instead, Boston started with a series of ads that tried to clear the highest bar of all: imagining the outsider as presidential material. They asked the viewer to imagine, "What would a Romney presidency be like?" The answer, in the first round of ads, was to repeal health-care reform and balance the budget. The answer in the second round was again deficit reduction and a President Romney who "stands up to China on trade." The promise to challenge China came just a few days after the *Post* story on Romney's record of outsourcing jobs to countries like China.

When Romney's China ad surfaced, along with the outsourcing story in the *Post*, the message team was more than ready. Mark Putnam, the brains behind Obama's thirty-minute TV special in the 2008 election, cut an ad that served as a brutal response on China, but couched in terms of Romney's words and the *Washington Post's* reporting.

"The Chinese are smiling all the way to the bank," said Romney, "taking our jobs and taking a lot of our future. And I'm not willing to let that happen." Then the narrator kicked in, saying Romney "made a fortune letting it happen," citing the *Washington Post* story. "Mitt Romney's not the solution," the ad ended. "He's the problem." The Obama team loved using tape of Romney, not least because the focus groups talked about how his own manner and words led them to question his credibility. It was two for the price of one: they could hit him on China at the same time as hitting him on his authenticity.

Another member of the message team landed another aggressive blow. Mike Donilon, a Biden adviser and admaker, created the line that demolished the *Day One* ads, by once again citing the

Post story. "Romney's never stood up to China," the ad said. "All he's ever done is send them our jobs." Axelrod called the line "artfully brutal," crediting the series with turning the corner on the outsourcing message.

But the final blow was the most dramatic. Axelrod was looking for a moment that would recall one of his own ads from a previous cycle in another kind of contest. Alan Dixon was a moderate Democratic US senator for Illinois, but he had a probusiness record and was facing an intense primary challenge from Al Hofeld and Carol Moseley Braun. Axelrod was Hofeld's strategist, and he created an ad showing an American flag rotating to the sound of "The Star-Spangled Banner." As the music grew distorted, the narrator told the story of Dixon's link to companies that outsourced American jobs. "When our senators are for sale, America is, too," the narrator concluded, as the camera zoomed in on a label on the flag that said Made in Taiwan. Dixon was from downstate Illinois, but that was where many manufacturing jobs were disappearing. He was soon defeated in the primary by Moseley Braun, not Axelrod's candidate, in a shock result for moderate Democrats.

One early summer day, Axelrod was listening to Romney deliver his regular stump speech. One of the stranger parts of Romney's campaigning style was that he liked to sing a song that was popular not just at election events, but inside the Mormon church, too: "America the Beautiful." The Mormon church celebrated America as not just a patriotic ideal but as a source of its early messianic belief that Christ would return to the United States, and specifically to western Missouri. "When I heard Romney singing 'America the Beautiful' everywhere," said Axelrod, "I thought: I'd love to see a spot where he's singing and we're telling the story of all of his outsourcing, his offshoring."

Inside Obama's message team, one person was obsessing about the China challenge. John Del Cecato was a partner at Axelrod and Plouffe's old firm AKPD, and had worked under Plouffe on Democratic congressional campaigns in the 2000 election. He was later part of the consulting team that took Obama from a Democratic primary in Illinois to the US Senate and the presidency beyond. This time around, as part of the sprawling ad team for the reelection, he was deeply concerned that the China issue would be an obvious way for Romney to try to peel off working-class white voters in the Rust Belt battlegrounds like Ohio.

Del Cecato set about creating the ad with Romney singing and it swiftly took hold in the media as well as online, building on an earlier concept by Obama admakers David Dixon and Rich Davis. *Firms* was simply unlike anything else on the air. Like Reagan's *Bear* ad, the sight and sound of Romney singing left many focus group interviewees confused. There was no voiceover to the spot, just the sound of Romney warbling his way through the classic song. "I'm not sure that it was our strongest spot," said Axelrod. "I think some of the other voiceover spots were actually stronger. But it was our most creative spot."

As Romney began singing of the spacious skies, the ad showed empty factory floors and text that said simply: "In business, Mitt Romney's firms shipped jobs to Mexico." As he sang about the majesty of purple mountains, this text was added: "And China." In an empty office, to the sound of Romney singing about fruited plains, the text said: "As Governor, Romney outsourced jobs to India." And as he hit the soaring chorus, the ad demonstrated where he kept his money by showing a Swiss flag flapping in the wind, an idyllic beach scene to evoke Bermuda, and another to evoke the Cayman Islands. "Mitt Romney's not the solution," the ad concluded in bold white letters on a black background. "He's the problem."

Inside the White House, David Plouffe loved the sharp definition the ad brought to the characterization of Mitt Romney. "I loved the 'America the Beautiful' ad because I think it grabbed people," he said. "Mitt Romney may have had an easier time if this wasn't the first election after a recession caused by Wall Street's misbehavior. He was not well-suited for the times."

But inside Obama's team there was real concern that the ad was too hard-hitting. Margolis, as the head of the ad team, believed the concerns were misplaced. "This ad did real business for us because it cut through," he said. "It also did a lot of work for us with the base—which was important at that point." So they tested the ad in focus groups, and they retested it to see what independent voters thought. President Obama himself feared the ad was going too far, so the team tested it once again. The results from each focus group were unequivocal: Romney was singing about his love for this country while taking steps to undermine it. The ad stood up to the testing, and it stood out among the dozens of commercials filling TV screens every night in the battleground states. "Part of what you're trying to do is create advertising that people pay attention to," said Margolis, "and this spot, people paid attention to. If you're in the other room and you hear Mitt Romney singing on the TV, you're gonna come take a look. If it's another announcer-driven ad, maybe not so much."

Getting people to pay attention represented nine-tenths of the battle. It was the reason why Obama chose to spend his money early: TV ads later in the campaign would be drowned out by the noise of a thousand attacks and counterattacks in the final weeks of an intense election. It was the reason why thousands of volunteers knocked on doors in battleground states: to bypass the media that undecided voters chose to ignore. And it was the reason why Obama's communications team decided to press the case against Mitt Romney to its logical conclusion.

By mid-July, the Romney campaign could barely keep up with the documents and disclosures about Bain Capital. Was their candidate telling the truth when he said he had left the company in 1999? How could he square that with official paperwork filed with the Securities and Exchange Commission that listed him, after that date, as the CEO and owner of various Bain entities? If he was responsible for job gains after he left the company, was he also responsible for job losses after he supposedly left the company?

Each round of revelations and interrogations took the campaign further away from a debate about the state of the economy and closer to an internal examination of the shady ownership structures of private equity vehicles. At a time of economic struggle, even the benign explanation of Romney's record seemed out of touch: this kind of shenanigans was the way business took place in a world where handsome fortunes could be conjured out of financial reengineering.

But the Obama campaign was not interested in sounding benign. To underscore their case—and to extend the pile-on by the news media—the communications team staged a conference call with reporters. The lead on the call was Bob Bauer, Obama's former White House counsel and trusted friend, and now his top campaign lawyer. Bauer was an election law expert who maintained a low profile and an understated tone. His answers to any question—about Guantanamo Bay detainees or campaign finance abuses—were almost always precise and fully conceived. Hosting the call was Stephanie Cutter, who preferred to maintain a higher profile and an overstated tone, if only to prompt a reaction from her audience.

Bauer told reporters that the situation was "serious," as it was reported by the *Boston Globe*: Romney's timeline of departure from Bain did not mesh with his public statements. Cutter took the argument to its logical conclusion. "Either Mitt Romney, through his own words and his own signature, was misrepresenting his position at Bain to the SEC, which is a felony," she began. "Or he was misrepresenting his position at Bain to the American people to avoid responsibility for some of the consequences of his investments." Among those consequences were the layoffs and outsourcing that his campaign denied with righteous indignation. (The *Globe* story was simply inaccurate, the Romney campaign insisted.)

Cutter's accusation of a felony prompted something that was all too rare from Boston: a same-day response by a senior campaign official. Campaign manager Matt Rhoades issued a statement that seized on Cutter's comments to argue that Obama's team was not conducting itself in a presidential manner. "President Obama's campaign hit a new low today when one of its senior advisers made a reckless and unsubstantiated charge to reporters about Mitt Romney that was so over the top that it calls into question the integrity of their entire campaign," he said. "President Obama ought to apologize for the out-of-control behavior of his staff, which demeans the office he holds. Campaigns are supposed to be hard fought, but statements like those made by Stephanie Cutter belittle the process and the candidate on whose behalf she works."

Rhoades was working the refs: the media liked to rule whether certain plays were in or out of bounds. He was also trying to undermine the reformist brand that Barack Obama had fashioned from his first campaign. In 2008, Obama had prided himself on his refusal of dollars from lobbyists and political action committees. At one point he had scolded his own staff for suggesting that Hillary Clinton was so close to Indian-American donors that she was a senator representing the Indian state of Punjab. He claimed that politics did not have to be a case of tearing down the other side. And he promised to unite red and blue America through compromise and common sense.

If the focus groups blamed Obama for anything—beyond his inability to fix the economy—it was his failure to unite the country and shift the political dynamic of partisan trench warfare. Now his own campaign was escalating the political attacks by accusing his political opponent of not just bending the truth, but breaking the law. The Romney campaign had turned an attack on Romney's character into a challenge to Obama's reputation.

Stephanie Cutter took pride in the exchange. She believed she had shifted the dynamic single-handedly. Yes, she took some heat from conservatives and pundits. But who cared? Nobody on her side had the guts to tell her—to her face—that she had stepped out of line. She stormed off the call predicting that the Romney campaign would respond, and they did. It was their move now, and she ordered all Obama surrogates off the air. When Boston put Mitt Romney on TV to talk about Cutter's felony accusation, the deputy campaign manager felt vindicated. She was a soldier on her tour of duty and she had just completed her mission: to sustain a story that most reporters found complicated to cover. The structure of private equity deals and the nature of SEC filings were all hard to follow. But an angry exchange about credibility and values between a presidential candidate and a deputy campaign manager? Now that was easy to enjoy. Cutter's work was done.

However, the White House felt less than proud of her work.

There was such a thing as an Obama brand, and Cutter was threatening to weaken it. Two of the president's closest aides believed the felony charge was a huge mistake and were deeply troubled by it. Valerie Jarrett, who served as the keeper of the Obama spirit of 2008, believed it undermined the president's position. She had heavyweight support from chief of staff Jack Lew, who believed the felony accusation was unbecoming, unpresidential, and strategically unwise.

Cutter won rare support from David Plouffe and Dan Pfeiffer, who argued that the public nature of her job would sometimes lead to such trip-ups. Axelrod himself had tripped up at several points in 2008, including one memorable exchange with reporters when he suggested that Hillary Clinton had some connection to the assassination of the former Pakistani prime minister Benazir Bhutto. Cutter had a high batting average, they claimed. Besides, what was the point of fretting now? The damage was done.

The debate about Cutter's performance did not happen in isolation. It was the latest twist in a long tale of internal doubts and disputes about her role and abilities, and whether she was helping or harming the president's reelection effort. At the heart of the message machine, Cutter stood out as one of the most visible elements. She was also one of the most controversial players on the team.

There were, in effect, two message machines at work at any given time on the Obama campaign. One was located in Chicago, at campaign headquarters, where Cutter controlled the press shop and was its highest-profile surrogate on TV. The other was located inside the White House, where the president's aides were theoretically keeping their distance from the messy work of campaigning to focus on the people's business of governing.

The campaign's real decision-making power about the message resided with David Plouffe inside the White House. His director of communications was Dan Pfeiffer, and between the two, there was no real room for the kind of job nominally held by Stephanie Cutter. Inside the West Wing, Obama's aides admired Cutter's smarts, productivity, and fearlessness. They liked her focus on the regional media that the pundits ignored or disdained. They even feared her anger and her relationship with the First Lady—not least because Cutter reminded anyone and everyone of how Mrs. Obama had often called for her help. Few people wanted to cross Cutter; nobody wanted to cross the First Lady. Still, Obama's closest aides believed that Cutter micromanaged too much, had delusions of power, and strayed out of her lane. That indiscipline was one of the root causes of the disastrous event on the steps of the Massachusetts legislature, as well as the felony accusations over Bain. With time, the whole Chicago team might settle into more comfortable, disciplined roles. But did they really have the time or luxury to wait?

The dysfunctional dynamic in Chicago was itself a worrying sign that the spirit of the first Obama campaign had disappeared. "I do think that there was some concern on behalf of some people that this sort of collegial, no-drama atmosphere that was so necessary to our success in 2008 did not exist," said one senior Obama aide. "It seemed more like Hillary '08 than Obama '08, and that was troubling. At first there wasn't enough happening out of Chicago in a message and communications way until the Republican primaries were over. So you didn't know how it affected execution. It just made conference calls awkward. The fund-raising stuff was going well. The field and technologies stuff was going well, so it didn't seem to impact. It wasn't until later when we began to see what consequences it had."

So they hatched a plan to push Cutter out of the picture. To those involved in the plot to sideline her, the plan would lead to her losing control of the press shop to focus exclusively on TV and video work as a spokesperson.

The president's dismay at the Axelfraud event in Boston triggered a series of interventions. The West Wing team decided they needed to exert more control and discipline. Plouffe had been one of the biggest advocates of moving the reelection headquarters to Chicago, unlike previous presidential reelection efforts that stayed in the Washington area. Now Obama asked Plouffe to spend time each week in Chicago, and he became far more deeply involved in the day-to-day decisions of the campaign. Messina once again took the role of Plouffe's chief operating officer, executing the West Wing strategy rather than acting as campaign manager in any traditional sense. Messina was himself exasperated by Cutter— by her hostility and independence—and he conspired with Plouffe to work around her.

Cutter's abrasive manner continued to weaken her position. She clashed with Axelrod over minor matters like meeting invitations where she felt she was getting frozen out. And she clashed with Messina over their respective management styles. As the campaign manager, Messina took it upon himself to be direct with Cutter about her manner and tried to correct her behavior. "No one enjoyed that process," said one senior campaign official. Cutter was not shy about responding to his suggestions in similarly frank ways. She had no respect for Messina, for what she saw as his spinelessness and indecision. She had been on the losing side of an election in 2004, and the losing side of the internal debate inside the campaign. She was determined not to lose either contest this time around.

So Messina tried to organize support for a bigger intervention. He gathered a small group together at a White Sox baseball game, where Grisolano, Axelrod, and Plouffe spent half the game talking about the Cutter question. Pfeiffer needed to take over the communications staff after the convention in September. Cutter's role would be confined to TV. The only remaining challenge was this: who would tell Cutter of her effective demotion? Messina offered, but that was rejected as an impractical move that would rupture Chicago. Plouffe wanted to keep his distance. There had already been several stories about how few women there were in Obama's inner circle, and nobody wanted to be involved in a story that could leak about the demotion of the only high-profile woman inside campaign headquarters.

When they consulted the president, he made it clear that he wanted Cutter to stay in some role. "Do what you want," he said, "but she better not quit."

Cutter's guarantor was, in fact, the most high-profile woman of all in Obama's inner circle: Michelle Obama. "Given Michelle Obama, she's not going anywhere," said one of the plotters. "The First Family feels very strongly that Stephanie is an asset. When things have gotten bad, especially for Michelle, people go to who they trust. When anything goes bad in the East Wing world, she looks at all of her staff and says, 'Go get me Cutter.'"

Soon Plouffe would be traveling with the president and could not maintain regular travel to Chicago. "There was only one Plouffe, and the president wanted Plouffe on the road with him," said one senior West Wing official. Besides, Plouffe preferred to be seen as a kind of godfather to the Chicago operation. There were too many disputes to referee, and he cared little for morale problems: he just wanted to focus on winning. Axelrod, his former partner, was clashing with Messina, his protégé. Messina was clashing with Cutter, who had never gotten along with his other protégé, Pfeiffer. He needed them all to work together seamlessly for the president's reelection, and he didn't want to take sides explicitly, or even call the balls and strikes. So he and Messina asked the White House communications director, Dan Pfeiffer, to start traveling to Chicago two days a week to exert some control—or, as they called it more diplomatically, improve coordination. Pfeiffer could manage the long-term planning, while Cutter could deliver the message on TV.

Pfeiffer and Plouffe were similar characters—low-key strategic thinkers with a worldview similar to that of the president they had served for six years. Inside the West Wing, staffers saw them as interchangeable: one from Delaware, the other from Rhode Island, both with too many *P*s and *F*s in their names. Under the guise of coordinating the president's scheduling, they sought to wrest control of a campaign that seemed to be heading off the rails. Alyssa Mastromonaco, the president's first scheduler and now deputy White House chief of staff, would control his movements, not Chicago. "For the first year of the campaign the president just did fund-raisers for them," said one senior Obama aide. "They did nothing else. Then all of a sudden now the bulk of his travel and activity is being run out of Chicago, and they weren't prepared for that. It was a bigger burden. Other than Axelrod, the folks out there were not as steeped in the Obama ethos: how he wants things done, how we do things, how we did things in '08."

Cutter herself was exasperated with Messina. She felt that he lacked strategic direction. She questioned his effectiveness, and she believed she needed to work around him to plan and execute the message in a deeply challenging election. She dismissed

Pfeiffer's arrival as a minor irritant that changed nothing about her job.

To the Obama campaign staffers around the senior leadership, the many disputes between Cutter and Messina were mystifying. It was painfully obvious that the two disagreed frequently and bitterly. But the origins of the dispute were unclear. And the topics of any given argument seemed small. They could clash over the timeline for a rollout of a new phase of the communications plan. They could clash over the wording of a press release. They could argue whether he had the right to communicate directly with her own staff, without going through her. Sometimes the arguments were bad enough that Cutter would leave the office to go home. Few of the clashes seemed to deal with the strategy of the campaign. Their open disputes were the opposite of the faux friendship between Messina and Axelrod, who papered over their rift with excessive and effusive praise of one another in meetings and on calls. In reality, Axelrod felt that Messina lacked the ability to see the big picture and had too small a worldview for such a big job. For his part, Messina seemed insecure with his own lack of stature: he would never be the equal of Plouffe and Axelrod, and he overcompensated by locking horns frequently with Cutter and jealously guarding his conversations with Plouffe.

At the heart of the personal disputes, there were the missing figures of David Plouffe and Barack Obama. Messina claimed to speak for Plouffe, and Plouffe claimed to speak for Obama. But in their absence, nobody could be sure that Messina was telling the truth. It was unclear to the staff if Axelrod spoke to Plouffe very often, and if Cutter spoke to Plouffe at all. None of them much enjoyed talking to one another in Chicago, either. The chief strategist and candidate were absent, and so was the sense of direction and cooperation. "Remember, in '08, we have the president 24/7.

We have each other 24/7 and there is no other," said another senior Obama aide. "This time, people in the White House feel removed from what's taking place in the campaign. People outside feel like we can't get through to the White House. Everything's still too much 1600 Pennsylvania Avenue. They're driving the bus to the point where they're 80 percent of the game. But they're also out of the spotlight."

The irony was painfully clear inside the Prudential building: the senior communications team could not communicate with each other. One of their greatest successes was to hide their own dysfunction from public view through most of the election cycle. "There was a general weirdness," said one senior Obama aide. "None of them would talk directly to each other, and they used other people as vessels to try to get information about what was actually going on. It became so hard to decipher. Everybody else gets thrown in the middle to try to communicate something to the other person and that's where all of this gets muddled. Stephanie didn't think Messina was actually running the campaign, so that is where psychologically she was willing to walk all over him. All of this is very passive-aggressive. This all exists, but it exists through indirect communications. It almost never exists face-to-face. And that's the weird part about it."

After all the plotting and machinations, Pfeiffer's arrival changed little. Cutter had wanted to be communications director inside the White House, and she wasn't about to concede that ground in Chicago. She continued to exert control over the strategic direction of Chicago's communications. In spite of their earlier dispute over a TV show appearance, she found an ally in her old mentor, David Axelrod, who decided to oppose the efforts to oust her. Cutter was not just useful as a surrogate for the campaign;

she was as exasperated with Messina as Axelrod was. Besides, the plotters and decision makers did not have the courage of their convictions. "A decision had been made to change Stephanie's job and bring Pfeiffer in," said one senior campaign staffer. "But everybody was too scared to tell her. And then Axe saved her. So Dan comes in to take control, which still annoyed the shit out of her, but it became sort of a nothing. It's not like they're talking that much. Of all the people who spent years complaining behind closed doors, no one will actually ever deliver the news to the person they're complaining about. That will just never happen. They'll completely avoid it. They made a decision and just didn't have the balls to carry it out."

The plan to reshape the message team did not stop in Chicago. The president needed a campaign spokesperson on Air Force One and on the road, as he barnstormed the battleground states. White House press secretary Jay Carney needed to remain focused on the serious policy pronouncements of the presidency. Moreover, Plouffe wanted to maintain the fiction that the two sides of Obamaland—the presidency and the campaign—were separate and distinct, rather than following the same strategic direction: his own. The role of traveling press secretary needed to be filled, and Plouffe had no intention of allowing Cutter to control that person. So he sought out and hired Jen Psaki, who had only recently departed her position as deputy communications director to Dan Pfeiffer. Psaki, a veteran of the campaign plane in 2008, would express the message spelled out by Plouffe, and only Plouffe. "He's the guy who pulls all the strings," said one senior Obama official. "He had his own vision of how everything would work on every aspect of the campaign, and specifically the message piece, which flows into everything." Psaki was rarely in Chicago. When she wasn't on the plane, she worked out of the Democratic National Committee offices in Washington.

There was no real precedent for two spokespeople traveling on Air Force One, and there was no clear plan on how they should deal with reporters. So on the first day, Carney and Psaki approached the small pool of reporters to ask their advice: would it be better to brief the media together, or one after the other? They decided to try to brief together, switching from serious foreign policy questions in the Middle East to less-than-serious questions about Rafalca, the Olympic dressage horse co-owned by the Romneys. On one Air Force One flight in mid-July to Jacksonville, Florida, Carney was pressed on the failing peace plan advanced by the former UN secretary general Kofi Annan. Less than a minute later, Psaki was interrogated about a DNC video lampooning Rafalca. The White House press pool reporter wanted to know if the White House had intervened—not in Syria, but on the DNC video. "There wasn't involvement from the Obama campaign or anyone, of course, in the White House along those lines," said Psaki. "We are rooting for the Romney horse in London."

By midsummer, the balance of power had moved firmly away from Chicago back to the West Wing. A White House that centralized power—controlling most policy decisions itself, rather than trusting cabinet secretaries and agencies—had lost confidence in its own campaign headquarters. "Essentially decisions about what the president did and when he did it—how all of his personal time was used and the messaging he did—along with all events and travel, basically shifted," said one senior Obama adviser. "A decision made in Chicago became a decision that was made in Washington with Plouffe. That was a frustration to the campaign, that it happened that way, but it was what the president wanted in terms of his comfort level that his time was being used wisely and strategically. He felt like he had so little time for the campaign, relative to '08, that you couldn't waste a trip."

Their saving grace was how their rival wasted his trips. While Chicago kept its dysfunction out of view, Boston could not stop its unforced errors from spilling into the news media. Much of that contrast boiled down to a dramatic difference between the discipline and self-awareness of the candidates themselves.

In 2008 then-Senator Barack Obama took a huge gamble: he flew his campaign plane overseas, to message to voters that he could handle foreign policy and pass a key presidential test. His advisers believed there would be significant crowds wanting to see him in Europe, and his popularity would represent a vivid contrast with President Bush's low standing across the world. Obama made a foreign trip look relatively easy, even without the support of a White House travel operation or diplomatic resources on the ground. He made no gaffes and attracted a vast crowd of more than two hundred thousand in Berlin.

But such foreign trips were not, in fact, easy. Presidential candidates do not have a ready command of foreign policy, and there are few votes to capture from ex-pats living overseas. Overall, sensible candidates tend to avoid a high-profile trip overseas at a time when they need to concentrate on reaching voters at home.

Romney made a different calculation. He flew first to London, where the city was making its final preparations for the 2012 Olympics. There he questioned whether the city was ready to host the games and voiced concerns about security. Those comments prompted a sharp response from the conservative prime minister David Cameron, who noted that it was much harder to host the Olympics in one of the world's busiest cities rather than "in the middle of nowhere." Everyone assumed this was a reference to Romney's beloved Olympics in Salt Lake City. Romney later breached protocol by revealing that he had met the head of Britain's spy agency, MI6. For all that, the conservative British tabloid the *Sun*, owned by Rupert Murdoch, dubbed him "Mitt the Twit."

From the UK, Romney traveled to Israel, where he managed to offend Palestinians by suggesting that the reason for their economic hardship was cultural, rather than years of occupation and violence. Comparing the GDP of Israelis and Palestinians, Romney said the "dramatically stark difference" was similar to the gap between Americans and Mexicans. "Culture makes all the difference," he said in Jerusalem. Palestinian officials condemned the remarks as racist. "It seems to me this man lacks information, knowledge, vision, and understanding of this region and its people," said Saeb Erekat, a senior aide to the Palestinian president Mahmoud Abbas. Romney was fortunate that Mexican officials did not react in a similar fashion.

The press covering Romney's trip grew obsessed with the gaffes, not least because the candidate and his aides refused to answer their questions. As the trip ended in Poland, Romney visited the Tomb of the Unknown Soldier in Warsaw, where reporters shouted their questions at the candidate. Romney's traveling spokesman Rick Gorka told the journalists to show some respect for the place, but reporters complained about the lack of a chance to ask questions anywhere. "Kiss my ass," Gorka snapped back, before telling another reporter to "shove it." Diplomacy was not the most obvious quality of the Romney team overseas.

What the Obama message team lacked in coherence and cooperation on their own, they gained in unity against a common enemy. Romney's disastrous performance brought the Obama campaign—in all its warring factions—together. His foreign trip tied the campaign to the White House, as policy issues merged with Chicago's goals. At headquarters, the press shop carefully tracked how local media in battleground states were reporting Romney's foreign blunders. Local TV in places like Toledo, Ohio, and Harrisburg, Pennsylvania, happily spread the news of the gaffes. The *Detroit Free Press* ("Britain Riled by Mitt Romney's Doubts Over Its Olympic Readiness"), the *Arizona Daily Star* ("Romney's Remarks on Olympics Have Brit Media in a Frenzy") and the *Richmond Times-Dispatch* ("Romney Rankles Brits at Start of European Tour") all focused on Romney's stumbles in London.

On board Air Force One, Obama's staffers could not believe what they were seeing. "There was a logistical pride we had because it's an incredibly difficult thing to pull off when you don't have the infrastructure of government. And we did that, four years ago. They did not," said Jen Psaki. "There were a lot of ways it could have gone. He could have survived it, and it would have been a nothing-burger. He could have, with the Netanyahu visit specifically, given their friendship, just looked like he was a greater choice. Especially because we were worried about the Jewish community and the message that would send. But it was an unmitigated disaster at every stop. We had already begun to see the impact of the attacks on Bain a little bit, in specific communities and anecdotally. This was an opportunity to cut the credibility on his preparedness to be commander in chief. It was not that the top people on the campaign believed the American people were suddenly voting on foreign policy issues, but it was a character and leadership issue, and that's how we talked about it. And it just made him look disconnected."

Plouffe treated the campaign and its messaging as if he was running a dozen governor's races across the country. The national and international stories that crossed his radar were only relevant in terms of how they were viewed through the prism of the state-by-state media, the state-by-state grassroots operation, and the state-by-state polling. The daily exchanges between reporters in Washington and campaign officials tended to focus on strategic and tactical questions about polling, ads, and next steps. Plouffe was far more interested in how voters in the battleground states were forming their opinions about the candidates' character and values. To the national press, this seemed like an effort to bypass their tough questions: a diversion of attention to the smaller, easier game of state politics. To Plouffe, the drill-down was an ambitious and sweeping concept. "I think that in those states he was not giving a small message," he said. "The truth is, one of the things we tried to do throughout the campaign is raise the stakes: that this is a big choice and it's going to have a big impact. When I say governors' races, it wasn't like we had different messages for different states; just that's the way we viewed it. Yes, we engaged in a little bit of the national media ping-pong. But we were swimming in the data from the states."

There were now just one hundred days to the election, and Obama was consistently tracking at 50 percent in the battleground state polls at the heart of his campaign's focus. Romney was trailing by 4 points, at 46 percent. The two-month-long attack on Romney's image and record—combined with his own fumbles and flaws—had left Obama with a solid foundation for the end of the summer and the home stretch of a long election. Even as Obama's team spirit was disintegrating, Romney's incompetent messages served to divert attention away from Chicago's structural problems. As a result, Obama's own poll standings were rising at a time when the unemployment rate remained unchanged. Romney had just two shots left to change his message and his numbers: his convention and the debates. Both were prime-time TV events that might just rewrite his own message to the biggest possible audience across the country. To do that, he needed to reinvent himself as something other than Mitt the rich, heartless, clueless Twit.

EIGHT

THE CHOICE

For the first few intensive weeks on the campaign trail, in May and June, President Obama found the election a liberating experience. His mood was unusually light and breezy on Air Force One, and his longtime aides thought he was barely taking the election seriously. He moved from occasional travel to the intensive schedule of daily trips, with outside events and what they called "real people introducers." Unlike in 2008, there were lots of day trips that returned to the White House for the night. Four years ago, the cheap charter plane had seemed like a flying frat house, with the same people on the road together for weeks on end. Now, the plane was Air Force One, and Obama came into contact with only a few staffers. Back then, they could barely believe their good fortune that they survived the primaries. This time around, they could barely believe they felt the nagging sensation that failure was a very real possibility.

"At the beginning of the summer, the president was just getting into the groove of the campaign," said Jen Psaki. "It was also a fun period because he was back on the trail for the first time in a long time and enjoying the whole thing. It wasn't that there were intense tracking polls every day or that he was locked in a room preparing for debates. In some ways it was a break from the everyday being in the White House, because he was out there a lot, but it wasn't very intense campaigning."

The president's mood was helped by the transformation in his wife's attitude. Back in 2008, Michelle Obama was still ambivalent about her husband's grand political ambitions. Unlike his previous elections, she threw herself into campaigning for him. But she was deeply frustrated by the blown chances to end the primaries, and she suffered personally from the public criticism of her stray comments about being proud of her country for the first time.

Four years later, the competitive juices of Michelle Obama kicked in. "She really wanted to win," said her friend Valerie Jarrett, a senior adviser to the president. "I'm not saying she didn't want to win last time, but she *really* wanted to win this time. I think everyone felt that the contrast between the president and Governor Romney and the direction Governor Romney would take our country was really terrifying, and I know certainly the First Lady felt that way, too. The stakes felt higher, and four years in, she's really comfortable on the campaign trail. She is immensely popular, and she wanted to do everything possible to help her husband. She didn't want to leave anything on the field. She campaigned with a lot of confidence, and it was very, very helpful."

The First Lady was much more confident and comfortable on the campaign trail than she was in 2008, when she was shocked by the conservative caricature of her as angry or unpatriotic. Her poll numbers were solid and high, which helped build her self-confidence. "I think she was inoculated from what they did to her last time because of her popularity," said Jarrett. "So it made it easier this time to go out there knowing that she was campaigning from a position of strength, and if they did come after her like they did last time, it would be at their peril. She was very at ease, very comfortable, but most intense about doing everything within her power to get her husband reelected. It was fun."

Like her husband, Michelle Obama found it liberating to be out of the gilded cage of the White House, talking to real people with real concerns about their lives, not the members of Congress whose concerns seemed far less straightforward. For both Barack and Michelle Obama, life on the campaign felt invigorating and authentic, compared to three and a half years inside the perimeter fence of 1600 Pennsylvania Avenue. It reminded them of their pre–White House life, while still enjoying all of the comforts of White House travel, including clear roads for motorcades and Air Force executive jets. At their destinations were hundreds or thousands of supporters who cheered them on, rather than dozens of unhappy pundits and politicians who critiqued their every move.

If they turned on a television in any of the battleground states they were visiting, the Obamas would have seen heavy repetition of their own campaign ads. Between July and August, they spent more than $100 million on TV commercials alone. To put that into context: in the final two months of the 2004 election, President Bush spent around $75 million. As astonishing as these two months of spending were, Obama was still getting outspent by Romney and his outside groups. Over the same period, the Republicans poured more than $175 million into defeating the president with TV ads. For most of August, the Obama campaign was getting outspent by a margin of two to one.

Sitting on a three- or four-point lead in the battleground states, Obama's message team shifted into a new phase. They had already spent almost $100 million on ads that mostly tried to destroy Romney's economic record in Massachusetts and his business record at Bain. Now they wanted to frame the policy choices that Romney and Obama represented, ahead of the party conventions in late August and early September.

Obama's ad team knew that at least half of August would be hard to break through with any kind of message. The London Olympics would dominate the news and TV viewing in general, no matter what Romney suspected about the city's preparations for the games. They needed to anticipate the post-Olympics conversation in late July, which would lead in to Romney's biggest opportunities to shift the election's dynamic: his choice of vice president and his own party's convention. Chicago wanted something big, so they deployed their leading player in his most effective position.

The Choice was the first campaign ad of the cycle to feature Barack Obama addressing voters face-to-face by talking directly to the camera. "Over the next four months, *you* have a choice to make," Obama began, pointing directly at the camera, as a background track of gentle piano began. "Not just between two political parties, or even two people. It's a choice between two very different plans for our country. Governor Romney's plan would cut taxes for the folks at the very top. Roll back regulations on big banks. And he says that if we do, our economy will grow and everyone will benefit." At this point, the camera cut to a close shot of Obama's face, and the piano music grew more insistent. "But you know what? We tried that top-down approach. It's what caused the mess in the first place. I believe the only way to create an economy built to last is to strengthen the middle class," he continued, as the image switched to Obama talking to voters at a kitchen table with his sleeves rolled up. The pictures changed again: he was working at a desk as he talked about paying down the federal debt, then in a classroom as he talked about investments in education, and even hugging an autoworker as he talked about manufacturing. He only returned to his original frame, talking directly to the camera, for the final line of the long, sixty-second ad.

"Sometimes politics can seem very small," he said without apparent irony, after months of his campaign indulging in dozens of small attacks. "But the choice you face, it couldn't be bigger."

A week later, they followed up with *Stretch*, which turned the choice into something much more personal for working families. In its style and form, the ad was a traditional thirty-second attack on Romney's tax policies and his low personal tax rate. But in its framing, the ad was designed to make the voters' choice as skewed as Romney's tax plan: why would you want to vote for a tax plan that favored people like Romney over yourself? "You work hard. Stretch every penny," the voiceover began, as a generic mom compared two cans of tuna in a supermarket. "But chances are, you pay a higher tax rate than *him*." At this point, they didn't even need to name *him* when his photo first appeared on screen. Over a portrait of him in what looked like an expensive boardroom, the voiceover continued: "Mitt Romney made $20 million in 2010 but paid only 14 percent in taxes. Probably less than you." After a five-second summary of his tax plan—less taxes for millionaires like him, more taxes for working people like you—the ad ended with this kicker: "Mitt Romney's middle class tax increase: he pays less, you pay more."

Romney's own choice was the boldest of his campaign. After tacking to the right in his primaries, he could easily have moved to the center for the general election, starting with his pick for the vice-presidential slot on his ticket. He could have selected another governor or entrepreneur to double down on his proposition that Obama's Washington needed an overhaul by someone with real-world experience as a job-creating executive. In 2008, Obama chose a relatively safe deputy in Joe Biden—with decades of experience in government to reassure voters that he, as a younger, freshman senator would not be clueless in the White House. But Romney did not play it safe, shift to the center, or reinforce his core message of change. Instead, he took a risk with a younger congressman, who was a committed conservative with no claim to being a Washington outsider. Paul Ryan was a darling of the conservative press for his radical efforts to reform the federal finances as chairman of the House Budget Committee. His proposals hinged on turning Medicare into a voucher program, a subsidy for private insurance premiums, leaving seniors a significant shortfall. Because his budget also cut taxes down to two low brackets, it would not in fact come into balance until close to 2040.

Ryan's selection was a gift to Chicago. It opened up an age-old line of attack that Democrats had exploited all the way back to Johnson's demolition of Goldwater on Social Security in 1964. Like Ryan, Goldwater insisted he wanted to privatize a popular social welfare program solely to keep it solvent. The LBJ campaign demonstrated how voters preferred to keep Social Security unchanged, and there were no signs that Medicare in 2012 was any different. In fact, polls showed that almost two-thirds of voters—and even a plurality of Republicans—believed that Medicare was worth the costs to the federal taxpayer. This reality led the GOP to some difficult and contradictory messaging. In the 2010 midterms, they argued that they were opposed to Obamacare precisely because it promised to cut Medicare costs by several hundred million dollars. Yet they also argued that Obama did not go far enough in cutting the deficit by reining in Medicare costs.

So Romney found himself in a quandary with his bold new veep pick. Less than a week after his announcement, Romney tried to push back against the Obama message in one outdoor press conference in Greer, South Carolina. In true Bain Capital fashion, he took a black marker pen to a whiteboard to argue his case in simplistic ways. One column was titled Obama; the other Romney. One row addressed seniors; the other, what he called "next gen." He filled out several items under Obama's approach to current seniors: a supposed $716 billion cut, 4 million people losing coverage, a 15 percent cut in nursing homes and hospitals accepting Medicare. Under his own name, he wrote "no change" and underscored the words. For the next generation, he simply wrote "bankrupt" under Obama and "solvent" under his own name. He underscored both words with a small line, as if his case were proven. "So the differences in our Medicare perspective could not be more stark and dramatic," he said, snapping the top of the marker back on. "As the seniors in America understand what the president's plan is doing to Medicare, they're going to find it unacceptable, and we're going to get a lot of support from people who understand that Medicare should be protected for current seniors and the next generation."

The whiteboard stood on a shaky easel in front of two flags, making it a strange cross between a boardroom and a politician's rostrum. And although he wanted to change the debate about Medicare, Romney could not avoid questions about his own taxes. Two weeks earlier, the Senate's Democratic leader, Harry Reid, said that he had heard, from a Bain investor, that Romney had paid no taxes for the last ten years. It was a scurrilous charge, without any proof. But it drew Romney into yet another question about his taxes, in front of his whiteboard.

"Given the challenges America faces—23 million people out of work, Iran about to become nuclear, one in six Americans in poverty—the fascination with taxes I paid I find to be very small-minded compared to the broad issues that we face," he said. "But I did go back and look at my taxes, and over the past ten years I never paid less than 13 percent." Romney had just buried his Medicare message under another round of news coverage about his personal taxes.

The next day, Romney woke up to a new Obama ad called *Facts*. A whiteboard would not be enough to rewrite a generation-long debate about the solvency of Medicare and Social Security. The ad, narrated by a woman's voiceover, leaned heavily on an AARP analysis of Obama's Medicare plan ("strengthens guaranteed benefits") and Romney's plan ("higher costs for seniors"). Only they didn't call it Romney's plan; they called it Ryan's plan, while showing a photo of both men waving shoulder-to-shoulder on stage. Ryan's plan could cost future retirees another $6,400 a year, the ad warned, over a photo of a woman who was plainly a current retiree. "Get the facts," the ad ended.

Romney was losing the message war on Medicare and taxes, and his efforts to reclaim any advantage—at a time when he was outspending his rival—were failing to gain traction. Instead, the news media took its cue from an unscripted outburst by an obscure Republican Senate candidate in Missouri. In an interview with local TV in St. Louis, Todd Akin answered a question about abortion for rape victims by claiming that rape does not result in pregnancy. "It seems to be, first of all, from what I understand from doctors, that's really rare," he began. "If it's a legitimate rape, the female body has ways to try to shut the whole thing down."

The comments were not just uninformed and outlandish; they tied directly back into the Republican overreaction to the new contraception coverage under Obamacare. It allowed the Obama campaign to revisit February's issue of women's reproductive rights, an issue that threatened to extend a gender gap among voters that could be fatal to Romney's chances.

Within twenty-four hours of the video appearing online, the Romney campaign called the comments "inexcusable." President Obama took the condemnation one step further by saying "rape is rape" and arguing that the comments only demonstrated why politicians should not make health-care decisions for women. Barely thirty-six hours after Akin's interview, Romney issued another condemnation, this time in stronger terms, calling the comments "deeply offensive." There was only one week to go before the biggest Republican messaging opportunity: their party convention in Tampa, Florida. It looked like Romney could not catch a break: there was no clear period for him to set the terms of the debate.

The Obama campaign bookended this preconvention period with another ad, delivered direct to camera, by another president: Bill Clinton. While Hillary Clinton had long since expressed her loyalty and support for Obama, President Clinton remained an independent figure. Behind the scenes he had offered advice to Obama's aides in his Harlem office, but in public he seemed closer to President Bush—at least at their joint speaking gigs—than the current Democratic president. Obama's message team knew that he could reach Democrats and independents in ways that their own candidate could not. He could attest to the political and economic realities that Obama had faced, and he could do so with style and charisma.

So Jim Margolis arranged to shoot several spots with President Clinton at the Jefferson Hotel in downtown Washington, DC, in the early summer. Clinton was uncharacteristically on time and well-prepared: he had read the scripts already and started scribbling on them to make changes just before they taped. He wanted to make sure the ads drove home the importance of cutting spending, and he nailed the ads in rapid order. Then they shifted to an interview style, which was less formal than a scripted message. Clinton started riffing about how his time in office was tough, but Obama's was much tougher. He enjoyed comparing Obama's agenda to his own, portraying Romney as the latest incarnation of his own opponents—and by extension, Obama as the latest version of his own presidency. The Clinton ads tested supremely well with the campaign's focus groups. His credibility was exceptional, which was no small feat for someone once impeached for perjuring himself. Clinton could convincingly deliver the message that Obama was on the right track because it was the Clinton track that was so successful in the 1990s.

The first Clinton ad to air was called *Clear Choice*, and it used many of the same images of the Obama ad *The Choice*. There was Obama talking to voters at the same kitchen table, and looking over the same solar panels. "This election to me is about which candidate is more likely to return us to full employment. This is a clear choice," Clinton began. "The Republican plan is to cut more taxes on upper-income people and go back to deregulation. That's what got us in trouble in the first place. President Obama has a plan to rebuild America from the ground up, investing in innovation, education, and job training. It only works if there is a strong middle class. That's what happened when I was president. We need to keep going with his plan." The ad was both a personal endorsement of Obama's approach and an effective attack on Romney's approach. Obama's choice of his chief surrogate was not his own vice president, but a former president and personal rival.

After more than a quarter of a billion dollars' worth of ads on both sides through August, the battleground polls were unchanged. On the eve of the Republican convention, with a new vice-presidential pick in place, Romney was still languishing four points behind Obama at 46 percent. He had made no dent in either the nature of the choice in front of voters, or the president's steady 50 percent level of support. To Obama's aides, this was the result of the president's innate popularity: after four years of watching him closely, voters believed he was likable enough. There was little room for Romney to message the president into being someone else. On the other hand, Obama's aides believed they could and would tell Romney's story in powerfully negative ways. The warring message teams successfully created a cold war of campaign advertising: a costly standoff that made no real advances and achieved a billion-dollar status quo.

The Republican convention in Tampa, Florida, did not start well. Tropical Storm Isaac, on a direct path to hit Tampa, forced the organizers to cancel the entire first day of business. It was an uncanny repetition of the severe weather that forced John McCain to postpone the start of his convention four years earlier, in Minneapolis. This time around, Day One was supposed to be themed "We Can Do Better," when they staged the roll call for Romney to secure his own party's nomination.

The second night fared much better, as Ann Romney, the candidate's wife, delivered a passionate speech testifying to her marriage and her husband's qualities. She made a direct appeal to the women voters who were recoiling from her party's positions on reproductive rights. "We're the mothers, we're the wives, we're the grandmothers, we're the big sisters, we're the little sisters, and we are the daughters," she said. "You know it's true, don't you? I love you women!"

If Ann Romney was trying to deliver an Oprah Winfrey–style message of women's empowerment, Paul Ryan's speech the following night was more like Sarah Palin's: Obama was little more than a socialist whose rhetoric was as empty as his record. "College graduates should not have to live out their twenties in their childhood bedrooms, staring up at fading Obama posters and wondering when they can move out and get going with life," Ryan said. "None of us—none of us have to settle for the best this administration offers: a dull, adventureless journey from one entitlement to the next, a government-planned life, a country where everything is free but us."

With just one more big night ahead, the messaging of the Republican convention had failed in at least two important tasks. There was no effective rebuttal to Obama's attacks on Bain and Massachusetts, and there was no compelling tale about Romney's character. Those challenges fell to the final night, when Romney's acceptance speech would begin with a long bio movie, to be aired on national television. The movie was powerful and insightful, even to the hostile eyes of Obama's message team. It brought to life the stiff-shirted Romney by telling the touching story of his romance with Ann, his admiration for his father, his own parenting of his five boys, and his business leadership at the helm of the Staples office supply store. Sadly, very few people outside the convention hall got to see it. Instead of airing the movie in the appointed hour on national television, Romney and his strategist Stuart Stevens were convinced they had a better idea. The veteran actor Clint Eastwood would deliver the introduction of the candidate, with no rehearsal, no teleprompter, and a handful of talking points. Eastwood simply asked for a chair on stage. It wasn't clear, until he began to ad lib, that he wasn't interested in sitting on the chair. Instead the empty chair was meant to represent an imaginary President Obama, whom Eastwood admonished at various points in his rambling monologue. The spectacle on the convention stage looked like Dirty Harry had lost his mind.

Romney's speech picked up where the bio movie would have left off, if anyone had seen it. The new nominee spoke touchingly of his parents' romance and more prosaically of his commitment to hiring women in senior jobs when he was governor of Massachusetts. He spoke of missing his children now that they were grown up, and he made a rare reference to his Mormon church as a community that welcomed his family. He rejected Obama's criticism of Bain, saying there were always some failures in business alongside the successes. And he launched into an attack that Obama's own focus groups made clear was the most potent of all: disappointment in the president for failing to live up to a nation's high hopes. "America has been patient," Romney said. "Americans have supported this president in good faith, but today the time has come to turn the page. Today the time has come for us to put the disappointments of the last four years behind us, to put aside the divisiveness and the recriminations, to forget about what might have been, and to look ahead to what can be."

It was a fine speech, but there were two gaping holes. First, Romney failed to mention the troops fighting in Afghanistan. He said nothing about those on the battlefield, which was a sharp contrast to the last two Republican acceptance speeches—by Bush in 2004 and McCain in 2008. Second, he barely mentioned his time as governor of Massachusetts: the one job that he could credibly argue had prepared him for the presidency. Pollsters later revealed that the most memorable part of the night was Clint Eastwood's dialogue with an empty chair. The battleground polls inside the

Obama campaign showed precisely no movement in Romney's numbers through his own convention.

Where Tampa was lackluster and its message was confused, the Democratic convention in Charlotte, North Carolina, was an energized and determined affair. After introductions from elected officials heartily endorsing the president's record, the first night belonged to Michelle Obama. During the day, the First Lady had been rehearsing her speech in several run-throughs in her hotel room. She was a perfectionist; this was her biggest speaking event to date, and she was determined to nail it. Her rehearsal performances were emotional in and of themselves. Her brother, Craig Robinson, came in the room for one practice run and grew tearful, even though he missed much of the speech. "You couldn't help but to be moved that day," said Valerie Jarrett. "She was just extraordinary."

She went on stage and delivered the same emotional speech just as flawlessly. She told the story of how they tried to keep their daughters grounded inside the White House, of how she loved their old life in Chicago and didn't want her husband to change. She told how her family was just like Obama's: they worked hard and didn't have much money. Her father was a pump operator at the water plant, and he suffered from multiple sclerosis. Watching him struggle to and from work was her inspiration, and he was proud to pay a small amount toward the college tuition of his son and daughter. "You see, for my dad, that's what it meant to be a man," she said. This was no tale of privilege or political dynasty. Even as First Lady, Michelle Obama was saying that she could relate to the struggles of blue-collar, working families.

Above all, she framed the great political debate about government and fairness in terms of the values of working Americans. "We learned about dignity and decency," she explained, "that how hard you work matters more than how much you make; that helping others means more than just getting ahead yourself. We learned about honesty and integrity—that the truth matters, that you don't take shortcuts or play by your own set of rules, and success doesn't count unless you earn it fair and square." In spite of the trappings of power and privilege inside the White House, she insisted Obama remained connected to the voters trying to survive a tough economy. "In the end, for Barack, these issues aren't political," she said. "They're personal. Because Barack knows what it means when a family struggles."

Michelle Obama was only overshadowed by someone whose testimony counted even more among undecided voters. President Clinton was the highlight of the second night and he knew it. Back at the 1988 convention, Clinton's keynote speech was twice as long as scheduled and the networks cut away from him. Two decades later, he pulled off the same stunt, speaking for forty-nine minutes—twenty more than allotted—but none of the networks dared to drop him. He delayed the nomination vote to the point where broadcast TV viewers would never see the historic moment, ad-libbing more than two thousand words in a speech that was only supposed to amount to little more than three thousand.

Clinton's force came not from his personal affirmation of Obama's qualities: the two remained distant from one another. Instead, his power came from his head-on demolition of the most challenging Republican message of all: that Obama had his chance to fix the economy, and despite everyone's best hopes, he wasn't up to the job. "In Tampa, the Republican argument against the president's reelection was actually pretty simple, pretty snappy. It went something like this: We left him a total mess. He hasn't cleaned it up fast enough. So fire him and put us back in," Clinton began.

"Now, look. Here's the challenge he faces and the challenge all of you who support him face. I get it. I know it. I've been there. A lot of Americans are still angry and frustrated about this economy. If you look at the numbers, you know employment is growing, banks are beginning to lend again. And in a lot of places, housing prices are even beginning to pick up. But too many people do not feel it yet. I had the same thing happen in 1994 and early '95. We could see that the policies were working, that the economy was growing. But most people didn't feel it yet. Thankfully, by 1996 the economy was roaring, everybody felt it, and we were halfway through the longest peacetime expansion in the history of the United States.

"But wait, wait. The difference this time is purely in the circumstances. President Obama started with a much weaker economy than I did. Listen to me, now. No president—no president, not me, not any of my predecessors—no one could have fully repaired all the damage that he found in just four years. But he has laid the foundations for a new, modern, successful economy of shared prosperity. And if you will renew the president's contract, you will feel it. You will feel it. Folks, whether the American people believe what I just said or not may be the whole election. I just want you to know that I believe it. With all my heart, I believe it."

Whether voters believed Clinton's message was, in fact, the whole election. It had nothing to do with the assertions of a former president, but it was nonetheless at the heart of the reselling of President Obama. It looked like the reincarnation of hope: the belief that in spite of the hardship of the last four years, the economy would get better under Obama to the point where you could feel it.

Obama's message team recognized the power of Clinton's words. Many of his themes tracked the ads he had already cut for them: that he had seen the same debates before in the 1990s, and that Republicans were as wrong today as they were back then. But his most important assertion was something they knew Obama could not argue for himself: that nobody, no president, could have done any better with this economy. Not even the great Bill Clinton himself.

After the convention, pollsters found that voters rated Clinton's speech far more memorable than those of either Michelle or Barack Obama. The president's own acceptance speech, on the final night of the convention, fell into two halves. One was the political message of his campaign consultants, tailored precisely to cover a hole in their internal research; the other was the political message of a president who used to teach community organizing and constitutional law.

Obama's internal polling and focus groups showed that voters, especially undecided voters, wanted to hear specifics of his policy proposals. After more than a year of intensive advertising and arguments, they needed the details. So Obama's speech started off in workmanlike fashion, checking off his policies on the list of some master focus group.

No wonder Clinton's speech rated so much higher than Obama's. It wasn't until the final third of his acceptance that the forty-fourth president of the United States articulated his vision for his country, his philosophy of government that he distilled into a single word.

"Citizenship," he explained. "A word at the very heart of our founding, a word at the very essence of our democracy, the idea that this country only works when we accept certain obligations to one another and to future generations." This was his personal message to counter the widespread conservative idea that he was an alien, a socialist, an un-American aberration.

He summed up his approach to citizenship with a Kennedy-esque turn of phrase. Just as Ted Kennedy had passed the torch to Obama when he endorsed him in the middle of the primaries in early 2008, just as he had passed health-care reform inspired in part by Kennedy's example, now he was trying to revive the spirit of JFK on the new frontier. "As citizens, we understand that America is not about what can be done for us," he said. "It's about what can be done by us, together—through the hard and frustrating but necessary work of self-government. That's what we believe."

After all the millions of dollars of advertising, and all the wasted press releases, Obama was finally voicing the message he wanted to deliver. It was not a message about his opponent's character or record. It was not a message about his own record or slogan. It was an earnest discussion about the nature of government. He initially wrote a much longer section on citizenship, but his aides hacked it back and later used the leftovers in his speeches on election night and his second inauguration. "It's a very Obama thing that citizenship isn't just about rights, it's about responsibilities, and that cuts both ways," said Jon Favreau, Obama's chief speechwriter for two campaigns and the entire first term. "Republicans think it's individual rights and Democrats, since the '60s, have focused on equal rights and civil rights. Sometimes it's at the expense of community, obligations, and responsibilities."

Obama's political aides wanted him to drop it. Axelrod worried that the citizenship discussion was too esoteric, too disconnected from the lives of real people. Perhaps he could lose the word *government*, he suggested.

"If we don't use the word *government* to discuss this, then what are we talking about?" asked Obama. "If we can't talk about it in a serious way, then why are we Democrats?"

Despite his abstract discussion about government, Obama's convention speech rated higher than Romney's. Women voters gave the president's speech a 62 percent approval rating compared to 50 percent for Romney's. Independents preferred Obama's speech by similar margins (57 to 46 percent). The rhetorical success wasn't enough to end the contest, but the numbers strongly suggested that Romney had missed one of his final chances to break through the noise with a new message about his character and campaign. Obama's battleground state polling remained stubbornly unchanged: after all the speeches, all the confetti, and all the hours of live TV, the president still held a 4-point lead.

The numbers would change only with an unscripted clip of video far from the sound and lights of a convention center. Back in May, a bartender took his camera to a $50,000-a-head fund-raiser in Boca Raton, Florida, in the hope of snatching some photos with a presidential candidate. He set it on his bar to record the proceedings but was disgusted by what he was hearing from Mitt Romney behind closed doors. He then posted what he felt was the Republican candidate's most outrageous comments—about Chinese working conditions—on YouTube. Nobody paid much attention to the video until David Corn at *Mother Jones* magazine saw the whole video and posted its more newsy clips.

The video was not some revelation of Romney's secret policies. It was rather an insight into his frustration with his message: voters were not listening to him because they were bribed with government services. Republicans understood that success was to be applauded, he explained. The rest of the country would have to wait for the debates, because people weren't paying attention. Politics was a transaction, and 47 percent of the population was already bought off.

Romney recounted how delivering this message was part of his daily work on the campaign trail. "In every stump speech I give, I speak about the fact that people who dream and achieve enormous success do not make us poorer. They make us better off," he said. "And the Republican audience that I typically speak to applauds. I said that tonight, and the media's there, and they write about it. They say that Romney defends success in America and dreamers and so forth. So they write about it. But in terms of what gets through to the American consciousness,...I have very little influence on that in this stage, as to what they write about. And that will happen, and we'll have three debates. We'll have a chance to talk about that in the debates. There will be ads which attack me; I will fire back....I wind up talking about how the thing which I find most disappointing in this president is his attack of one American against another American, the division of America based on going after those who have been successful."

Romney continued to walk his audience through his message strategy. He did not agree with the thinking behind Obama's early ad spending. People weren't watching right now, and wouldn't through the summer. "After Labor Day, in September and October, that's when it'll get fun," he promised.

Then came the follow-up: how, in the two months before the election, could he convince people to take care of themselves?

"There are 47 percent of the people who will vote for the president no matter what," he answered. "All right, there are 47 percent who are with him, who are dependent upon government, who believe that they are victims, who believe that government has a responsibility to care for them, who believe that they are entitled to health care, to food, to housing, to you name it. That that's an entitlement. And the government should give it to them. And they will vote for this president no matter what. And I mean, the president starts off with 48, 49, 48—he starts off with a huge number. These are people who pay no income tax. Forty-seven percent of Americans pay no income tax. So our message of low taxes doesn't connect. And he'll be out there talking about tax cuts for the rich. I mean that's what they sell every four years. And so my job is not to worry about those people. I'll never convince them that they should take personal responsibility and care for their lives. What I have to do is convince the 5 to 10 percent in the center that are independents that are thoughtful, that look at voting one way or the other depending upon in some cases emotion, whether they like the guy or not, what it looks like."

Perhaps there was a time when presidential candidates cared more about their policies than the mechanics of messaging. But the election cycle of 2012 was not that kind of campaign. Obama faced the challenge of repackaging his record and reframing an economic debate as a choice between two worldviews. Romney could not comprehend why his message was not resonating, and he shared his political marketing strategy with the people who were paying for it. His frustration with breaking through would turn into the first real time that his message broke through. Of course, this wasn't exactly the message that he wanted to deliver to the entire voting population.

The "47 percent" video dominated the election cycle through September. It was the 2012 equivalent of the Reverend Wright video that almost sunk Obama's campaign in the primaries, or the Howard Dean scream that finished off the Vermont governor in 2004. Since it came directly from the candidate's mouth, the video carried more immediacy and credibility than the sermons of Obama's former pastor. And unlike the Reverend Wright sermons, this fund-raiser video carried the irresistible tease that it was secret: part of the hidden world of money in which our politicians spend most of their time campaigning, with tuxedoed waiters tending to superwealthy donors.

The video went into an endless loop on cable news. It featured prominently on broadcast news programs at the national and local levels. Obama's polling showed that up to 80 percent of voters knew about the video within two weeks of its posting. Those were numbers that most news developments—like North Korea threatening war—could never reach. Chicago could sit back and let the news media run with it.

Romney dodged the immediate demands for an apology. In an unusual and hastily arranged session with reporters, he called for the release of the full video and tried to put his remarks in context. "It's not elegantly stated, let me put it that way," he explained. "I was speaking off the cuff in response to a question. And I'm sure I could state it more clearly in a more effective way than I did in a setting like that."

Obama's message team had their own ideas about how to state Romney's case in a more effective way. Once voters had heard about the story for a little more than a week, they delivered two simple ads. The first was the subject of a press release to the media and looked like a traditional attack ad. *Fair Share* pointed out that the 47 percent of voters, whom Romney felt he could never reach, paid more in taxes than he did. The second ad, *My Job*, was not announced to the media but was far more damaging. There was no voiceover, and no footage of the dinner. Just Romney's voice, played over photos of American voters: a single mother with two children, a woman wearing safety goggles in front of heavy machinery, two elderly veterans, a Latino worker, and finally another woman working in a factory. On screen throughout were a few words: " '47 percent' of Americans."

It would take another two weeks before Romney would apologize for his comments, telling Fox News he was "just completely wrong." By that time, the *Onion* had turned the sentiment into satire: "Romney Apologizes to Nation's 150 Million 'Starving, Filthy Beggars.'" In the days after the tape emerged, Romney's support softened, while Obama's stayed steady. What had been a 4-to-5-point race in the battlegrounds became a 6-to-7-point race.

The video emerged just as early voting was beginning across the country. To mark that moment, the Obama campaign moved into what it hoped was its closing argument, with a long, two-minute ad called *Table*. The message team knew this was their most effective type of ad, and they used it sparingly. "They had the biggest impact for a couple of reasons," said Larry Grisolano. "First, because he's good. And when people see him, they like him. Romney didn't have that asset to play, and we were very careful about how we played that. Second, because there is such a tight, continuous story being told, and you can just see the link from one ad to the next ad to the next ad. These things always tested through the charts for us."

Fully a half of *Table* consisted of the president talking directly to the camera: "During the last weeks of this campaign, there will be debates, speeches, and more ads. But if I could sit down with you in your living room or around the kitchen table, here's what I'd say," he began. The other half of the ad was a numbered walkthrough of a four-point plan for what he called "a new economic patriotism" in his second term. It ended with a simple call to action: "Read my plan. Compare it to Governor Romney's, and decide for yourself."

In the first cuts of the ad, which was shot in the White House, there were no numbers on screen to show that this was a four-point plan. As soon as they added the numbers, the focus groups believed the plan was more substantive. Undecided voters especially like the self-confident ending: *go look for yourself to see how much better my plan will work out for you.*

At this point, Obama and his inner circle were oozing self-confidence. Early and absentee voting was beginning in some states just as Romney was imploding. The message war had been won, and the gamble on early advertising had paid off. They had not, in fact, run out of money in the fall. Donors big and small had stepped up, and Obama's spending was running at parity with Romney's in the last half of September.

On the eve of the presidential debates, there was little that could stop them.

NINE

INSIDE HIS HEAD

When he first ran for the White House, Barack Obama preferred to stay at Caesars Palace on his frequent visits to Las Vegas. The grandeur and opulence were preposterous, but he loved it. In fact he loved Caesars so much that it became a running joke: when his aides saw the overwrought stage at the Denver convention that year, they quipped that the Greek columns were meant to evoke his favorite Vegas resort. It was only half in jest. Obama's love of Caesars, like the set in Denver, spoke to his overinflated sense of self.

His supersized ego was not just the product of the presidency, although four years in the Oval Office had done nothing to add to his sense of humility. In 2004 he rehearsed a walk-through at the Boston convention to get a sense of the space where he would soon deliver his breakthrough speech about uniting red and blue America. As he took to the stage, he couldn't resist comparing himself to LeBron James: the young star who was finally ready for the big time. "I'm LeBron, baby," he told a reporter alongside him. "I can play on this level. I got some game." Presidents and presidential candidates are not known for their demurring nature, and voters are hardly likely to vote for modest leaders. His conservative critics seemed to think that an arrogant president named Obama was far more offensive than an arrogant president named Bush. It was hard to avoid the suspicion that those critics expected an African-American leader to be more careful about his confident attitude than all the other forty-three presidents of the United States.

Still, his overconfidence was a problem, just as it was for Bush. His aides were concerned by his lack of preparation and disengagement at vital times for his candidacy and presidency. They feared that he seemed to have some sort of near-death wish; some desire to fly them into a tailspin of failure before hauling them out of disaster just before the final moment of impact. After surviving the failure in the New Hampshire primary and the Reverend Wright onslaught, he still won his party's nomination. After the Sarah Palin panic, he still won the presidency. After the loss of Ted Kennedy's seat, he still passed health-care reform. Success seemed to follow swiftly on the heels of failure, and Obama seemed to be unfazed by either experience. He enjoyed the clutch moment, turning likely defeat into victory with his shot at the buzzer. "This is a guy who pulls a rabbit out of a hat a lot," said one longtime aide.

But first, he needed to take himself to the brink of failure, and in his Vegas-like confidence, this looked like the gambling moment. For those who had seen this pattern before, they recognized the point of greatest risk when they saw the "47 percent" video. "My fear at the time after seeing it was the way this was going to play itself out was Romney was going to hit bottom and bounce back up," said Dan Pfeiffer. "He was already falling apart when this happened. He had been through a horrendous six weeks from the Olympics all the way through. Basically, I said, now if he doesn't drool on himself and insult half the country, he will be declared a winner in the first debate. I've been known to take the dark view of things, but we'd been waiting and waiting and waiting. We knew it was coming, we just didn't know when."

That moment started with debate prep, when President Obama returned to Vegas but not to Caesars. His hotel was a cookie-cutter Westin in the suburb of Henderson, and he had work to do. Obama made no secret of the fact that he hated debates. He felt they were phony theater, and he had forced himself to play along with the general election debates against John McCain. But that was only after flubbing most of his primary debates before that. Looking back, he explained away his poor performances in 2008 with some self-analysis: his political philosophy was to bring people together, to find common ground. Those skills were precisely what he needed to avoid in presidential debates, where there was a premium on focusing on pointed differences on stage. He was prone to the long-winded disquisitions of someone who once taught constitutional law; not the precise verbal punches of a trial lawyer. Still, knowing his flaws and the outsized prominence of the debates, Obama began his debate prep early in 2012: fully five months before the first encounter on stage with Mitt Romney. From mid-May onward, Obama's debate team started shipping materials to the president, and he replied with specific requests.

"I know my record," he told his team. "I'm interested in learning Romney's record because I really haven't followed the stuff that closely. But at the end of the day what I really need from you guys is just how to frame this thing up. What do I respond to and when do I let go?"

The debate team included his regular message team plus a

couple of former White House aides: Anita Dunn, formerly his director of communications; and Ron Klain, formerly Biden's chief of staff. Both had years of debate experience and knew how to sharpen any candidate's performance. But the debate team did not focus on how to frame the candidate's message. Instead they began with huge notebooks that detailed Romney's policy positions and public statements. Obama responded with long lists of questions in a ceaseless search for a vindicating fact about his own record to refute a likely Romney attack.

The debate team was concerned from the get-go. Obama seemed to be falling into the classic incumbent trap. Vindication tours looked terrible to voters: they sounded whiny, arcane, and defensive. Besides, the challengers always looked better on stage standing next to incumbents. The combination—as President Bush found in 2004 and Al Gore found in 2000—was usually disastrous in the first debate.

Vegas was not the first time Obama had worked on his debating skills. Before leaving for Nevada, he and his debate team had secretly staged three rehearsals at the headquarters of the Democratic National Committee in Washington. The DNC was a great location to hide the prep: at the White House, they would have needed to move in equipment, whereas at the party's offices there was a studio ready for debate work. But the sessions did not go very well: over the course of three mock debates, Obama found himself in a defensive crouch, responding to every Romney attack, as delivered by his combative stand-in, John Kerry. The team was not too worried by the dismal performance. They wanted him to get it out of his system, to ask them for a way out.

Obama felt his first mock debate went pretty well, considering that Kerry had been prepping for four months, while he had spent no time getting himself ready. He indulged in lengthy responses to Kerry's attacks on the deficit, taking the chance to rebut years of misinformation about the budget hole he inherited from President Bush. And he spent too much time relitigating the Recovery Act stimulus, correcting every distortion the Republicans had propagated for the last three and a half years.

The second mock debate coincided with a shift in strategy as the dynamics of the contest changed. When the prep began in early summer, the team's focus was to highlight the choice between Obama and Romney—rather than accepting that this election was a referendum on Obama. "A huge part of our strategic thinking around the first debate was that the president would have to go in there and really force the choice," said one senior Obama aide. "That he would be very aggressive about making sure it was a choice between two policy paths, two paths for the American people. That he needed to be very aggressive in prosecuting that, because Romney would be trying to make it a pure referendum on him."

However, by the time the first debate neared, the choice was already clear. Romney had picked Paul Ryan as his vice-presidential partner and tied himself to Ryan's budget. The "47 percent" video had shifted the focus entirely to Romney, crystallizing the choice between the two candidates better than any messaging from the Obama campaign. So the message team made a big decision. They all thought they were LeBron, baby. "We decide that we can take the foot off the gas and that we really don't need to make it a choice any longer," said the senior aide. "He doesn't really need to be aggressive anymore because it's kind of baked in there. And instead he can use as much of the time as he can, realizing he needs to respond to a few things, but comfortably really making his case to the American people about what comes next." They agreed with the public criticism that Obama had yet to explain what would happen in his second term. So they decided that the first debate would be the ideal place to outline that vision. Instead of sharpening the choice between the two candidates on stage, Obama would explain what he wanted to do if he won.

They staged one final mock debate in Washington, shortly before heading out to Vegas. But the final session was even worse than the first two. By chance, it was scheduled on the same day Obama attended the return of the bodies of four victims of the terrorist attack on the United States diplomatic post in Benghazi, Libya. One was the US ambassador to Libya, Chris Stevens; two were former Navy SEALs working as CIA security officers; the fourth was a State Department computer specialist. Obama was visibly preoccupied and downbeat after the ceremony at Joint Base Andrews, where he would normally board Air Force One. His debate team realized too late they should have canceled the rehearsal altogether.

Vegas was not an ideal place for debate prep. Although the Vegas suburbs were ground zero in the contest for Nevada's six electoral college votes, it was not in the right time zone for the first debate at the University of Denver. Still, Obama's first question-and-answer session went well. He broke for dinner, and returned for a full debate rehearsal, when his performance was more mixed. Obama seemed confused by the strategy.

"When do I respond?" he asked, repeating his question from several months ago. "When do I let it go?"

The debate team found it hard to be precise, caught between the risk of losing their poll lead and the risk of flunking the debate test. Obama said he didn't want to let Romney get away with anything he wanted to say. So what should he do in case Romney said something outrageous, or tried to interrupt?

"When do I attack?" he followed up. "How do I attack?"

The answer was to ignore Romney and pivot to the choice between one of two futures. Their best advice was to avoid the here and now.

There were two obvious areas of attack: the "47 percent" tape, and Romney's lack of clarity on Bain. Obama was ready to land a punch on his rival for the "47 percent" comments, but his debate team did not tell him that it was an absolute requirement. In addition, their best advice was to avoid Bain altogether: it was the one subject where Romney knew more than Obama. If Romney was likely to be prepared for anything, it was to push back against attacks on Bain and the 47 percent.

Obama hated the prep, for sure. He rejected lines that his team suggested, laughing at the absurdity of the theater. He seemed to think of the debate as a joint press conference with a foreign leader. Those he could handle without breaking a sweat. On one trip to a campaign office, he half-joked that it was all too much work. "Basically they're keeping me indoors all the time," he told one volunteer. "It's a drag. They're making me do my homework."

Obama looked unusually flustered from his first words on camera in Denver. "There are a lot of points I want to make tonight, but the most important one is that twenty years ago I became the luckiest man on Earth because Michelle Obama agreed to marry me," he began. "And so I just want to wish, sweetie, you happy anniversary and let you know that a year from now we will not be celebrating it in front of 40 million people."

Mitt Romney was more than prepared, even for the simple opener about the Obamas' anniversary. "Congratulations to you,

Mr. President, on your anniversary. I'm sure this was the most romantic place you could imagine, here with me."

Watching on TV, Robert Gibbs—Obama's one-time message shaper—was stunned. "Oh shit," he said out loud, as he suffered flashbacks to the worst debate performances of the 2008 primaries.

"It was so emblematic of the debate problems in 2007 and 2008," Gibbs later recalled. "We used to drill in him, 'The first sentence out of your mouth has to be the basis on which you build the rest of your answer.' My theory on this is if you give Barack Obama two minutes to answer a question, the one thing you can assuage yourself is that he isn't going to give back any time."

Sitting down in the crowd, next to Michelle Obama, Valerie Jarrett was worried from the start. "I knew it was painful," she said. "He was not on top of his game. I thought that Governor Romney was very strong. Very, very strong." They had been planning to return to the hotel to celebrate the Obamas' anniversary, and a great first debate. Instead, Obama seemed caught between what he wanted to say on stage and what his agreed strategy was. He couldn't attack in case it destroyed his own popularity. But he needed to attack to show he had some backbone. He looked indecisive and weak because his game plan was itself conflicted and weak. So when Romney backed away from his own tax plan— calling the president's charges "inaccurate"—Obama avoided an extended clash and quickly pivoted to talking about investments in education and energy.

The debate team was blindsided. "We had expected Romney to lie about Obama's record," said a senior Obama aide. "But we had not expected Romney to walk away from his own recent record. We were used to seeing him walk away from his positions on abortion, gay rights, and all of that. We had not expected him to actually deny his tax cut position. That was nowhere in our playbook for the simple reason that it was just inconceivable to us, since it was the centerpiece of his economic plan. So that was something the president was totally unprepared for." The only glimmer of hope was that Romney also lied about his own health plan, saying that preexisting conditions were covered in his proposals, not just Obamacare. Obama's aides could at least walk into the press spin room to declare that Romney was plain wrong about his own agenda. "That was really helpful because we were in a meltdown about what to say," said a senior Obama aide.

Obama's message team was split between Chicago and Denver, but when they joined a conference call fifteen minutes before the end of the debate, the reaction was the same in both places. It was a disastrous performance. The message team was following the reaction among journalists on Twitter, and they were expecting a firestorm of criticism. They watched in dismay as MSNBC's commentators ripped the president's performance apart in ways, they felt, that Fox News would never do to Romney had he debated so poorly. The conference call threatened to descend into a pit of gloom, with each Obama aide complaining about how bad the situation was. Only a couple of voices suggested going aggressive with the argument that Romney was a simple liar.

The digital media team kicked into salvage mode, making a series of web videos arguing that Romney did not tell the truth. But their biggest success, getting more than 3 million views on YouTube alone, picked on Romney's debate line pledging to cut funding for PBS and Big Bird from *Sesame Street*. As a target, Big Bird seemed so harmless compared to other challenges facing the US economy and the federal government. It was the only lifeline for the Obama campaign, and it was better than wallowing in defeatism.

The next day Obama returned to campaigning in Denver

and used all the debate lines he had neglected to roll out the night before. He countered on Romney's abandoning of his own tax plan, as well as his assault on the innocuous yellow figure of Big Bird. He even landed a line about the 47 percent. "From the day we began this campaign, I always said real change takes time," Obama told supporters. "It takes more than one term. It takes more even than one president or one party. You certainly can't do it if you've got a president who writes off half the nation before he even takes office. In 2008, 47 percent of the country didn't vote for me. But on the night of the election, I said to all those Americans, 'I may not have won your vote, but I hear your voices, I need your help, and I will be your president, too.'"

"What the fuck?" said one senior Obama aide, astonished at how easily the candidate delivered the very messages he had forgotten at the debate. "Why is he doing this to us?"

Inside Obama's inner circle, there were flashbacks to the New Hampshire primary in 2008. At the time they seemed to be on a glide path to victory, after their big win in Iowa. Everyone predicted a quick second win in the Granite State, and the nomination would soon be his. Instead, they lost to Clinton, and the long march to the nomination took several months. New Hampshire was the night Obama delivered one of his best-known speeches, rallying a dejected crowd with the refrain "Yes We Can." And Denver the next morning, when supporters were fired up for four more years, seemed to echo those days. "I think it was a wake-up call to everyone that we shouldn't take anything for granted," said Jarrett. "And the next morning, that cold morning in Denver, the crowd came out and people were yelling: 'We've got your back!' And I think it actually energized the campaign and the folks, his supporters, in an important way. It was a painful ten days between the two debates. But as he said, he tends to not make the same mistake twice, and he had every confidence that he could get it right."

Back in Chicago, the digital team was finding it hard to strike the right tone. They couldn't send out e-mails saying, "We've got your back," because it was an admission that the president was in trouble. Reporters would have no trouble writing stories about an e-mail that tried to rally Obama's base in such a desperate way. "In difficult moments like the first debate, you really have to ground yourself in what that story line is and what the individual's role is and how they're feeling," said Joe Rospars. "Versus how reporters feel or how the bed-wetting high-dollar donors feel. You have to thread the needle because the press is reading the e-mail, too. So you've got to figure out how to thread it in a way that's meaningful and authentic for the supporters."

The needle-threading answer was an e-mail from Jim Messina, the morning after the debate, that simply referenced the newfound confidence of the other side. "Here's the first thing Mitt Romney said to his supporters this morning: 'Victory is in sight.' Stand with President Obama for a second term. Chip in $5 or more today." It ended with a photo of a crowd of thirty thousand supporters who showed up to see the president in Madison, Wisconsin, that afternoon. The e-mail message was a rallying cry without telegraphing the deep fear that dominated the thoughts of Obama's aides in the Prudential building and the West Wing.

The polls started to move almost immediately, but the movement was not nearly as dramatic as the media reaction. In Obama's battleground state surveys, the president lost 1 point while Romney gained 1 point, turning a 6-point contest back into a 4-point race. Expectations for Romney's performance were so low that he won back some of his softer support by simply looking confident, competent, and inoffensive.

Obama met with his debate team in the Roosevelt Room back in the White House, and he apologized. "Don't feel bad," he told them. "It was my failure. I didn't do a good job." The team disagreed. They had served him poorly and failed to foresee Romney's tactics. The question now was what to do with the next debate. Everyone in Democratic politics weighed in with advice for the second debate. Bill Clinton warned Obama's team not to go negative because the second encounter was a town hall format, with voters visible in the background and on the sides of the set. But they all agreed that was a nonstarter as a strategy for a comeback. The debate team at least shifted their own approach to the prep. In place of the big notebooks, they handed Obama a one-page sheet of everything he needed to say. Another page spelled out how he needed to respond to attacks, distortions, and downright lies.

Plouffe knew the media was ready to write the Romney comeback story. No presidential contest would ever be finished a month before election day. But he had no idea the comeback would be this forceful. Obama would need to wait for some new development before he could write his own comeback story. That might be the vice-presidential debate; more likely, it would be his own second debate against Romney. In the meantime, all they could do was hang tight and prep for the next encounter.

Biden's performance was strong, but not flawless. He avoided looking weak, like his boss a week earlier. But he overcompensated as he tried to shut down Paul Ryan's arguments: he laughed, smiled, and shook his head through Ryan's claims of bipartisanship or his critique of Obama's foreign policy. It wasn't pretty, but Biden's performance reassured the Democratic base that the presidential ticket was ready to fight back.

For the first time in the 2012 cycle, Obama's team was concerned about the messaging of their rivals. Until now, they had been running against the economy, the threats to the middle class, and the radical Republicans overall. Now Romney's team was cutting ads that repackaged the first debate, and Obama's aides were troubled. One targeted the hardship endured by the middle class under Obama's term; the other focused on those struggling to find jobs. A week later, the Romney campaign was turning their candidate into an updated version of Obama from 2008: a figure who could unite red and blue America. "We have to work on a collaborative basis," Romney said from the debate stage, in an ad called *Bringing People Together*. "Republicans and Democrats both love America. But we need to have leadership: leadership in Washington that will actually bring people together and get the job done and could not care less if it's a Republican or a Democrat. I've done it before. I'll do it again."

In Chicago, Larry Grisolano had been planning an entire campaign around the economy. He was more than prepared for the argument that the economy was so bad it was time for a new man in charge. That was precisely why the Obama message team had shifted the argument to a debate about the survival of the middle class. Now, right at the end of the campaign, the Romney team hit upon the most potent argument against Obama. Once Romney rushed to the political center in the first debate, he could try to reclaim the bipartisan mantle that Obama had been denied after almost four years of Republican obstruction. "The one vulnerability we had that we kept seeing in our focus groups that we did a fair amount of message work to try and be prepared for—but it still concerned me—was this whole argument that he promised to change Washington, and it's worse than it ever was before," said Grisolano. "Romney governed in a bipartisan way with a Democratic legislature, and he could do a better job. Obama let us down on that. It was after the first debate, he started using this in his speeches and they ran an ad on this, which I thought was pretty good. But I honestly think in retrospect it was too little too late."

The wait for the second debate was painfully slow. Gibbs traveled to the White House to lunch with his old boss just days before the next showdown. "He knew he had this near-death experience," Gibbs said, dialing back his critique. His advice was to concentrate on the ordering of his answers. In reviewing the first debate, Gibbs said Obama had ultimately groped his way to the right response. But the start of his answers was uniformly poor. His advice to the debate prep team and to the president was to practice the first thirty seconds of each answer, not the full two minutes.

All the anxiety of Obama's inner circle was focused on his second debate prep, at a resort in Williamsburg, Virginia. If his team was hoping for a better candidate on day one, they were in for a shock. The president's first mock debate was once again defensive and ineffective.

The next morning, Plouffe, Axelrod, and Klain met with the president alone. Plouffe told him he could lose the election if he suffered another poor debate, because voters in their focus groups were willing to make excuses for his first debate. There was no such cushion for a second bad debate. They handed him his one-page briefing and advised him to execute it. "He gave up on the idea that these were going to be debates that were actually useful to the American people in terms of expanding their knowledge about how government works," said one senior Obama aide.

To do that, he needed to drop the Washington language of legislating. Obama called Gibbs a few minutes before walking on stage for some last-minute guidance. "Remember: your thesis has to be at the beginning of your answer," Gibbs said. "And don't talk about this the way people in committee talk about this. Live where people live. Talk about things the way people do when they're sitting around the kitchen table."

Obama's message team knew they had one immediate goal. They needed to shift the press narrative on Twitter as soon as the debate opened at New York's Hofstra University. This time around, they could not afford to lose the first twenty minutes to a Twitter pile-on about the president's performance. "You have to use your first answer to lean into the pitch on what your antici-pated press narrative is," said one senior Obama aide. "Going into the second debate, it was: 'Which Obama is going to show up? Is he going to be passive again?' So his first answer, no matter what the question was, had to be very aggressive. Then everyone's reac-tion was: 'Definitely an aggressive Obama showed up tonight. Different Obama here tonight.' That's your narrative."

It was hardly a sophisticated plan, but it worked. The first question came from a twenty-year-old college student worried about getting a job. Romney delivered the very response that Obama's team feared: that he was a Massachusetts moderate who supported Pell grants at a time when the middle class was suffer-ing. Obama himself looked and sounded like the scrappy under-dog he was in the press accounts, if not the polls. He immediately drew his rival into a debate about the auto-industry bailout and whether or not Romney had wanted Detroit to go bankrupt, as he wrote in a *New York Times* op-ed column. Romney took the bait, insisting it was Obama who let the companies go bankrupt.

The president followed with the kind of succinct punch that eluded him entirely in the first debate. "Governor Romney says he's got a five-point plan? Governor Romney doesn't have a five-point plan. He has a one-point plan. And that plan is to make sure that folks at the top play by a different set of rules. That's been his philosophy in the private sector. That's been his philosophy as governor. That's been his philosophy as a presidential candidate."

If Obama was indeed a clutch player, this time he had left his signature move until well into the fourth quarter. When Romney tried to attack the president for his response to the Benghazi attacks, Obama faked him. In basketball, he liked to pretend to be a right-hander before crossing the ball to his left and driving to the hoop. On the debate floor, and finally on his game, he let Romney believe he knew where he was headed. Obama had reviewed his own comments in the Rose Garden and knew them better than Romney—especially his reference to the attacks as part of a generic "act of terror." Romney had repeated his own talking points so often that he was unaware of the details of the Rose Garden statement. "I think it's interesting the president just said something which is that on the day after the attack, he went in the Rose Garden and said that this was an act of terror," Romney said hesitantly.

"That's what I said," Obama replied.

"You said in the Rose Garden the day after the attack, it was an act of terror. It was not a spontaneous demonstration. Is that what you're saying?" It was never a good debating tactic to ask your opponent a question whose answer you doubted.

"Please proceed, Governor," said Obama.

"I want to make sure we get that for the record because it took the president fourteen days before he called the attack in Benghazi an act of terror," Romney said, repeating his stump speech lines.

"Get the transcript," Obama said simply.

At this point, the moderator, CNN's Candy Crowley, engaged in some instant fact-checking: "He did in fact, sir."

"Can you say that a little louder, Candy?" Obama asked innocently.

"He did call it an act of terror," she confirmed.

Obama returned to the White House exhausted after the second debate. He was drained by the experience of trying to reverse the momentum on the debate stage, while still hitting the road to rally supporters as if nothing were unusual. He got back to the Executive Mansion to find a camera crew ready to shoot a final ad with him: the ad that would inspire people to get out the vote. For all the vaunted strength of the field operation, and for all the digital organizing tools at their disposal, people still needed a reason to go to the polls. That reason was one man and his message.

The camera crew was waiting for him in the state dining room: one of the few places inside the White House where campaign video could be shot, under the rules Congress allowed. But Obama was downbeat and drained.

"I am dead tired," he said. "Let's do this in one take."

"Well, of course, sir," said Jim Margolis, his leading adman. "We can do this in one take if you want. Just so you know: we're going to put $30 million behind this spot. So maybe you want to do two or three just to make sure we kind of get it right."

"Okay," Obama replied. "Pretty persuasive argument."

Over the next hour of takes, Obama worked on the final ad, intended to push people off their sofa and into the voting booth.

"After all we've fought through together these past four years, will we go back to the top-down economic policies that got us into this mess? Or will we move forward with the policies that are getting us out of this mess and strengthen the middle class together? The choice is yours," he said, as the screen cut from one still of

Obama voters to another. "It's up to you now. But if you want to make your voice heard, you've got to show up." He pointed them to a website with voting details, before ending the minute-long plea with a simple transaction: "I will always have your back. Thanks for getting mine. Now let's get out there, and vote!"

The final debate, on foreign policy, was held in Boca Raton, where Romney had spoken so memorably about 47 percent of America's voters. It was by far the challenger's weakest performance. He congratulated the president on killing Osama bin Laden and much of the leadership of Al Qaeda, but he warned that "we can't kill our way out of this mess." After warning repeatedly that Obama was weak on Iran and its nuclear ambitions, he now acknowledged that "we have to do as the president has done." Back in Chicago, Obama's debate team was beginning to chuckle. They had predicted Romney would agree with Obama on five out of six questions, but it turned out they were wrong about the sixth. To Chicago, Romney the unpredictably fearsome debater had become Romney the predictably poor closer. "The biggest thing he had going after the first debate was that people actually felt he came across as presidential," said one long-standing Obama aide. "And then in the last debate he looked so weak the whole time and tentative. It wasn't even what he said. It was just that he came across as not ready to be president when it came to foreign policy."

By this point, the ad operation was so sophisticated in its buying strategy that Obama's team could pinpoint its targets with TV. There were ads for women, for Latinos and African-Americans, short ads and long ads. In the Jewish community of Shaker Heights outside Cleveland, as well as some of the retiree communities in Florida, the campaign found smaller cable providers to place an ad with Obama riffing on Israel in the final debate. He talked about visiting Yad Vashem, the Holocaust museum, and then touring a border town to see rockets fired on family homes. In the over-crowded, overheated media market of the fall, the Obama team needed to work harder than ever to find value for money spent in quieter corners of the cable universe: more obscure shows, smaller cable providers, more targeted ads. Anything to break out through the cacophony of the final weeks of the election.

After the first debate, the Romney campaign dedicated its efforts to a single message about momentum: the polls were moving rapidly in his direction, and Democrats were panicked. Polls taken after the first encounter gave Romney leads of between 1 and 4 points. Obama's own battleground polls—where he remained in the lead by 4 points—were of no use in changing the story line in the press.

The Romney team tried to push ahead with a series of ads and messages to make up ground in the Rust Belt states. They told reporters they were making a play for Pennsylvania's electoral college votes, despite the fact that the state polls gave Obama an average lead of five points. And they released an ad that attempted, in the final days of the campaign, to rewrite the well-worn narrative that Obama had saved the auto industry. "Who will do more for the auto industry?" the voiceover began. "Not Barack Obama. Fact-checkers confirm his attacks on Mitt Romney are false." It wasn't clear which attacks the ad was referring to, or why the fact-checkers in question rated the attacks only "mostly false."

"The truth: Mitt Romney has a plan to help the auto industry. He is supported by Lee Iacocca and the *Detroit News*. Obama took GM and Chrysler into bankruptcy, and sold Chrysler to Italians who are going to build Jeeps in China. Mitt Romney is going to fight for every American job."

The ad was such a stretching of the truth that Obama's ad team was easily able to turn the attack on its head. The newspaper fact-checkers said the Romney ad was itself false, pointing out that Chrysler had already issued a statement saying it was not shifting production of Jeeps out of the United States, but instead building up production in China to serve the Chinese. "I think the ad ran in Toledo where everybody knew that there were more people working because of Jeep, so it just kind of backfired," said Axelrod. "It looked like a cheap and unfair shot."

There were at least three factors that made Romney's task even harder than usual. The first was the improving economy itself; after selling himself as the candidate to fix the economy, the falling unemployment rate was not exactly consistent with his message. On election day, the rate stood at 7.8 percent: a drop of half a point over the year, and precisely the same rate that welcomed Obama to the Oval Office in January 2009. The second factor was Romney's own record of outsourcing jobs and investing in China. Finally, Obama had already filed the World Trade Organization complaint against China for illegal subsidies for its own car exports and car parts. At the time, his aides insisted the WTO case had nothing whatsoever to do with the election. On the face of it, that was hard to believe. Many executive actions were delayed because of the election; this one, perfectly suited to a battleground state like Ohio, just had to move ahead on time. Obama's 2009 trade action against cheap Chinese tires was already the subject of an ad that featured prominently on TV stations in Akron.

The Jeep ad seemed to Obama's message team like a sign of overreach by their opponents at a time when they were feeling more confident about their own pitch about the economy. "There's no doubt that as the economy got a little bit better through the fall, we would be a little bit more forward leaning," said Plouffe. "We were able to say, always cautiously, 'But we can't turn back because people were really feeling like things were getting better.'"

How much more confident was Chicago? They could even indulge in a message joke at the media's expense. For months the campaign's slogan had been Forward with a period at the end. At the end of July, the *Wall Street Journal* had spent good time and newsprint on a story dedicated to the period at the end of the word. Did the punctuation add emphasis or interrupt the forward flow of progress? Would a comma have been a disaster? Would they ever introduce a semicolon?

As they embarked on a sleepless forty-eight-hour, coast-to-coast tour of eight states, in the closing days of the election, Plouffe thought it was time to return to the *Wall Street Journal* story. He suggested an exclamation point. Back in 2008, he would have been too cost-conscious to waste money on printing new signs just to mess with the media. This time around, with the battleground polls stuck firmly in the 3-to-4-point range, he decided to go crazy with the punctuation. "It's almost like an inside joke basically," said Pfeiffer. "And also we knew it would be like a cool thing that people would talk about online." The *New York Times*, among others, obliged. "On placards and banners at Mr. Obama's stops during a two-day, round-the-clock swing through eight states, the newly punctuated slogan made its debut," wrote the *Times*. "The campaign called no special attention to the change, made no announcement, and yet there it was." It was hard to tell what was smaller: the microscopic focus of reporters, the media obsession of Obama's senior aides, or the punctuation itself.

In the final days of the election, the mix of ads was remarkably varied. The targeted ads for distinct segments of voters—women,

Latinos, African-Americans—were supposed to end with the summer. Instead, they carried through the fall because they still had an impact as they dealt with social issues, women's health, and the economy. By the end of September, Obama's team was spending close to $30 million a week on ads, and in the last two weeks of the election they spent a total of $100 million. Throughout this closing phase, they were heavily outspent by Romney and his allies. In those last two weeks, Romney's team spent $160 million. It is worth repeating: just eight years earlier, President Bush spent a grand total of $75 million in his entire general election.

With such overwhelming numbers of ads on the air, Obama's team shifted the tone to cut through the noise. There was the legendary actor Morgan Freeman narrating, in his Voice of God, how "the last thing we should do is turn back now." There was a get-out-the-vote ad that reminded supporters of the 537 votes that changed the course of history in Florida in 2000. "So if you're thinking that your vote doesn't count, that it won't matter," the narrator said, "well, back then, there were probably at least 537 people who felt the same way." Back in Chicago, Messina wanted to see the return of *Firms*, in which Romney sings "America the Beautiful." But the focus groups did not like the ad as much at the end of the cycle as at the earlier phase.

What was left in the edit suite, never to air, were a number of ideas that crossed a nominal line of taste. There was an unaired spot featuring Ronald Reagan speaking to high school students, talking about the way tax loopholes meant that millionaires were paying nothing in tax while bus drivers were paying more. "Do you think the millionaire ought to pay more in taxes than the bus driver or less?" Reagan asked the students, who promptly shouted out: "More!" That ad died, just like a similar ad in 2008, featuring Reagan asking his classic question in front of Carter: "Are you better off than you were four years ago?" With both ads, Obama's team decided against airing them out of deference to Nancy Reagan. Concerned by her poor health and the prospect of offending her, Obama's team felt the ads were not worth the likely controversy.

The week before election day, a unique confluence of extreme weather and politics produced the extraordinary scenes of Superstorm Sandy. As a hurricane, it first made landfall in Jamaica and Cuba before spending the next five days working its way north. Rather than drift east into the Atlantic, it collided with a Canadian system to turn west, into the most densely populated part of the eastern seaboard: New Jersey and New York. While the winds had slowed since its Caribbean journey, Sandy was still carrying a hurricane's force at eighty miles per hour. The storm surge rose thirteen feet, demolishing the Jersey Shore, entire neighborhoods on Long Island, and flooding the streets and tunnels of Manhattan.

Campaigning by the presidential candidates briefly stopped. In its place were pictures of devastation, rescue, and recovery, and finally the traditional tours by elected officials. After all the figurative storms of election rhetoric and campaign messaging, Sandy's aftermath was a real-world demonstration of the power of government and the presidency itself.

It was also a political tableau of something denied the president for most of the last four years: bipartisanship. Obama toured New Jersey with the state's conservative firebrand governor, Chris Christie: a man shortlisted to be Romney's vice-presidential pick, who delivered the keynote speech at the GOP convention just two months earlier. While campaigning for Romney, Christie derided Obama as someone who was lacking leadership skills, or as he put it, "blindly walking around the White House, looking for a clue." Now he could not praise Obama's leadership highly enough. He was outstanding, deserved great credit, and couldn't be thanked enough.

"Believe me, I'm aware of all the atmospherics," Christie told reporters, as he casually leaned on the podium at a news briefing. "I'm not in a coma. But the fact is I don't care. Like I told you all the other day, I don't care.... The president of the United States came and offered help for the people that I am sworn to represent. And I accept his help and I accept his goodwill and I accept his great efforts that he has put forward on behalf of our state. There will be some folks who will criticize me for complimenting him. Well, you know what? I speak the truth. That's what I always do. Sometimes you guys like it, sometimes you don't. Sometimes politicians like it, sometimes they don't. But I say what I feel and what I believe."

In a world of heavily packaged politicians, of hundreds of millions of dollars' worth of television ads, of e-mail spam asking for money and a manipulated political press, Christie's bluntness—his readiness to upset the partisan conventions of an election—was unusually refreshing. It was also, as they liked to say in the Obama White House, a case of good policy being good politics. New Jersey, a Democratic-leaning state, needed the help of the federal government. But Christie could have been less effusive in his praise of Obama, not least if he wanted to run in the Republican presidential primaries in 2016. By heaping compliments on Obama, he effectively undercut four years of Republican messaging that Obama was personally unreasonable, ideologically unworkable, and suspiciously un-American. Sandy and Christie did not lead to any detectable movement in the battleground state polls. The events may have been too late to register, or they were simply viewed as local stories by voters in other states unaffected by the hurricane. Obama's internal polling ended at a 3-point margin in the battlegrounds, with the president steady at 50 points and Romney stuck, ironically, at 47 percent.

As devastating and emotional as Sandy was, Obama and his inner circle were moved even more by their final journey together. The last trip represented the end of the road after almost five years of what felt like an endless campaign. He would never do this again, and there was a bittersweet sense of relief and regret. Campaigning represented some of the highest moments of Obama's career, and some of his greatest disappointments. He and his friends and aides felt the weight of campaign fatigue, of White House stress, and the rapid aging that was the result of both. He also felt exhilarated by the crowds, and the memories, and the friends who had become his political family.

The campaign trail, especially in its earlier and later stages, represented a simpler world than either Washington or Chicago. There was no time or space for clashing egos among Obama's message team; no difficult strategic choices for him to game out; no room for him to withdraw into the cocoon of introspection and wonkery that he inhabited inside the West Wing. He loved to perform on the campaign stage and fed off the energy of the crowds.

Two of his best friends from Chicago, Marty Nesbitt and Valerie Jarrett, joined him for the last day of campaigning in Wisconsin, Ohio, and Iowa. Jarrett had spent the weekend in Florida, rallying the spirits of early voters waiting hours in line to exercise their basic right to choose the next president of the United States. She would typically go to the back of the line to tell them

to hang in there. But she found her encouragement was unneces-
sary. There were DJs and celebrities who showed up to keep the
crowds entertained, and their spirits were already high. "Don't
worry, honey," said one voter. "We're not going anywhere. We'll
stay here as long as it takes."

There were twenty thousand people in Madison, Wisconsin, at the start of Obama's last day of campaigning for president.
Bruce Springsteen joined him for the rally and the following flight
to Columbus, Ohio, for his next gig with Jay Z. On board Air Force
One, Obama talked to officials about the Sandy recovery operations, before continuing that conversation with Springsteen himself in the conference room on board. It was the Boss's first trip on
the president's plane, and he thought it was pretty cool.

Jarrett cried at each stop that day, especially the last two.
"Tears were streaming down my face. It was just overwhelming,"
she said. "I think it was the electricity and the energy. I felt like the
lightning in the bottle from 2008 was clearly back." By the Obama
campaign's count, the news from the early voting states was very
positive. In Wisconsin, he was up 15 points among early voters; in
Ohio, he was up 24 points; in Iowa, his lead was 23 points. Those
numbers were big leads that Romney would have to work excep-
tionally hard to overcome.

In Columbus, Obama made an unscheduled stop at a campaign office, where he performed his election day ritual: he picked
up the phone to encourage voters to get out and vote, and to
encourage his volunteers to carry on their work. He hugged and
kissed volunteers, before telling them how important they were.
"This is the foundation of this campaign," he said. "All the ups and
downs, the TV stuff, doesn't matter because you guys are what
make this campaign."

They flew on to Des Moines, where the president waited for

his wife's plane to land so he could surprise her at the bottom of the steps. In the presidential limo, the Obamas and their Chicago friends talked about how this was his last campaign stop ever. He was overjoyed to end the journey where it all began, in Iowa.

"We have to remember in a second term that campaigning outside of DC is good for my soul," the president told the First Lady.

"We're going to make sure we get you out of DC a lot," she agreed.

It was a cold night in Des Moines: winter was already closing in. But the old gang of campaign aides was there: Axelrod, Messina, and the Iowa staff themselves. Close to the corner of East Fourth and East Locust, where the first campaign office opened its doors almost five years earlier, Michelle Obama took the stage to thank first the Boss and then Iowa. For her, Iowa remained not just a place where a presidential future took shape but where she and her daughters began to come to terms with a distorted life at the center of politics. She talked about the house party in Sioux City where she kicked off her Jimmy Choo heels and stood barefoot in the warm grass of a summer afternoon to talk to two dozen women about her unknown husband. She mentioned her daughter's July 4 weekend birthday, when they celebrated in small-town diners and the backyards of clapboard homes. Iowa in 2007 was the last time they could be a private family in public view.

"As you know this is a pretty emotional time for us, because this is the final event of my husband's final campaign," she began. "So this is the last time that he and I will be on stage together at a campaign rally. And that's why we wanted to come here to Iowa tonight, because truly this is where it all began, right here. And I have so many fond memories of this state—the house parties in

Sioux City and Cedar Rapids, celebrating Malia's birthday in Pella, and seeing my husband's face carved in butter. Believe me, we still talk about that at Christmas. But I will never forget the kindness and warmth and love that you all showed me and my family, especially our girls. That is truly what made the difference back in those early days when I wasn't so sure about this whole process, back when I was still wondering what it would mean for our girls and our family if Barack got the chance to serve as president."

Obama took the stage and expressed none of the same reservations about running for office. "I came back to ask you to help us finish what we've started," he began. "Because this is where our movement for change began. Right here. Right here. Right behind these bleachers is the building that was home to our Iowa headquarters in 2008. I was just inside, and it brought back a whole lot of memories." He spoke of the young people who worked for little money, little sleep, and sometimes no heating. He spoke of the American Gothic mural they painted to cheer the place up; of the marching band at the steak fry (the only one in Iowa, they believed at the time); of the passionate supporters at the Jefferson-Jackson dinner where he eviscerated Hillary Clinton's candidacy.

He told how they organized themselves and their neighbors, and their efforts spread across the country.

"And when the cynics said we couldn't, you said, 'Yes we can.'"
The audience echoed his call.

"You said, 'Yes we can.' And we did. Against all odds, we did."

He talked about the choice facing the country, what it meant to fight for change, and what true change looked like. And he left his audience—including millions watching live on TV—in no doubt that the power to change the country lay in their hands.

"Iowa, after all the months of campaigning, after all the

rallies, after the millions of dollars of ads, it all comes down to you," he said. "It's out of my hands now. It's in yours. All of it depends on what you do when you step into that voting booth tomorrow."

To get them into the voting booth, he told one more story: about the little lady in Greenwood, South Carolina, who got him all fired up and ready to go, when he was tired and downbeat four years ago.

He had asked Edith Childs to do one more chant and response, one more *Fired Up! Ready to Go!* He was ready to fly her from South Carolina to Iowa just to hear her one more time on the campaign trail.

"You know what Edith said? She said, 'I'd love to see you, but I think we can still win North Carolina, so I'm taking a crew into North Carolina to knock on doors on election day. I don't have time just to be talking about it. I've got to knock on some doors. I've got to turn out the vote. I'm still fired up, but I've got work to do.'

"And that shows you what one voice can do. One voice can change a room. And if it can change a room, it can change a city. And if it can change a city, it can change a state. And if it can change a state, it can change a nation. And if it can change a nation, it can change the world. And, Iowa, in 2008, your voice changed the world."

It surely did. And just like Edith Childs, Iowa's voice got bigger and louder with each retelling. When his spirits needed lifting, President Obama told and retold the story of his original transformation—from an unknown senator into the best-known leader in the world. For a brief moment, he wasn't the commander in chief, the resident of the Executive Mansion at 1600 Pennsylvania Avenue. He was just another candidate, another hopemongering hopeful: alternately tired and grumpy, energized and inspirational. The man who had emerged from an Iowa cornfield, styling himself part Lincoln and part King. Because amid all the overpaid, overblown message men in politics; amid all the squabbling, self-important staffers; amid all the hundreds of millions of dollars in screechy TV ads; amid all the focus groups and opinion polls; there was no better message, from no better messenger, than the candidate himself telling what sounded like a simple story.

TEN

THE OFFICE

t happened at the start of the first term, and they made the same mistakes at the start of the second.

Within weeks of entering the White House in 2009, President Obama and his inner circle capitulated in the message war against Republicans on jobs and the stimulus spending. They lost control of the narrative on health care for most of a year through its tortuous passage, and even after its signing into law.

At the start of their second term, it took a little longer for Obama's team to lose control of communications: around three months, rather than three weeks. But the second time around, it was a sudden collapse rather than a slow, grinding disintegration. First they could not muster enough support to get gun control out of the Senate; then they were deluged with four controversies in quick succession: the continued dispute over the attack on Benghazi, the aggressive media investigation around national security leaks, the hostile IRS approach toward political groups seeking tax-free status, and revelations about the extent of online surveillance by the National Security Agency.

How could a team that was triumphant at messaging their way out of a bad economy find such smaller challenges so overwhelming?

The simple answer is that the White House team was not made up of the same people as the campaign. David Plouffe, the de facto campaign manager, left the West Wing at the start of the new term. His sidekick, Dan Pfeiffer, took his place as the first among equals of the senior advisers. But the rest of the team had little to do with the election messaging.

Indeed, there were no plum jobs offered to anyone senior from campaign headquarters in Chicago. In other campaigns, after previous elections, there were always senior positions found for the people who had toiled so hard to reelect the president. But for the Obama reelection campaign, there was no payoff in the new administration. A small handful of midlevel campaign officials, like polling director David Simas, found similarly midlevel jobs inside the new administration. "At the end of 2008, there was a long list of campaign staff landing administration jobs through the presidential appointment office. They made sure they looked after them," said one senior campaign official. "Where is that list now? It never happened. They just moved on."

Most moved on to create consultancies where they could make money from their experience on the Obama campaign. Whether or not they had ever worked on the digital or analytics side of Chicago's operations, many marketed themselves as if they were instrumental in the more innovative side of the message. Stephanie Cutter survived the attempts to push her aside to set up a consulting firm with Teddy Goff, one of the leaders of the digital media team. Her abrasive nature found its natural home as one of the cohosts of the confrontational CNN talk show *Crossfire*. David Axelrod cemented his position as an elder statesman of messaging by founding the Institute of Politics at the University of Chicago, and by sitting down to write his memoirs. Jim Messina joined the speaking circuit and became head of Organizing for Action, a long-shot effort to turn the campaign's database of donors and supporters into an activist group across the nation. Larry Grisolano repurposed his ad-buying strategy into a business model for a new data-driven firm called Analytics Media Group. Robert Gibbs joined with Ben LaBolt to start the Incite Agency, a communications firm that promised to deploy the strategies behind "one of the most successful startups in history." In public, they all professed to have respected one another and enjoyed the triumph of reelecting the president. In private, their emotions remained raw and far more complicated. The campaign disputes continued to gnaw at them, as rivals claimed credit for each other's work and their careers developed at different paces.

Inside the White House, the senior officials kept their jobs whether or not they were washed out. In fact, the ex-aides, who had either left or been pushed out previously, were regularly brought in for advice. As the IRS story dragged on, and House Republicans threatened long investigations, Obama's fifth chief of staff, Denis McDonough, convened two groups of outside advisers to help shape their message strategy. One group included Clinton-era aides, like Paul Begala and Mike McCurry, whose advice amounted to ridiculing the small scale of these so-called scandals. Compared to the suicide of the deputy White House counsel, fraud charges against an associate attorney general, or a presidential affair with an intern, the Obama White House was barely in trouble. The rumors, intrigue, and investigations that surrounded the stories of Vince Foster, Web Hubbell, and Monica Lewinsky engulfed much of the Clinton era. What Obama's team faced would have been treated like a minor road bump in the 1990s.

The second group included Obama aides who had barely left: David Plouffe himself, Robert Gibbs, Anita Dunn, and Stephanie Cutter. Their advice was to release information quickly, return to the economic and middle-class agenda of the election, and to get out of Washington as much as possible. "We spent less time talking about the IRS and more time strategizing about the stuff that is dominating the public conversation right now, which is the economy, improving education, and preparing the workforce for the twenty-first century," said Gibbs. Their advice elicited a great ho-hum from the West Wing: with all the experience gathered in the room, they managed to come up with no fresh ideas. Besides, the president's approval ratings had barely moved since his election, hovering at or slightly under 50 points.

All four stories—the IRS, the leak investigations, Benghazi, and the NSA—involved agencies that, by their very nature, were either hard to discuss or impossible to control. The independence of the IRS was codified into law after Watergate; the Justice Department's investigations were strictly secret until filed in court; and the Benghazi attacks involved CIA officers and a CIA safe house. The real challenge facing the White House was how they handled the message around those stories. Did they know about the IRS overreach earlier than they initially suggested? Did the attorney general know about the aggressive nature of the investigation into journalists' work? Did they minimize the role of terrorists in Benghazi in their public statements ahead of the election? Three stories were metascandals: disputes about the message—and what it said about transparency and credibility—rather than underlying wrongdoing by the president's aides. The fourth sparked a genuine policy debate about transparency itself: there was simply no communications solution to the secret efforts to monitor all communications across the globe.

For White House officials, there could not have been any greater contrast to the campaign, where the so-called events of an election were manufactured and preplanned. Everything was in public view in an election, and the message was supported by hundreds of millions of dollars of advertising.

Could they have reacted any better, or faster, once the stories emerged? "You want to be fast, but it's not worth the ten- or twelve-hour jump you would get on the news cycle, if you're going to be wrong or you do something that gets you into bigger trouble," said Jennifer Palmieri, the White House communications director who also served in the Clinton White House at the depth of its scandals. "One of the things people don't appreciate about the IRS story is: yes, this was flagged up and people knew it had the potential to be really bad. But we get lots of warnings like this, with Inspector General reports. When you hear the IG side of it, they may have a theory that sounds pretty spectacular. But when the report comes back, you often find there's nothing to it."

The White House waited for the IG report before it took action against the leadership of the IRS, but the wait—in today's Twitter-timed news cycle—seemed like an eternity to the media. The following Sunday, Pfeiffer took to all five talk shows for the first time to explain their approach. He tripped up at least once, telling ABC's George Stephanopoulos that "the law is irrelevant" because the administration would take action regardless. He meant that the question about the law was irrelevant, but the sound bite further enraged the already angry cohort of conservative commentators.

Events were unpredictable, but presidents were less so. Even before his second inauguration, President Obama chose to invest his considerable political capital in an issue on which he had never campaigned nor commented on at any length: gun control. After the massacre of elementary schoolchildren in Newtown, Connecticut, in mid-December, the president took the executive decision to throw everything behind reasonable gun laws to restrict some semiautomatic guns and large-capacity magazines of bullets. Obama's aides knew they had a less than 50 percent chance of getting a successful vote out of the Senate, but they were ordered to try anyway. "There honestly wasn't a ton of analysis that went into the decision," said Palmieri. "The president really wanted to do it. We all thought it was either important to get it done or get caught trying. This is a time when getting caught trying is fine."

They justified the narrow defeat in the Senate—they were five votes short of breaking the filibuster on expanded background checks, and two votes short on gun trafficking—by blaming the terrorist attack in Boston. The pressure cooker bombs and the ensuing manhunt sucked up the nation's attention and the media's focus just two days before the gun control votes. "We were building momentum, and the bombing took attention away," said a senior White House official. President Bush suffered the same fate when he tried and failed to reform Social Security in the first year of his second term: he was struggling before Hurricane Katrina made landfall, and Social Security reform never recovered afterward. His much vaunted political capital was spent.

Much like his predecessor, the problem for the newly elected President Obama was that the gun control failure and the three pseudoscandals left the impression that he was a weak and ineffective leader. Maureen Dowd at the *New York Times* infuriated the West Wing by writing a column that chided Obama for failing to twist arms or schmooze senators. She yearned for a leader like President Andrew Shepherd of Aaron Sorkin's 1995 movie *The American*

President, starring Michael Douglas. Obama's aides believed the gun control debate was immune to arm-twisting and schmoozing. Besides, they had tried the strategy in health-care reform and it had backfired badly: voters who did not understand the legislation were very clear in disapproving of sweetheart deals to buy a lawmaker's affection. The White House felt the most powerful message came from the Newtown families themselves: if senators were prepared to ignore them, they were prepared to ignore anybody.

This kind of passive fatalism was common in the first term, as well as the start of the second. Obama's team felt they faced issues—in the recession and gun control—that they could not message their way out of. That was not their approach during the campaigns of 2008 and 2012, when they confronted huge personal and political challenges, including a struggling economy that threatened to overwhelm them. When faced with an apparently insurmountable obstacle, they sought to redefine the opposition and the nature of the obstacle. They did not give up the fight at the thought of high unemployment; instead they ran against an economic system that hurt the middle class, and redefined their opponent as part of the problem.

The message team could make that play when millions of voters were the ones to decide on the merits of the debate. Inside Washington, the Obama White House was much more leery of redefining the opposition in the kind of caricatures used against Romney. There were only one hundred voters they cared about, and all of them were United States senators.

However, this was the same trap they fell into with health-care reform. By playing an insider's game, they could not afford to alienate anyone who might be a gettable vote in the Senate. Public events were powerful, but they did not translate into effective pressure on individual senators. The grassroots remnant of the Obama campaign—Organizing for Action—proved far less potent that the grassroots campaign of the National Rifle Association.

Playing an outsider's game would have required different staffers, a greater focus on a single message—backed by real ad dollars—and a swarming response to the other side. Instead, Obama returned to the White House after the election to his old team, slightly reshuffled. The tough offense and the ad dollars were in the hands of outside groups, like Michael Bloomberg's Mayors Against Illegal Guns. In that sense, with a reliance on outsider messaging, Obama's White House looked more like the Romney campaign than his own.

Obama's single most effective aide in political strategy and messaging was David Plouffe, and he left the White House as the new term began, to pick up private-sector consultancies and rejoin the speaking circuit. Plouffe was so effective at controlling the message that the president had to keep secret his farewell remarks at an event to announce his new chief of staff. "I had to hide this in the end of my remarks because I knew he wouldn't want me to bring it up. So we had some Secret Squirrel stuff going on here to avoid him thinking that we were going to talk about him," Obama said in the East Room of the White House. "But as many of you know, David has been with me from the very start of this enterprise running for president. I can't tell you how lucky I have been to have him manage our campaign back in 2008, then join the White House during these very challenging last two years. He's built a well-deserved reputation as being a numbers genius and a pretty tough combatant when it comes to politics. But what people don't always realize—because he doesn't like to show it—is the reason he does this stuff is because he cares deeply about people. And he cares about justice, and he cares about making sure that everybody gets a shot in life. And those values have motivated him to do incredible things, and were it not for him, we would not have been as effective a White House and I probably wouldn't be here."

Plouffe was a great asset to the president, but he wasn't flawless. His decision to base the campaign in Chicago, while effectively running the campaign from the West Wing, was questionable. Obama's inner circle insists it allowed the campaign to maintain its focus on the grass roots and to ignore the Beltway conventional wisdom on messaging. But the field operation would have stayed focused on its metrics, regardless of location. And the message team was stuck in a quagmire of infighting and suspected conspiracies, not least because Plouffe was out of view. Some of these tensions would have also knotted themselves into being at a DC headquarters: there were inevitable overlaps between a campaign and a White House, designed to stay separate under election laws. And some Obama aides believed a Washington headquarters would have suffered even more from internal rivalries than Chicago did. Still, Plouffe's absence—like that of the president—left a vacuum that others filled poorly. There was no way for the campaign staffers to bring their election spirit to a new term, because those staffers were essentially frozen out of the biggest decisions during the election itself. Besides, many of them were dispatched to the campaign precisely because they were already frozen out of the administration's decision making in previous jobs.

That dynamic underscores the cliquish nature of Obama's presidency. Despite his confidence on stage, Obama has governed with a very small circle of decision-making aides, and his circle barely expanded through his first term in office to take in a handful of Clinton-era aides. His new chief of staff, Denis McDonough, was one of his original Senate staffers in 2005, alongside his senior adviser and former chief of staff, Pete Rouse. Another senior adviser, Valerie Jarrett, had hired Michelle Obama into Chicago city government and been a personal friend to both Obamas for several years. And the fourth senior adviser, Dan Pfeiffer, was a relative newcomer, having joined the first Obama campaign in early 2007.

Real outsiders fared badly inside Obama's West Wing. Bill Daley, the president's second chief of staff, never fit in and was considered hopeless and lost by Obama's aides. The first director of communications, Ellen Moran (who was previously executive director of Emily's List), lasted barely three months. His first chief of staff, Rahm Emanuel, was a known factor from Chicago. But Emanuel's Clintonesque, calculating, and tactical style epitomized the inside-Washington mentality that Obama's closest advisers felt was a betrayal of the campaign spirit of 2008.

Unlike the Bush administration, Obama's White House did not suffer from deep policy splits between doves and hawks, or moderates and their ideological rivals. Their rivalries were personal and spiritual: whether they truly believed in the ethos of 2008, or whether they preferred the realpolitik of the Washington system. The outsiders were ironically seen as the ones who didn't comprehend the outsider's nature of the Obama brand.

Such contradictions were part of the warp and woof of Obama himself: a newcomer who promised to upend the status quo but seemed all too ready to live within its conventions and limitations. Inside the White House, he never resolved those tensions, especially if they involved the personal conflicts on his political team. He centralized decision making around himself and his inner circle, but his decisions were often painfully slow in coming. He erred on the safe side of big decisions for too long before edging into the risk-filled choices that presented themselves inside the Oval Office. Whether it was his decision to arm the rebel forces in Syria or to support same-sex marriage, Obama was a constant source of frustration and mystification for his supporters inside and outside the administration. On Capitol Hill, even Democratic members complained that his absence and coldness left them struggling to understand his motives and his management style: if they didn't love him or fear him, why should they take a bullet for him? They were unclear about where he was headed, so they focused on the lack of personal outreach. But the reality was that personal contact left them no clearer about his true identity and purpose.

There were two rare exceptions to the notion that outsiders could not thrive inside the White House: Obama's previous chief of staff, Jack Lew; and White House press secretary Jay Carney. Both were low-key, pragmatic, and effective at executing their given mission. They stayed inside their lanes and the status quo, which helped them to fit in to an often fractious team. But that low-key style did little to challenge an often-complacent commander in chief, who was quick to resent outside criticism and felt perennially misunderstood and underestimated by the political class that sat in judgment of him.

What changed, beyond all recognition, in 2012 was the nature of a presidential campaign. The election transformed the message machine through the vast scale of spending and through the unprecedented use of technology. Long gone are the days when candidates and pundits fretted about the notion that you could sell a president with a cornflakes campaign. Long gone are the days when voters had qualms about giving cash to wealthy candidates and their well-financed campaigns. The Obama campaign found it easier to get their supporters to hand over their credit card details than access to their list of Facebook friends.

In their use of e-mail and social media, as well as advertising analytics, the Obama campaign broke new ground in message targeting. In the next election cycle, campaigns will combine set-top-box data with their voter files to deliver specific ads directly to the gettable voters they are most interested in reaching. Less useful voters will not see those so-called addressable ads, even if they are watching the same shows at the same time. The accuracy of Obama's modeling was striking even to those who were working with it every day. "On election day, my friend called me up from Iowa and he said they had just counted the Polk County absentee ballots," said Larry Grisolano. "There are forty-seven-something thousand ballots, and the model said we'd come out of this thing with about a twelve-thousand-vote lead. He gave the precise numbers, and it was off by a hundred votes. They were spot-on, and that is just a golden thing to have."

For the GOP, the Obama revolution demonstrated just how much ground they needed to catch up in the four years before the next presidential contest. They lagged far behind in technological capabilities, and their early efforts to build complex voter modeling were fragmented and faltering. Even their core message seemed to ignore the immediate lessons of 2012, as the House Republicans rapidly returned to voting for abortion restrictions rather than economic opportunity.

Such targeting may be important to the political professionals, but it's far from clear that the hundreds of millions of dollars they spend are particularly effective. According to Obama's internal battleground state polls, the election was a 3-point race when it began, and it was a 3-point race when it ended. In between, Obama spent $430 million on ads and his allies spent another $90 million. Romney spent $225 million and his allies spent some $425 million. In total, that put Obama and his allies at $520 million versus Romney and his allies at $650 million. Together they easily cracked the $1 billion mark and had no lasting impact on the polls. Along the way, they shaped our understanding of the candidates and their agendas in profound ways, but not to the extent that they were worth more than $1 billion. Obama's ad team produced around 500 ads and ultimately aired some 150 of them. Their ads certainly burnished the popularity of the president's own personality and probably helped his approval numbers to survive, in Teflon style, the controversies and failures that were so prominent in the first months of his second term.

For Obama's team, the ads were not a debatable question: if they hadn't spent their money early, they could not have beaten Romney so handily, no matter what the poll movement suggests. In fact, the only question about the ads was how much they cost at a time when other types of online communication were taking over. Obama embraced digital media the way FDR embraced radio: his team set aside concerns about privacy and intrusion in their desire to establish a seemingly more intimate conversation with voters. "There's a viral nature to our communications that didn't exist in the past," said David Axelrod. "So ads are important if you have a revealing moment in a debate or on the stump—and by the way, everything you say now, someone is reporting, putting online instantly, and shooting it around the country and around the world—so I think that the balance is shifting some. My problem isn't so much about selling presidents like soap, because there's so much scrutiny given to these candidates. People know who they are by the time election day comes around. I don't think they are solely reliant on ads to find that. The problem with ads is that they cost too much and they are the prime driver behind the rising cost of elections. And I think that is an insidious thing."

Insidious but unavoidable: Obama's 2008 campaign was the

groundbreaker in demolishing the public financing of presidential campaigns at the general election stage. "I am a believer in the spirit of campaign finance laws. I'm not a believer in their efficacy," said Axelrod. "All we've done is create a cottage industry for lawyers to try to circumvent the system."

Obama was highly unlikely to confront the legislative challenge of campaign finance reform in his final few years in office. He wanted to pass immigration reform as the major new law of his second term, because he saw it as his contribution to the civil rights movement: helping to bring equality to the country by welcoming undocumented residents out of the shadows and into full participation in their own communities. Beyond that, he hoped to return to the middle-class agenda he campaigned on, even as he was buffeted by congressional investigations and the immediate failure of his gun control efforts. He and his staff faced continuing struggles to message and implement his sprawling health-care-reform legislation that was the centerpiece of his administration, alongside the economic recovery that was still under way. Still, his senior staff was relieved to see the economic indicators move significantly upward in 2013—from employment to the long-suffering housing sector. They felt that few of these challenges were as daunting as the task of winning reelection after the worst recession in eighty years.

In reality they knew that time was short. Their first-term honeymoon ended after a year in office, when health care seemed doomed with the loss of the Massachusetts seat—and the sixty-vote count—in the Senate. But even then, health-care reform passed, as did the repeal of the restrictions on the open service of gays in the military and the extension of unemployment benefits.

Within weeks of his reelection in 2012, Obama fulfilled an election promise by raising taxes on the wealthiest Americans, at least on their income above $400,000 a year. It was clear inside the West Wing that any second-term honeymoon would be shorter than the first, with far less to show in legislation from a divided Congress.

The real beginning of the end was the start of the 2016 primaries, and the early moves were already beginning in the first six months of Obama's second term. Hillary Clinton was repositioning herself on domestic issues with a public statement about her shift on same-sex marriage. Meanwhile, Vice President Joe Biden was already traveling to early voting states. Aides to both blockbuster candidates were openly discussing the hopes and dreams of their mentors. On the Republican side, 2016 politics were also encroaching on Rand Paul's travel schedule, Ted Cruz's Tea Party critiques of the GOP, and Marco Rubio's playing Hamlet on immigration reform.

For the Democrats, it was not clear that Obama's legacy would be all that helpful. David Plouffe long believed that many Obama voters felt personally connected to the candidate, identified only loosely with the Democratic Party, were infrequent participants in elections in general, and would not easily transfer their support to others. Obama's closest aides—including most of his message team—were highly unlikely to join other campaigns in 2016, because they were largely burned out. However, the midlevel and lower-level staffers—especially the experts in analytics, digital media, and field operations—would surely go on to lead political campaigns for the next decade or more.

Back in 2008, as he traveled westward across the country between primaries, Obama made it clear that his real goal—what he hoped would be his lasting legacy—was focused on the process of politics, as much as the policy that he could turn into reality. Yes, he wanted to pass health care, improve education, and end the wars in Iraq and Afghanistan. But what he valued as much as that, if not more, was the notion that he could inspire a new generation to take part in politics and campaigns. That was the kind of change he could believe in: change from the bottom up that would overhaul the political system as a whole.

"It has been a running theme in my political career—the notion that there's something about our democracy that is broken that prevents us from solving real problems," Obama told me. "I think throughout my career I have tried to describe that, about what in our broken political process needs to be fixed. Divisions based more on ideological or racial or religious constructs than they're based on deeply rooted beliefs—that's part of the change I've talked about. The dominance of special interests and money in politics—that's part of the change I've talked about. The lack of participation and involvement in decision making—that's part of the change I've talked about. The need to cut through the spin and PR and to be able to present things honestly to the American people—that's part of the change I've talked about. These have been constant concerns that I have had without doubt back to my community-organizing days. But it also had to do with my diagnosis of why so many problems are left unsolved."

Obama could not overcome the ideological divisions in American politics: they seemed at least equal to the divisions that President Bush experienced in office. The demographic gap between the two parties was one big reason why immigration reform could stand a chance of success. And it wasn't clear Obama had made any progress in changing the "religious constructs" that threatened his own reelection effort.

As for cutting through the spin and PR, Obama had one of the biggest, most expensive, and most successful groups of spin and PR experts ever gathered in American politics.

On one measure of change, Obama's record matched his life-long ambitions and the vision he mapped out in 2007 and 2008: participation.

For the first time ever, the rate of African-American turnout surpassed white turnout, at almost two-thirds, and the jump was especially high among black women. While the overall voting rate was down, the actual number of people voting was up across the nation as the population continued to grow. The growth in voters was especially significant among African-American, Latino, and Asian voters, while the number of white voters declined. In that sense, President Obama represents a transitional figure as the United States grows into an increasingly diverse nation with a majority of its population made up of a coalition of minorities— something that is projected to take place over the course of the next generation.

Just as important as the percentages of voters, Obama's campaign inspired vast numbers of volunteers to urge people to vote. Through nineteen months of organizing, the campaign registered 1.79 million voters, which was almost twice the number Obama's volunteers registered four years earlier. The campaign made more than 125 million points of contact with real voters— either phone calls or knocks on doors—to persuade them to show up, not counting direct mail and leaflet drops. That was almost the same number as the total count of people who voted for either Barack Obama or Mitt Romney.

For Obama, that participation was vital not just for his election but for change itself. "Ensuring that the American people trust what their government says, that they are part of an honest debate, that money isn't completely skewing the process," he told me, "all these things are necessary to deliver on better housing, better schools, better health care, affordable college education."

The message of the 2012 election was a colossally expensive and successful exercise in repackaging. It overcame obstacles that the political statisticians deemed insurmountable: not the least of which was a stubbornly and historically high unemployment rate. It succeeded in spite of the deep internal disputes that threatened to disrupt and destroy the entire message team. It triumphed over the missteps and fumbles of not just the challenger but also the president himself.

Without the message, there would have been no reason to go knock on doors; no compelling conversations on all those phone calls; no reason to stand in line for hours to exercise the basic right to vote. The message wasn't worth more than $500 million in television advertising; but it was worth the invaluable effort to convince all those hundreds of thousands of voters to register, or to vote, for the first time in a long time. For it was more than a collection of ads, e-mails, slogans, and press calls. And it was bigger than the petty disputes of overinflated egos in Chicago and Washington. The message was the medium of change, and it touched more people in more ways than seemed possible at its mesmerizing start.

NOTES

This book was based on contemporaneous reporting, several dozen interviews with the key players (many of whom wished to remain anonymous), and the following published works:

One: Vindication

White House transcript, "Remarks by the President on Election Night," McCormick Place, Chicago, Illinois, 11/7/12; President Obama: "I'm Really Proud of All of You," YouTube (barackobama dotcom channel), 11/7/12.

Two: The Deep End

Interview of Paul Ryan on CNBC's *Squawk Box*, "Rep. Ryan's Economic Message," cnbc.com, 5/17/11; Transcript of CNN debate at Saint Anselm College, Manchester, New Hampshire, cnn.com, 6/13/11; Transcript of *The Rush Limbaugh Show*, "Boehner Should Reject Obama's Request for Joint Session Speech," rushlimbaugh .com, 8/31/11; Editorial, "Oh, Grow Up," *New York Times*, 9/1/11; Jake Tapper, "POTUS Has Coffee with Progressive Media Stars," abcnews.go.com, 12/19/11; Jennifer Steinhauer, "The Vote That Delayed Obama's Speech," *New York Times*, 9/8/11; White House transcript, "Address by the President to a Joint Session of Congress," 9/8/11; Joe Conason, "Obama Campaign Chiefs Meet Quietly with Clinton in Harlem," *National Memo*, 11/14/11; "Barack Obama's Speech at Nasdaq," *New York Times*, 9/17/07; Text of President Teddy Roosevelt's New Nationalism speech, whitehouse.gov, 12/6/11; White House transcript, "Remarks by the President on the Economy," Osawatomie High School, Osawatomie, Kansas, 12/6/11; "President Obama: The Economy, the Congress, the Future," *60 Minutes*, cbsnews.com, 12/11/11; Kathleen Hennessey and Ashley Powers, "Why Sen. Harry Reid Is Pulling for a Conservative Republican," *Los Angeles Times*, 6/5/10.

Three: Team of Rivals

Joshua Green, "Obama's CEO: Jim Messina Has a President to Sell," *Bloomberg Businessweek*, 6/14/12; Noam Scheiber, "What's Eating David Axelrod?" *New Republic*, 9/27/10; Reid Cherlin, "Stephanie Cutter: 'I Know How to Throw a Punch,'" *Marie Claire*, 3/1/12; "Obama Answers 1996 Gay Media," *Windy City Times*, 1/14/09; Jeff Zeleny, "On Sundays, Tight Obama Circle Sizes Up Election," *New York Times*, 5/4/12; Robert Pear, "Obama Reaffirms Insurers Must Cover Contraception," *New York Times*, 1/20/12; Helene Cooper and Katharine Q. Seelye, "Obama Tries to Ease Ire on Contraception Rule," *New York Times*, 2/7/12; Helene Cooper and Laurie Goodstein, "Rule Shift on Birth Control Is Concession to Obama Allies," *New York Times*, 2/10/12; Adam Serwer, "The GOP Plan to Give Your Boss 'Moral' Control Over Your Health Insurance," *Mother Jones*, 2/14/12; Sabrina Tavernise and Erik Eckholm, "Ultrasound Abortion Bill Nears Vote in Virginia," *New York Times*, 2/20/12; Jeff Zeleny and Jim Rutenberg,

"G.O.P. 'Super PAC' Weights Hard-Line Attack on Obama," *New York Times*, 5/17/12.

Four: The American Dream

Jackson Lears, *Fables of Abundance: A Cultural History of Advertising in America* (BasicBooks, 1994), p. 90; Kathleen Hall Jamieson, *Packaging the Presidency: A History and Criticism of Presidential Campaign Advertising* (Oxford University Press, 1984), pp. 9–11; Lears, *Fables of Abundance*, pp. 218–21; Roland Marchand, *Advertising the American Dream: Making Way for Modernity 1920–1940* (University of California Press, 1985), pp. 18–21, 88–94; Jamieson, *Packaging the Presidency*, pp. 19–21, 82–87; Barbara Kiviat, "The Bastardization of the American Dream," *Time*, 8/17/10; Jamieson, *Packaging the Presidency*, pp. 158, 176–8, 193–4, 212–14, 249; Museum of the Moving Image, *The Living Room Candidate: Presidential Campaign Commercials 1952–2012*, www.livingroomcandidate.org; Presidential job approval data from gallup.com; NBC News/Wall Street Journal polls, 10/16–18/04 and 11/1–3/12; Richard Wolffe and Susannah Meadows, "In Bush's Shadow," *Newsweek*, 9/12/04; The Institute of Politics, John F. Kennedy School of Government, *Campaign for President: The Managers Look at 2004* (Rowman and Littlefield, 2006), pp. 124–6, 182–4, 214–21; Jane Mayer, "Attack Dog," *New Yorker*, 2/13/12.

Five: Definitions

Jim Provance, "Obama Kicks Off Re-election Campaign in Columbus," *(Toledo) Blade*, 5/5/12; White House transcript, "Remarks by the President and First Lady at a Campaign Event," Value-City Schottenstein Center, Columbus, Ohio, 5/5/12; Pew Research Center for the People and the Press, "Auto Bailout Now Backed, Stimulus Divisive," 2/23/12; Democracy Corps memo by Stanley

Greenberg, James Carville, and Erica Seifert, 2/23/12; Jeremy W. Peters, "Aggressive Ads for Obama, at the Ready," *New York Times,* 5/8/12; John Heilemann, "Hope: The Sequel," *New York,* 5/27/12; Michael D. Shear and Ashley Parker, "Axelrod's Anti-Romney Message Gets Drowned Out," *New York Times,* 5/31/12; Glenn Thrush and Jonathan Martin, *The End of the Line: Romney vs. Obama, the 34 Days That Decided the Election* (Random House ebook, 2012); Daniel Fisher, "The Truth About Bain: Inside the House That Mitt Built," *Forbes,* 10/22/12; Alexander Burns, "The Bain of Mitt Romney's Campaign, *Politico,* 7/14/11; Glen Johnson, "President Obama's Campaign Shifts Attack on Mitt Romney to Story of American Pad & Paper," *Boston Globe,* 5/21/12; Andy Sullivan and Greg Roumeliotis, "Special Report: Romney's Steel Skeleton in the Bain Closet," Reuters, 1/6/12; Peter Grier, "Obama Ad Depicts Mitt Romney as Job-Killing 'Vampire.' Over the Top?" *Christian Science Monitor,* 5/14/12; NBC News transcript of *Meet the Press,* 5/20/12; White House transcript, "Remarks by the President at NATO Press Conference," South Building, Chicago, Illinois, 5/21/12; Aaron Blake, "Bill Clinton Sticks Another Fork in Obama's Bain Strategy," *Washington Post,* 6/1/12; Alexander Burns, "Mitt Video Defends GST Steel Deal," *Politico,* 6/27/12; Paul Blumenthal, "Priorities USA Action, Obama Super PAC, Says July Fundraising Dropped," *Huffington Post,* 8/20/12; Robin Bravender and Kenneth P. Vogel, "Pro-Obama Super PAC Raises $59K," *Politico,* 2/20/12; Joy-Ann Reid, "Obama Campaign Releases First Black Radio Ad," *Grio,* 6/11/12.

Six: The Digital Divide

Marcus Stern and Tim McLaughlin, "Analysis: Obama's Ad Team Used Cable TV to Outplay Romney," Reuters, 1/5/13; Zeke Miller, "#DRINK: Obama Campaign Launches GOP Debate

Watch Fundraising Game," *Business Insider*, 10/18/11; Michael Scherer, "Barack Obama's New One-Click Fundraising Trick," *Time*, 3/14/12; Alexis C. Madrigal, "When the Nerds Go Marching In," *Atlantic*, 11/16/12; Joshua Green, "The Science Behind Those Obama Campaign E-Mails," *Bloomberg Businessweek*, 11/29/12.

Seven: Summer Haze

Tom Hamburger, "Romney's Bain Capital Invested in Companies That Moved Jobs Overseas," *Washington Post*, 6/21/12; White House transcript, "Remarks by the President at Campaign Event," Hillsborough Community College, Tampa, Florida, 6/22/12; White House transcript, "Remarks by the President at Campaign Event," Westin Peachtree Plaza Hotel, Atlanta, Georgia, 6/26/12; Carrie Dann, "Biden Hammers Romney on Outsourcing, Wealth," msnbc.com, 6/26/12; Michael D. Shear, "Washington Post Rebuffs Romney on Retraction," *New York Times*, 6/27/12; Nicholas Shaxson, "Where the Money Lives," *Vanity Fair*, August 2012; Catherine Rampell, "Job Weakness Starts to Shape Election Tone," *New York Times*, 7/6/12; Michael D. Shear, "Republican Web Site Points to Obama as 'Real Outsourcer-in-Chief,' " *New York Times*, 7/10/12; "Romney Interview with CBS News: Full Transcript," cbsnews.com, 7/13/12; Jennifer Epstein, "Obama Team: Romney Committed a Felony or Lied to Voters," *Politico*, 7/12/12; White House transcript, "Press Gaggle by Press Secretary Jay Carney," Aboard Air Force One En Route Jacksonville, Florida, 7/19/12; Frank James, "Romney in London: Not a Smashing Success So Far," NPR.org, 7/26/12; Ashley Parker and Richard A. Oppel Jr., "Romney Trip Raises Sparks at a 2nd Stop," *New York Times*, 7/30/12; Sarah Huisenga and Matt Vasilogambros, "Romney Spokesman to Reporters: 'Shove It,' " *National Journal*, 7/31/12.

Eight: The Choice

Stephanie Condon, "Poll: Most Americans Say Medicare Is Worth the Cost," cbsnews.com, 4/21/11; Michael Falcone, "Mitt Romney's Whiteboard Blues," abcnews.go.com, 8/17/12; Sam Stein and Ryan Grim, "Harry Reid: Bain Investor Told Me That Mitt Romney 'Didn't Pay Any Taxes for 10 Years,'" *Huffington Post*, 7/31/12; Lori Moore, "Rep. Todd Akin: The Statement and the Reaction," *New York Times*, 8/20/12; Dan Balz and Philip Rucker, "Republican National Convention Cancels Monday Events Because of Tropical Storm Isaac," *Washington Post*, 8/25/12; "Anatomy of a Speech: Republican National Convention," *New York Times*, 8/29/12; James Rainey, "Advice to Romney: Show the Winning Bio Video Everyone Missed," *Los Angeles Times*, 9/28/12; Callum Borchers, "Bill Clinton Ad Libbed Some of His Most Memorable Lines in Democratic Convention Speech," *Boston Globe*, 9/6/12; Pew Research Center for the People and the Press, "Democratic Convention Highlights: Clinton Outshines Obama," 9/10/12; "Anatomy of a Speech: Democratic National Convention," *New York Times*, 9/5/12; David Corn, "Meet Scott Prouty, the 47 Percent Video Source," *Mother Jones*, 3/13/13; "Full Transcript of the Mitt Romney Secret Video," *Mother Jones*, 9/19/12; Associated Press, "Romney Offers No Apologies for 'Victims' Remarks," 9/18/12; MSNBC, "The Ed Show for Wednesday, March 13th, 2013," 3/14/13; Associated Press, "Mitt Romney: '47 Percent' Comments Were 'Just Completely Wrong,'" 10/5/12.

Nine: Inside His Head

David Mendell, *Obama: From Promise to Power* (Amistad, 2007), p. 2; Olivier Knox, "Obama: Debate Prep is 'A Drag,'" *Yahoo! News*, 10/1/12; Debate transcripts, Commission on Presidential Debates, 10/3/12, 10/11/12, 10/16/12, 10/22/12; Devin Dwyer,

"Obama Challenges China at WTO Over Cars," abcnews.go.com, 9/17/12; Glenn Kessler, "4 Pinocchios for Mitt Romney's Misleading Ad on Chrysler and China," *Washington Post*, 10/30/12; Carol E. Lee, "Punctuation Nerds Stopped by Obama Slogan, 'Forward.,'" *Wall Street Journal*, 7/30/12; Peter Baker, "Obama's Slogan Moves from "Forward." to "Forward!" *New York Times*, 10/26/12; White House transcript, "Remarks by the President and the First Lady at Final Campaign Event," Intersection of East Fourth and Locust Streets, Des Moines, Iowa, 11/5/12.

Ten: The Office

Philip Rucker and Juliet Eilperin, "On IRS Issue, Senior White House Aides Were Focused on Shielding Obama," *Washington Post*, 5/22/13; Sean Sullivan, "Dan Pfeiffer: Legal Questions in IRS Scandal 'Irrelevant' to 'Inexcusable' Actions," *Washington Post*, 5/19/13; Maureen Dowd, "No Bully in the Pulpit," *New York Times*, 4/20/13; White House transcript, "Remarks by the President at a Personnel Announcement, East Room," 1/25/13; United States Census Bureau, "The Diversifying Electorate—Voting Rates by Race and Hispanic Origin in 2012 (and Other Recent Elections)," 5/8/13.

ACKNOWLEDGMENTS

To paraphrase President Obama, I didn't build this book myself. It took a huge amount of help—from sources, coworkers, friends, and family—to get this to publication. I have learned, over the course of my last two books, that not all of them want to be acknowledged the same way: some prefer to remain anonymous, others want to minimize their role. So I hope I don't screw this up too much.

I am hugely grateful to those inside the White House and the Obama campaign who gave so freely of their time to inform this book: David Axelrod, Jon Favreau, Robert Gibbs, Larry Grisolano, Valerie Jarrett, Ben LaBolt, Jim Margolis, Jim Messina, Jen Palmieri, Dan Pfeiffer, David Plouffe, Jen Psaki, Harper Reed, Joe Rospars, and many more who asked not to be identified. Above all, I'm indebted to Jamie Smith who fielded my many requests with a ceaseless supply of good humor and grace.

I am truly lucky to work with the incredibly professional and talented team at MSNBC. They have been wonderfully encouraging and understanding throughout, not least as we worked on the complex and challenging launch of the new MSNBC.com. Phil Griffin encouraged me to write this book two years before publication, and the first digital team—Sharon Otterman, Denis Horgan, and Farra Kober—was enormously supportive. It's an honor to work every day with the whole senior leadership of MSNBC. And we could not come close to launch without the energy, enthusiasm, and leadership of Pat Fili-Krushel, Vivian Schiller, and their teams.

A huge thank you goes to my wonderful digital group, who pretended not to notice my lack of sleep. I am especially grateful to Michele Richinick, who saved me in the latter stages of the interviews. It is a privilege to work with the homepage editors, multimedia editors, show reporters, and national reporters who make up MSNBC.com; and I am incredibly fortunate to work with the shows that have built MSNBC into the brilliant TV that it is today.

My life as a book author would not have begun without the true friendship, wise counsel, and total professionalism of Kris Dahl. Kris rescued me, and this book, at so many stages. *The Message* would never have appeared in print without her tremendous skill, judgment, and experience.

I honestly cannot say enough to thank Sean Desmond and the whole team at Twelve. Sean has now edited all three of my Obama books, for which he deserves a chest full of medals. He is quite simply the best editor I have ever worked with, anywhere. Sean has the knack of knowing precisely when to intervene: when a word is clunky, a line is overwritten, a section is redundant, or a chapter is unstructured. And I have kept him very busy with all of those. I wrote this book with his voice in my head, so he was editing this well before he saw a word of it. My great thanks go to everyone at Twelve for the enormously skilled work involved in turning round this book so professionally in such short time: Deb Futter, Brian McLendon, Paul Samuelson, Kristin Vorce, Mark Long, Bob Castillo, and Libby Burton.

Having said all that, all errors in this book are mine.

In DC, my biggest thanks go to our friends who kept my family on track despite my many disappearing acts. To our Maret and Sidwell friends: we will miss you deeply. To the Reds, and the Frogs, the Purple Thunder, and the Porpoises, thank you for keeping us all sane. To Paula's Fab Three: your support means the world to us. To my pool sharks: I will get you back. To Cindy and Todd, Vicky and Jim, thank you for an unforgettable send-off. To Tichi and Jose, Michele and Broderick: you are family.

To my mum: Your spirit and your drive are inspiring, even though they feel ordinary to you. If your grandchildren can learn to keep a thimble's worth, they will surely find their way. To my dad: Your heart and your generosity are unbound. Your love of politics and community has always been contagious. To David: You are a rock. I have always looked up to you, and do so today more than ever.

To Paula, Ilana, Ben, and Max: I love you more than I can possibly write here. I am sorry I have been away for so long, in New York and in this book. One day soon, I will be the husband and father you deserve.

INDEX

Hamburger, Tom, 156–57
Hannity, Sean, 76
Harkin, Tom, 132
Harrison, William Henry, 81
Hayes, Chris, 29
health care reform (Obamacare), 46–47, 54,
    75–76, 158, 187–88, 242–43
    contraception rule, 69–73
Hofeld, Al, 162
Hofstra University, second presidential
    debate at, 220–22
Horton, William, 89, 94
Houdini, 146
House Republicans
    budget plan of, 75
    contraception rule and, 72–73
    debt-ceiling crisis of 2011 and, 17–18,
        19–20, 41–42
    Obama campaign's strategy of running
        against, 25–26, 27–28
    Romney and, 151
Hubbard, Glenn, 155
Huffington, Arianna, 28, 29
Huffington Post, 155
Hurricane Irene, 23–24
Hurricane Katrina, 24
Hurricane Sandy, 228–30
Huselton, B. C., 126

Iacocca, Lee, 224
immigration reform, 41, 74, 249
inauguration day of 2012, 14
Institute of Politics at University of Chicago,
    238
Iowa, 23, 63–64, 109, 231–35
Iraq war, 79, 91, 93, 116, 251
IRS, 236–40
Israel
    Obama and, 223–24
    Romney visit, 178, 179
Israeli-Palestinian conflict, 61, 178
It's the Middle Class, Stupid! (Greenberg and
    Carville), 33–34

James, LeBron, 206–7
Jarrett, Valerie
    campaign of 2008, 44
    campaign of 2012, 6, 56, 62, 122, 128
        last day of campaigning, 230–31
        presidential debates, 213, 215–16
    Michelle Obama and, 183–84, 195, 245
Jarvis-Shean, Liz, 152–53

Jay Z, 231
Jeep ad, 225–26
Jefferson Hotel (Washington, DC), 190–91
jobs plan (American Jobs Act) of 2011, 24–28
Johnson, Broderick, 128
Johnson, Lyndon B., 84–86, 95, 187
Journey (ad), 89–90

Keehan, Carol, 72
Kennedy, Edward M. "Ted," 14, 56, 58,
    120–21, 199, 207
Kennedy, John F., 84, 95
Kennedy, Robert F. "Bobby," 11, 48
Kerry, John
    campaign of 2004, 32, 40, 46, 55, 56, 95,
        116, 118
    Swift Boat ads, 92–93
    Obama debate prep of 2012, 209–10
King, Martin Luther, Jr., 48
Klain, Ron, 209, 219
Klein, Ezra, 29
Koch, Charles and David, 67–69, 125
Kroft, Steve, 37–38
Krugman, Paul, 28, 29–30

LaBolt, Ben, 74, 125, 152–53, 154, 238
Lambert Pharmacal Company, 82
leaks (leaking), 62, 107–9
Leno, Jay, 140
Let's Move campaign, 56
Lever, William, 130
Lew, Jack, 62, 168, 246
Limbaugh, Rush, 26, 72
Lincoln, Abraham, 81
Listerine, 82
London Olympics, 177–78, 185
Loopholes (ad), 88

Maddow, Rachel, 29
Mad Men, 96
Mankiw, Greg, 155
Margolis, Jim
    background of, 39–40
    campaign of 2012, 113
        ads, 39–40, 100, 102, 103, 105–6, 118,
            136, 139, 164, 222
        Clinton spots, 190–91
    New York Times profile, 107
Marie Claire, 58
Marshall, John, 29
Massachusetts Senate election of 1994,
    120–21

ABOUT THE AUTHOR

RICHARD WOLFFE is executive editor of MSNBC.com and an MSNBC political analyst, appearing frequently on *Morning Joe* and *The Last Word*. He covered the entire length of Barack Obama's presidential campaign for *Newsweek*, after reporting on President Bush as the magazine's senior White House correspondent. Before *Newsweek*, Wolffe was a senior journalist at the *Financial Times*, serving as its deputy bureau chief and US diplomatic correspondent. He lives with his wife and their three children in New York.